How Do I Help Him?

A Practitioner's Guide to Working with Boys and Men In Therapeutic Settings

By

Michael Gurian

Bestselling Author of *The Wonder of Boys,*
*The Minds of Boys***, and** *Leadership and the Sexes*

Gurian Institute Press, 2011

Books and other materials by Michael Gurian and the Gurian Institute can be accessed through most brick-and-mortar stores, most online outlets, and the websites: www.michaelgurian.com and www.gurianinstitute.com.

Printed in the United States

ISBN 978-0-9839959-0-6

Reviews of *How Do I Help Him?*

"In his insightful and practical new guide, *How Do I Help Him?*, Michael Gurian, explains why so many men and boys dislike traditional counseling. He argues persuasively that males may resist open-ended discussions of their 'feelings,' but they are hungry for mentoring, and eager to talk about their core issues of manhood and motivation. This guide is filled with many helpful examples for engaging the male brain. I recommend this book for any therapist who has ever been frustrated in his or her attempts to reach men and boys—that's all of us!

—Michael Thompson, Ph.D., author of *It's a Boy!,* and writer/producer of the PBS special *Raising Cain: Protecting the Emotional Lives of Boys*

In *How Do I Help Him?*, Michael Gurian eloquently captures the reason talk therapy is so often ineffective for males. Gurian's understanding of boys and men and his wisdom regarding how to alter our approaches can, and hopefully will, change the therapy landscape exponentially in the direction of being meaningful and effective. I highly recommend this book to everyone in the helping professions."
—JoAnn Deak, Ph.D., Author of *Girls Will Be Girls* and *How Girls Thrive*

"In *How Do I Help Him?*, Michael Gurian combines brain science, counseling theory, and case study into a readable and informative synthesis that is valuable for those seeking to address the needs of men and boys in therapeutic settings. Amidst all the rhetoric surrounding the 'boys' crisis', Gurian provides a clear voice of reason that clarifies the problems, and offers plausible solutions. His writing style, as always, is crisp and compelling. This book makes a valuable contribution to the ongoing discourse surrounding the issues that he presents."
—Frances R. Spielhagen, Ph.D., Director, Center for Adolescent Research and Development, Mount Saint Mary College, Newburgh, New York

"*How Do I Help Him?* is a powerful and practical book. It provides a great weaving of stories, statistics and research. While the book was written with therapists and social workers in mind, it actually helps anyone who wants a richer understanding of gender. This book energizes me! I hope everyone in the psychology, law, criminal justice, and mental health fields will read it."
—Michael Piraino, National Director, Court Appointed Special Advocates (CASA)

"*How Do I Help Him?* is a must have and *use now* book that gives professionals fresh direction, insights, and strategies for working with boys and men. Written by Michael Gurian, one of the world's foremost gender experts, this book empowers and equips us to alter counseling environments and theories to work well with males. As Founder of a Counseling and Treatment Center 27 years ago, I only wish this groundbreaking book had been available earlier."
—Gregory Jantz, Ph.D., Founder, the Center for Counseling and Health Resources, and Author of *Healing the Scars of Emotional Abuse*

Previous Books by Michael Gurian

Psychology and Gender
What Could He Be Thinking?
Love's Journey
The Invisible Presence (previously published as
Mothers, Sons and Lovers)
The Prince and the King

Child Development and Parenting
The Purpose of Boys
The Wonder of Girls
The Wonder of Boys
A Fine Young Man
The Good Son
What Stories Does My Son Need? (with Terry Trueman)
Nurture the Nature
It's a Baby Boy! (by the Gurian Institute,
with Adrian Goldberg, ACSW, Stacie Bering, M.D.)
It's a Baby Girl! (by the Gurian Institute,
with Adrian Goldberg, ACSW, Stacie Bering, M.D.)

Education and Gender
The Minds of Boys (with Kathy Stevens)
Boys and Girls Learn Differently!: A Guide for Teachers and Parents
(with Kathy Stevens, Patricia Henley, Terry Trueman)
The Boys and Girls Learn Differently Action Guide for Teachers
(with Arlette C. Ballew)
Strategies for Teaching Boys and Girls—Elementary Level
(with Kathy Stevens, Kelley King)
Strategies for Teaching Boys and Girls—Secondary Level
(with Kathy Stevens, Kelley King)
Successful Single Sex Classrooms
(with Kathy Stevens, Peggy Daniels)

Business-Corporate
The Leading Partners Workbook
(with Katherine Coles, Kathy Stevens)
Leadership and the Sexes (with Barbara Annis)

Spirituality
The Wonder of Children (previously published as
The Soul of the Child)
Ancient Wisdom, Modern Words:
Prayers, Poems, and Readings
The Sabbath: Poems and Prayers

For Young Adult Readers
Understanding Guys
From Boys to Men

Fiction and Poetry
The Miracle
An American Mystic
The Odyssey of Telemachus

Dedication

For Gail, Gabrielle, and Davita,

And for Phil,

With Deepest Thanks

Table of Contents

Part I: More Than a Feeling

Acknowledgments

For more than twenty years, I have counseled families, couples, children, adolescents, and adults. During this time, I have been in dialogue with many others in the field regarding what is happening in our mental health professions. A primary matter for discussion has been the lack of theory, practice, and training available to help professionals work best with boys and men. When I teach a workshop or seminar, I ask participants to raise their hands if they have received training in how to work with boys and men specifically. Rarely is a hand raised. However, when I ask, "Who needs or wants to know more about how to work with males?" nearly every hand gets raised, including my own!

How Do I Help Him? provides theory and strategies I hope you will use to change your institutions and individual practices toward greater effectiveness with males. I am a professional mental health counselor in private practice, and I am a social philosopher whose work combines neurobiological, anthropological, and psychological research with wisdom-of-practice and action research in the field. I have written this book from both a research-based and practitioner-friendly perspective.

In writing the book and promulgating strategies within it, I stand on the shoulders of many others working in the field of male development, to whom I owe my grateful thanks. Some of these colleagues include: Michael Thompson, Ph.D., Judith Kleinfeld, Ph.D., William Pollock, Ph.D., Warren Farrell, Ph.D., John Ratey, M.D., Terrence Real, M.S.W., Mary Pipher, Ph.D., JoAnn Deak, Ph.D., Dan Kindlon, Ph.D., Ruby Payne, Robert Bly, James Hillman, Ph.D., Robert Moore, Ph.D., Don Elium, M.A., David Feinstein, Ph.D., Jean Shinoda Bolen, M.D., Tom Golden, LCSW, Jack Kammer, M.S.W., David Kundtz, M.A., David Wexler, Ph.D., Louann Brizendine, M.D., Mark Kiselica, Ph.D., Leonard Sax, M.D., Arthur Horne, M. D., and Dave Verhaagen, Ph.D. Thank you all for your research and practice.

My deep thanks also extend to my collaborators and co-authors over the last fifteen years: Kathy Stevens, MPA, Kelley King, Patricia Henley, Ph.D., Adie Goldberg, ACSW, Peggy Daniels, M.A., Stacie Behring, M.D., Arlette Ballew, Terry Trueman, M.S., and Barbara Annis. You have constantly strengthened my ability to think strategically and practically about the needs of boys and girls, and women and men.

To all the other people, too many to name, who have aided us in the Gurian Institute's wisdom-of-practice research over the last fifteen years, I wish to express my deep gratitude. We could not conduct our research without your help.

In the mental health field, I offer my deepest gratitude to colleagues who have supported my work with their peer review and theoretical and practical suggestions, specifically Daniel Amen, M.D., Harold Koplewicz, M.D., Tracey Shors, Ph.D., Jeff Hedge, D.O., Lloyd Halpern, M.D., Gary Plep, LCSW and Sue Amende Plep, MFT, Frank DiLallo, M.S., Pam Brown, M.A., Alan Rinzler, M.S., Gene Dire, M.A., Jeannie Corkill, M.S.W., and my wife of twenty-five years, Gail Reid-Gurian, M.A. Your support and critique inspire me to keep pushing the envelope.

To all the people who have written letters (back when we did that!) and e-mails more recently, I express my deepest thanks. Among the many gifts your correspondence has offered me, one that influenced this book is your ongoing challenge: that I provide a resource for therapists and mental health professionals combining gender theory with leading-edge practice. I hope this book fulfills some of that challenge.

My deep thanks also extend to colleagues in publishing, including Russ Davis, of Gray Dog Press, my literary agent, Candice Fuhrman, and my editor of many years at Jossey-Bass/John Wiley, Alan Rinzler. Your gifts have made this book possible.

To my clients, I extend my profound gratitude. By letting me serve you, you have helped me become more effective with both women and men, and boys and girls.

To Gail and our daughters, Gabrielle and Davita, I extend the kind of gratitude that can barely be expressed in words. As women, you have insisted I work diligently for both under-served females and males, and, throughout this insistence, you have kept me focused on seeing diverse sides of various gender equations. Thank you for guiding my work in your many ways.

And to all of you who work with children and adults in your diverse settings, thank you for your work and service. The new millennium opens a new era in mental health care. By working with all children and adults in vigorous new ways, we fulfill our crucial professional role: we ensure a positive future for our civilization, one client and one patient at a time.

Note to Reader

In this book, in order to be inclusive of the greatest numbers of practitioners, practices, and organizations, I will use the words "clients" and "patients" and "therapy" and "counseling" alternately. Simultaneously, because I use the word "clients" in my private practice, you will find my narrative language leaning toward the use of that word. Please substitute, however, "patients" and other words as needed to fit your practice or organization. In nearly every case in this book, those substitutions will not affect narrative flow or meaning.

Introduction: How Do I Help Him?

"There isn't time to waste. Boys and men need us now more than ever. Our questions as professionals should be: 'Will we act now?' and 'Will we do what it takes to reach our males?'"
--Adie Goldberg, ACSW, M.Ed., Co-Author of *It's a Baby Boy!* and *It's a Baby Girl!*

I saw my first therapist in 1968, when I was ten years old. In that year, both Martin Luther King and Bobby Kennedy, Jr. were assassinated. My parents, ardent opponents of the Vietnam War, took my brother, sister, and me on a number of peace marches that year. Both my parents were academics who lived and taught a deep sense of public idealism, which remains strong in their progeny to this day.

At the same time, our home life was less than ideal. My father fought clinical depression and my mother's mental health issues led to physical violence against her children. In the '60s, if children were having problems, the problem was probably in the child. Because I acted out at home and in school, my parents and my school counselor decided I needed to see a psychiatrist and, most probably, to be placed on medication.

When my parents and I walked into the psychiatrist's office in downtown Honolulu, we walked into an office like any other—desk, desk chair, couch, love seat, book cases, end tables and lamps. Dr. Brown invited all of us to sit down. We talked for a while, and a plan for my treatment was agreed upon. Over the next weeks, I fulfilled the main part of the plan—coming to see Dr. Brown weekly. Within a few weeks, I started on Ritalin. Each week, the medication was supported by my sitting on the couch and Dr. Brown sitting in his chair so that I could talk with him.

While that sit-and-talk environment worked better for me than it would for many other boys (I am more verbal than many boys and men around me), sitting and talking about feelings did not end up being enough fodder for internal change in me or familial change in the Gurian house. Other issues ensued over the remaining weeks of our time together, and I left that therapist, beginning a boyhood pattern of leaving therapy soon after I started. The environment and approach of the therapist did not seem to work for me as a boy.

Yet I desperately needed therapy. I was hungry for assistance that would teach me who to be and how to live and grow successfully. I wanted therapy to work! But still, a pattern emerged quite quickly: whenever I entered therapy, I didn't feel at home in the strategies the therapist used. And on the faces of my therapists I saw a puzzled expression that I later realized in words, "How do I help this boy?"

Rarely was this puzzlement and sense of inadequate methodology clearer to me than when I entered therapy again as a 16-year-old hormone-driven, wounded, confused adolescent boy. I walked into the office of a very kind woman who asked me to tell her how I was feeling. When I couldn't answer, she asked again. I kept trying to answer, and those answers gave me some enlightenment, but within weeks, and like so many boys, I failed in therapy. Without realizing it, too, my therapist failed—her own internal question, "How do I help him?" went unanswered. Many years later I would look back on my time with her and realize that her failure to answer the question haunted millions of potential male clients and therapists over a period of many decades.

It was in my mid-twenties, in graduate school, that I discovered neurobiological research. I had already committed myself to feminism, an ardent supporter of women's equality, thus I had committed myself to the idea that gender stereotypes oppressed female development and repressed male emotional life. From this feminist frame, I kept trying to determine why I, as a young male, had been such a misfit in family, school, and therapy. My discovery of neurobiology gave me a nascent realization that I needed to expand my understanding of gender to incorporate the early feminist frame but also move beyond it to include research in gender biology and brain science.

By that time I had met my wife, Gail, and was finishing graduate school, I had become a young man in his late twenties who stopped to see where he was. At twenty-seven, I began to concertedly study available research on differences in the brains of males and females. This gender science was mainly available through self-study—it was not taught in any of the universities near me. In some academic environments in that era, the study of the gendered brain of males and females was considered, at worst, dangerous, at least, a distraction.

Adding brain science and genetics to the gender roles and gender stereotypes issues during the 1980s and 1990s, I focused on studying genetics, biochemical analysis, PET scans of the brains of men and women, and socio-anthropology. This study took me to Ankara, Turkey, where I pursued comparative research in gender dynamics in Turkish cities and villages, and began to develop an understanding of new gender theory and practice in the field of psychology: what I have called "nature-based theory."

Using Gender Science to Help Clients

In 1991, after my return to the United States, I began working as a mental health counselor, and saw my first client in September of that year. This led to the development of a college course, which I later taught at Gonzaga University and Eastern Washington University. As far as I know, the Psychology of Men and Gender course was the first of its kind to both emphasize the nature side of gender theory, and apply theoretical analysis of nature-based findings to specific gender innovations.

During this time, I also began to look carefully at how few male clients were coming to, or staying in, my own and my colleagues' counseling and therapy practices. Most therapists I knew were female, and many of those therapists openly discussed the fact that boys and men needed a great deal of help, but academic theory did not provide significant assistance in helping therapists serve the needs of males. As this dialogue evolved, I saw what we have all perhaps seen: males were "dragged to therapy by wives and girlfriends," and were "not interested in or able to stick with therapy." Our profession was hemorrhaging boys and men.

In 1996, my colleagues and I formed the Gurian Institute in order to organize and teach a science-based and nurture-and-nature gender approach. For the theoretical and early practical underpinnings of this theory and its gender specific solutions, please see *The Wonder of Boys, The Wonder of Girls, Boys and Girls Learn Differently,* and *Leadership and the Sexes.* Over a period of fifteen years, we have developed collaborative application models for theory and practice in a number of settings, for both boys and girls, and women and men. These settings include: family systems, therapeutic institutions, government agencies, preschools, K–12 schools, colleges, businesses, religious communities, and social service agencies.

The present book, *How Do I Help Him?*, specifically focuses research and strategies on effective systems and practices for helping boys and men in clinical settings, from therapeutic to social services to case management. I've written this book from a practitioner's point of view so that you can immediately apply its theory and practices to any individual or group therapeutic environment you might be working in right now. While, traditionally, psychological theory is meant to change everyday practice, sometimes, practice changes theory. That is often the case with gender effectiveness strategies. Prevailing gender theories often get altered by practice in the field. Thus, in writing a practitioner's guide to working with boys and men, I am narrating and presenting my material from a daily-work, strategic point of view.

At the same time, I will ask you to look at the very foundations of the psychology field and psychotherapy professions. I hope you will join me in asking together: "Does our profession understand boys and men as well as it understands girls and women?" "Have our psychological theories—from cognitive-behavioral to family systems to positive psychology to any other baseline theory—developed in ways that favor therapy with females, and leave males behind?"

I will argue that psychological theory, in general, and our psychology-based professions and practices, in particular, have inadvertently developed in ways that are not optimally effective for working with males in need. I will further argue that now, in the new millennium, we have neurobiological, psychological, anthropological, and sociological assets available to us that were not available in the last century. We can expand our gender theories and practices toward increased effectiveness with males, and the process of such expansion will be invigorating and rewarding in compelling ways.

Questions

Throughout this book, I'll provide new possibilities for setting up an office to be more male-friendly, and we'll look together at ways to alter your communications techniques, conflict style, behavioral judgments, and research base to more fully include male-friendly theory and practice. As you are inspired to make changes in your practices, I hope you will feel group cohesion with others who are branching beyond traditional therapeutic practices toward greater gender innovation.

Everywhere I travel, I meet someone who says, "I'm trying this....I'm trying that...." Wisdom-of-practice research is presently compelling our profession forward. As I try to capture some of that forward progress in this book, I do so in full knowledge that you and I are innovating experimentally. You may have already tried some of the things I suggest in this book, and you may have your own success data for your innovations. If you do, please share it. My job in this book is to present therapeutic innovations from a gender-brain lens, and feature practices, tools, and innovations that have borne fruit.

My intention is not to substitute a new psychological theory of personality disorder or pathology. I believe the innovations in this book can increase your effectiveness with male clients in any theory in which you now work—cognitive-behavioral, social constructivist, object-relations, Jungian, Adlerian, post-traumatic stress, addictions recovery, family systems, family of origin—no matter your defining theory or theories, I hope this book will aid your present work in gender-effective ways.

Furthermore, I hope *How Do I Help Him?* also provides a platform for answering these major societal questions:

*Because the fields and institutions of psychology intersect with nearly every social institution, how different might our whole culture be if the hundreds of thousands of counselors, therapists, social workers, case managers, nurses, doctors, psychologists, and psychiatrists serving adults and children inculcated knowledge and practice that included boys and men as effectively as present practices include girls and women?

*How much safer might our streets be if the boys and men in our care stayed longer in the safety of our offices and our psychotherapeutic "family," rather than leaving it quickly or relatively unchanged? Specifically, if we knew and adjusted to boys' and men's needs in psychotherapy—especially what they need when they are young and first facing difficulty and suffering—would our prisons fill up as fast as they do?

*From a business point-of-view, if we in private practice or in rehabilitation centers and other institutions fully understood the boys and men in our care, wouldn't each of us individually serve more clients, and thus, as more boys and men got the therapy they needed, wouldn't they stay in therapy for as long as they needed to stay (which would also increase our business)?

*Finally, wouldn't we as professionals and human beings feel a great deal more fulfilled if we felt that we were fully serving *all* our clients? Wouldn't we feel better about how we provided therapy, especially to the boys and men we can't seem to get through to, the ones about whom we so often throw up our hands? Wouldn't we experience less frustration and burnout?

As you read this book and explore its theory and practices, I hope you will try things for yourself to see if they work for you. As you use them to fit your defining theories and approaches, I hope you'll gather and collect your experiences and data. When they don't work, they won't work. That is good data, too.

This research approach has been my method in working with professionals on practitioner improvement in various settings over the last two decades. In six school districts in Missouri between 1998 and 2000, Patricia Henley and the school of Education at the University of Missouri-Kansas City field tested nature-based theory and science-based practical strategies in order to study the innovations from both a theoretical and practical viewpoint. Student success outcomes surpassed expectations, and the innovations and strategies far surpassed, in number and quality, the menu I had initially proposed for the study (For more results of this two-year pilot study, see *Boys and Girls Learn Differently!* 2010).

In working with gender, I have found it especially crucial to test innovations in the field. If you use, transform, or integrate suggestions from *How Do I Help Him?,* I hope you will reach out to me and let me know. You can contact me through www.michaelgurian.com. Over the last two decades, I have found this networking and innovation-sharing to be useful and necessary.

Especially as pertains to gender issues, I have found that some of our academic environments and our governmental agencies (as I'll discuss more fully in Chapters 1 and 2), are slow to see just how desperate life has become for boys and men. We who work with them every day must innovate in the meantime, and share our knowledge with one another, with rigor, with objectivity, and with compassion, for our boys and men need us urgently, and more and more every day.

A Hidden Focus

On the surface, especially given sentences like the previous one, it may seem that this book is only about helping boys and men. Actually, it includes a hidden focus and purpose—to help girls and women. Gender is not a zero sum game. More than half of my clients are girls and women, and I am the father of two grown daughters; I have also been husband of Gail, a family therapist, for twenty five years. The joke in my house is—"There's Dad and everyone else: female." Even our pets are female! From humor comes a truth: my life is surrounded by girls and women who drive me to do my best, always, for both genders.

Thus, in books like this, in which I focus on how to help our underserved boys and men, I have a tacit intention: to help our culture raise loving, wise and successful men who will treat girls and women, like my daughters, with equality and love. As a post-feminist man, I approach my work and writing from a female-friendly, female-positive point of view, and an equally male-friendly and male-positive point of view. Gender theory that includes neurobiology, as mine does, reflects the fact that human nature, whether male, female, or transgender, is evolving through genetics, biology, nurture, and socialization toward ever-greater intersection and overlap of the sexes—while also retaining significant modalities in which males and females are different.

Thank you for joining me in this book. We belong to a profession that has promised to help all human beings live better lives. We can deliver on that promise in the new millennium in ways we could only dream of doing before, if we will fully open both our psychological theories and our daily practice to the specific and profound needs of boys and men.

Part I

More Than a Feeling

"My son is not a 'person,' he's a *boy*. I am not a 'person,' I'm a *man*. What Jeremy needs and what I need is more than a feeling—we need the truth. We need you as a counselor to tell us the truth."

--Chris, 41, father of one boy and one girl, husband, CEO of a small business, and a counseling client

Chapter 1: The Other Second Sex

"I went into a rage and said, 'No! No! No! No!' And in order to give strength to my No, I stomped the earth so fiercely with my foot that my leg sank into the freshly turned earth up to my knee, and, like a wolf caught in a trap, I am now tied, perhaps for the rest of my life, to the grave of the ideal."

--Charles Baudelaire

Chris, Tanya, and Jeremy came to me when Jeremy, 14, was failing at school. He had received good grades until seventh grade, and he tested off the charts in math and science intelligence, but, gradually, he stopped doing homework, or did it but didn't hand it in, or he lied about doing it. His parents and teachers were saddened and frightened. This bright kid was getting F's, and ruining his future.

Chris said, "We've tried therapy for Jeremy once before, and I've been in therapy too. It doesn't work. It was all about 'feelings.' The therapists didn't 'get' guys, or what we go through. We need you to help us with something deeper than the usual feelings stuff."

Tanya said, "I hope you have better luck getting Jeremy to open up than other therapists. We don't know how to get him to tell us what's wrong. I'm scared for him."

Jeremy said nothing, rolled his eyes, frowned, withdrew. In later sessions I got to know this family on many levels, but in this first session I mainly heard what all of us hear when a child's future is at stake: parental fear. Woven through fear for the child was fear that counseling and therapy, which are touted by our profession as game changers, might not work. If they didn't, where would the family be? Like so many families, Chris, Tanya, and Jeremy walked into a counselor's office already worried that the office was not set up for the boy or man in the family.

Were these parents correct to want our profession to help them save their son? Of course, they were. Our role as therapeutic professionals is a profoundly important one. Was this family also right to suspect our profession of not fully understanding how to reach males? Unfortunately, I believe the answer is also, "Yes."

This situation is true enough of the time that we need to fix it, at both macro and micro levels.

Our Other Second Sex

In many professions, there is an inherent, historically calcified gender bias against girls and women. The book in your hands will ask you to consider that the therapy profession is not one of those. I believe that if we look at four elements of our profession, we will see an inherent gender bias against boys and men. We will see that the "other sex" or "second sex" in our profession is male.

Please consider these four points, all or most of which you have probably already noticed around you.

*Most therapists are female and most clients and patients are female. For example, men comprise only 10 percent of the American Counseling Association's membership. Men comprise only 20 percent of master's degree holders in psychology, and only 10 percent of new social work degrees. On the client side, boys and men need therapy as much as girls and women do, but they do not come to therapy as frequently as girls and women, nor do they, on average, stay as long. Thus, the vicious circle continues—females get more help from a female-centric profession than males do, and males leave the profession, skewing the long-term population in our offices toward females.

*Most of our professional strategic and tactical training in how to work with clients is related to how we use words and verbal communication to elicit responses from our clients that will help them heal their minds and bodies. Most of us know instinctively (and research I will provide in Chapter 2 supports this instinct) that girls and women are more facile with words and word-emotion linkage than boys and men (on average), but our profession, still, utilizes verbal interaction as our primary therapeutic strategy.

*The physical spaces of our offices are set up for the client to sit in a chair and talk with us in a sit-still modality. This is the case even though we know instinctively that boys and men find that modality much less comfortable than girls and women. In Chapter 2, I will provide neurobiological research to further support the instinct and intuition of gender bias against males in the sit-and-talk modality.

*When we gather at workshops or seminars to talk about our difficult clients--many of whom are boys and men--we avoid going too deeply into "what boys need" and "what men need" for fear that speaking on the subject will upset the gender political climate we work in, one in which most contemporary professional attention must be paid to what girls and women need, if we are to right past and present wrongs against girls and women.

Baudelaire's quote is instructive in this regard. It doesn't blame anyone, for there is no one to blame. Sometimes, things calcify unnoticed until noticed. I believe our profession has stomped its foot for so long into its own earth that now its foot is stuck in an ideal client: female. This "stuck-ness" and this calcification have profound consequences.

While we will go deeper into exploring these points throughout this book, it is worth noting immediately that our therapy profession runs parallel to our school systems. In our schools, most teachers are female, and the majority of successful students in schools are female (see statistics below). Just as with our therapeutic professions, many people, even people inside the profession, do not realize how problematic our schools have become for boys. Mothers and fathers of sons, like Tanya and Chris, do know, for they are living the systemic bias in our schools against boys, who, like Jeremy, now receive two-thirds of the D's and F's in our nation's schools, but only a minority of the A's.

As in our schools, our therapeutic misunderstanding of what boys and men need from therapy is not a result of malice from women. Both women and men want to be effective with all populations. Except for some women therapists who are angry at boys and men for personal or political reasons, the vast majority of female therapists are just as compassionate toward males as are the vast majority of male therapists. Women teachers love their boys as much as their girls. Women teachers and therapists want to provide deep compassion toward the boys and men in their care. It is mainly women therapists and teachers who come to me at a talk or workshop and say that the theoretical systems we have in place do not fully understand boys and men.

Here are some recent comments:

"Until today's workshop, I received no science-based training in how to help boys grow or learn differently than girls."

"I had never seen the brain scans that show how differently men process feelings than women. I was just taught that everyone is an individual, and I was taught theories to use on 'people.'"

"I knew I was losing the males, and I had instincts about what to do, but I didn't get training in boys and men, so I just fell into the inertia of being more effective with girls and women."

A Bias of Omission

By asking you to look at inherent gender bias against males in our profession, I want to clarify three perspectives:

1. I will not in this book claim that the gender bias against males in the psychology, education, and social services fields is equivalent to the patriarchal bias against females that we continue to fight all over the world. The gender bias we collectively call "patriarchal" was and is often one of degrading females. I do not believe our contemporary therapeutic and psychological bias against males is meant to be degrading. It is more a sin of omission than commission.

2. I will argue that we have systematically omitted full and diverse understanding of boys and men from our toolbox for both political reasons and for reasons of ease-of-service. Sitting-and-talking seems theoretically easier than any other method, so we have set up therapeutic systems to favor that method, and thus, without realizing it (and because we did not realize the science of the male and female brains) our methods mainly favor female minds.

3. In the same way that some people blamed girls and women for their "weaknesses" and "defects" during the patriarchy, now, in the post-patriarchal and post-feminist world, some people blame males. When boys and men don't succeed in therapy or personal growth, we unconsciously or consciously think of the male's defects, especially in his inability to access his feelings. We don't look hard enough at the therapeutic and mental health system itself for its flaws in dealing with one-half of our human population.

Chris, Tanya, and Jeremy

During our first session, Chris, Tanya, Jeremy, and I talked about family dynamics and other intake information. About thirty-five minutes into the session, I asked to speak with Jeremy without his parents present. When he and I were alone, I asked questions I often ask of intransigent or withdrawn males in a first session. These are questions of identity rather than of feeling or emotion, per se.

> *What does your first name mean?
> *What does your last name mean?
> *What are your family's ethnic origins?
> *What is your religion or spiritual path?
> *What do you like to do when you're not in school?
> *Who are your friends?
> *What music do you like?

I ask these questions not only to learn more about the boy, but also to signal to the boy that I "get" his maleness. For him as he walks into my office (especially in the wake of all his troubles), *respect* is crucial. Through my questions and interaction with him around those questions, I am signaling to him that "I respect you. I respect that you are a boy with an identity—I don't think of you as just some kid-with-problems." This respect-identity approach is often critical to males in a first visit to a new counselor or therapist. Already in a first visit, the male is deciding whether to report to his parents (or spouse, if he is grown) that "this therapy thing isn't getting anywhere, it's stupid."

As we continued to talk, I moved the conversation toward the presenting issue—homework/school/power struggle—asking him to recap what his parents had reported. As expected, Jeremy provided a minimalist recap of the situation (about twenty words).

When he finished, I asked, "So, what do you have to say about all the fear your parents are feeling about you?"

He shrugged.

"Nothing?" I probed.

Silence, then more silence, then, "I don't know."

"The homework, grades, the lying and fighting with your folks and your teachers…what's *your* point of view on all this?"

A shrug. Silence.

Jeremy, as a boy, was testing whether I was "not mushy." Much of his silence and minimalism was related to the alien quality of this sit-and-talk environment. Much of it was also related to his defiance, resistance, etc. But some of it was related to his testing me as counselor to see whether I would stay present, be an authority, remain engaged, or withdraw and give up on him.

Finally, after more probing by me, Jeremy said, "I guess everyone's freaking out."

"Yes. They are. But what about you? Are you freaking out?"

"Not really." A shrug.

From me, now, came silence of my own. ("Not really" actually meant "Yes," so I waited him out).

Looking downward, not at me, he finally said, "Are we just gonna talk about my feelings, like my dad said?"

"What do you think?"

"That's what counseling is, right?"

I shrugged my shoulders, settled in. "It's that, but a lot more than that, too. Especially with guys."

He looked up, made eye contact. "Whatdoyoumean—'with 'guys'"?

"I mean, counseling is more than 'feelings.'" My fingers made quotation marks in the air. "We won't just sit here and talk. Counseling is about what makes you, Jeremy, strong, and what makes you weak. This time together is about your destiny as a man. Are you a man, yet?"

He lowered his eyes again. "That's a lame question. Of course not."

I read him as wanting to assert some power, but in his change of lowered eye trajectory I saw that he felt dominated by my adult authority. He knew he was not a man yet, and could not pretend he was. This was helpful to me as his counselor. By his revelation of his boy-not-yet-man position in the hierarchy in the room, I learned that he was not as hardened as some 14-year-olds who will keep eye contact in the face of "Are you a man?" and lie, "Yeah, I'm a man," or become defensive, "Don't try that stuff on me," or try to one-up me with, "I'm a man as much as you are."

I asked: "Do you think you have a destiny, Jeremy? Something important you're meant to do with your life?"

He looked upward toward me again, but didn't hold eye contact, moving his eyes to the middle distance. "I guess so."

"That's good. I think you do. I'm going to help you find it. It's bigger than fighting over homework, but it could take some digging to find it. It's about more than a feeling--it's about being a man."

We will meet Jeremy, Chris, and Tanya again in this book. The wounds and difficulties this family brought to counseling were multifaceted, and can provide a great deal of insight into males. And as counseling continued, many feelings did come up, and their activation was liberating for the family. At the same time, we needed to go in other directions, as well.

For now, I hope you'll take away from this episode an immediate sense of approaching counseling and therapy with boys and men as being about, from the outset, looking at *male identity* and *manhood* more than *feelings*. To you and to me, feelings are very important, of course, but a subtext argument of this book will be that for most males, "feelings" are small, uninteresting, not the "heart of the matter."

"Duh!" you might say. "I didn't need you to point that out." Or, you might say, "No, I disagree. Even 'male identity' and 'manhood' are about feelings."

To either response, I would say, "Let's keep going deeper." The distinctions regarding emotion and functionality that males bring to our profession—a distinction, in a sense, between "feelings" and "everything else"—is an important one, and one I will keep developing with you throughout this book.

I believe that if we as a profession avoid dealing with the male point of view, we will lose the male client quickly. If we allow boys and men to think during our first session that we don't understand their point of view, we commit a major "sin of omission" that is gender bias at its core.

I say this knowing full well that there are exceptions to the "it's more than feelings for guys" generalization. There are seven billion people on earth, thus there are 3.5 billion ways to be a boy or man. Diversity and variety are a huge part of the gender puzzle, as we'll note throughout this book. Some boys and men are, from day one, supremely interested in their own, and other peoples', feelings.

And nearly every boy and man is empathic and compassionate in his own way, and cares about the feelings of the people he loves.

That said, and as a way of deepening our effectiveness with boys and men, I will present the view that most males are neither initially nor primarily interested in their own discreet and complex feelings. As you look around you at how boys and men are cared for, I hope you will come to appreciate the challenge Chris, Tanya, and Jeremy provided—their insistence that therapy be "more than about feelings," and "work for Jeremy as a *boy*, and Chris as a *man*." In the challenge this family made to our profession, I see them asserting two crucial things to us:

1. Males have a lot of inner intelligence regarding character and emotion, but they need us to know how to help them as *males* to elicit that intelligence in ways that fit their boy-energy and male identity, ways that do not necessarily involve the constant goal of discussing feelings.

2. Our profession hasn't really had much clear sympathy for males as boys and men, thus these males are intrinsically suspicious of us. From day one in our office, they and the women who love them ask us to prove that we actually know what makes males tick. If we prove that we do know, boys and men will open their psyches to us. If we don't, they won't.

In saying these things to us, Chris, Tanya, and Jeremy are hoping to inspire our bravery as practitioners, even while we are hoping to inspire the whole family to be brave inner searchers as clients.

Exploring Our Therapeutic Gender Biases More Deeply

Join me for a moment in looking at the second issue this family challenges us with: Does our profession have as much sympathy as it ought to for boys and men as it has for girls and women? Let's ask bravely:

    *In our homes, schools, streets, courts, prisons, workplaces, and businesses, do we know as much as we need to about boys and men?

    *Do we as professionals know as much about the core issues boys and men face as we do girls and women's issues?

    *Do our practices and ways of talking with boys and men reflect our deep knowledge of what they are suffering?

    Here are some statistics regarding the state of boyhood and manhood in America that may surprise you. We as a profession have long been so sensitized to the real and painful sufferings of girls and women, we often do not realize what their brothers, fathers, and husbands are going through as a group.

Did You Know?

    Tom Mortenson, senior scholar and policy analyst at The Pell Institute for the Study of Opportunity in Higher Education, has been tracking gender statistics for nearly four decades. He is author of "The State of American Manhood," published in *Post Secondary Education*, March 2011.

    Here are just a few of his (and the federal government's) findings. As I share these with you, I want to express my thanks to Mr. Mortenson for providing these statistics, and to the Pell Institute for pursuing its many goals of supporting our young people, both female and male. I have included the websites from Mr. Mortenson's report here, in the text, so that you can easily navigate original sources, should you want to look at each statistic further.

Mental and Social Health

For every 100 females ages 15 to 19 that commit suicide, 549 males in the same range kill themselves.
http://www.cdc.gov/nchs/data/dvs/LCWK1_2002.pdf

For every 100 females ages 20 to 24 that commit suicide, 624 males of the same age kill themselves.
http://www.cdc.gov/nchs/data/dvs/LCWK1_2002.pdf

For every 100 girls ages 15 to 17 in correctional facilities, there are 837 boys behind bars.

http://www.census.gov/population/www/cen2000/phc-t26.html

For every 100 women ages 18 to 21 in correctional facilities, there are 1,430 men behind bars.
http://www.census.gov/population/www/cen2000/phc-t26.html

For every 100 women ages 22 to 24 in correctional facilities, there are 1,448 men in correctional facilities.
http://www.census.gov/population/www/cen2000/phc-t26.html

Learning and Physical Disabilities

For every 100 girls diagnosed with a special education disability, 217 boys are diagnosed with a special education disability.
http://www.iteachilearn.com/uh/meisgeier/

For every 100 girls diagnosed with a learning disability, 276 boys are diagnosed with a learning disability.
http://www.iteachilearn.com/uh/meisgeier/statsgov20gender.htm

For every 100 girls diagnosed with emotional disturbance, 324 boys are diagnosed with emotional disturbance.
http://www.iteachilearn.com/uh/meisgeier/statsgov20gender.htm

For every 100 girls diagnosed with a speech impairment, 147 boys are similarly diagnosed.
http://www.iteachilearn.com/uh/meisgeier/statsgov20gender.htm

For every 100 girls diagnosed with mental retardation, 138 boys are diagnosed as mentally retarded.
http://www.iteachilearn.com/uh/meisgeier/statsgov20gender.htm

For every 100 girls diagnosed with visual impairment, 125 boys are visually impaired.
http://www.iteachilearn.com/uh/meisgeier/statsgov20gender.htm

For every 100 girls with multiple disabilities, 189 boys have multiple disabilities.
http://www.iteachilearn.com/uh/meisgeier/statsgov20gender.htm

Further Disabilities

For every 100 girls less than 15 years old with a severe disability, 191 boys have a severe disability.
http://www.census.gov/hhes/www/disability/sipp/disab05/ds05t1.xls

For every 100 girls less than 15 years old with a disability that needs assistance, 195 boys have a disability that needs assistance.
http://www.census.gov/hhes/www/disability/

For every 100 girls less than 3 years old with a developmental delay, 165 boys have a developmental delay.
http://www.census.gov/prod/2006pubs/p70-107.pdf

For every 100 girls 3 to 5 years old with a developmental delay, 154 boys are developmentally delayed.
http://www.census.gov/prod/2006pubs/p70-107.pdf

For every 100 girls 6 to 14 years old with a severe disability, 160 boys have a severe disability.
http://www.census.gov/prod/2006pubs/p70-107.pdf

For every 100 girls 6 to 14 years old who have difficulty doing regular schoolwork, 176 boys have difficulty doing regular schoolwork.
http://www.census.gov/prod/2006pubs/p70-107.pdf

For every 100 girls 6 to 14 years old who have difficulty getting along with others, 183 boys have difficulty getting along with others. http://www.census.gov/prod/2006pubs/

For every 100 girls 6 to 14 years old with a learning disability, 160 boys have a learning disability.
http://www.census.gov/prod/2006pubs/p70-107.pdf

For every 100 girls 6 to 14 years old with mental retardation, 302 boys have mental retardation.
http://www.census.gov/prod/2006pubs/p70-107.pdf

For every 100 girls 6 to 14 years old with other developmental disability, 212 boys have other developmental disabilities.
http://www.census.gov/prod/2006pubs/p70-107.pdf

For every 100 girls 6 to 14 years old with speech difficulty, 214 boys have speech difficulty.
http://www.census.gov/prod/2006pubs/p70-107.pdf

K-12 Education

For every 100 girls who repeat kindergarten, 194 boys repeat kindergarten.
http://nces.ed.gov/pubs2006/2006064.pdf

For every 100 girls ages 9 to 11 years enrolled below modal grade, there are 130 boys enrolled below modal grade.
http://nces.ed.gov/programs/digest/d08/tables/dt08_155.asp

For every 100 girls ages 12 to 14 years enrolled below modal grade, there are 120 boys enrolled below modal grade.
http://nces.ed.gov/programs/digest/d08/tables/dt08_155.asp

For every 100 girls ages 15 to 17 years enrolled below modal grade, there are 130 boys enrolled below modal grade.
http://www.census.gov/population/socdemo/school/TableA-

For every 100 tenth-grade girls who perform community service at least once a week, 68 boys do the same.
http://nces.ed.gov/programs/digest/d04/tables/dt04_138.asp

For every 100 tenth-grade girls who take music, art or language class, 52 boys take music, art or language class.
http://nces.ed.gov/programs/digest/d04/tables/dt04_138.asp

For every 100 twelfth-grade girls who participate in music, drama or debate, 70 boys participate.
http://nces.ed.gov/programs/digest/d04/tables/dt04_138.asp

For every 100 twelfth-grade girls who participate in vocational clubs, 71 boys participate.
http://nces.ed.gov/programs/digest/d04/tables/dt04_138.asp

For every 100 twelfth-grade girls who carried a weapon on school property, 276 boys carried a weapon.

http://nces.ed.gov/programs/digest/d10/tables/dt10_171.asp

For every 100 twelfth-grade girls who were threatened or injured with a weapon on school property, 175 boys were threatened or injured.
http://nces.ed.gov/programs/digest/d10/tables/dt10_171.asp

For every 100 twelfth-grade girls who engaged in a physical fight on school property, 226 boys got into a fight.
http://nces.ed.gov/programs/digest/d10/tables/dt10_171.asp

For every 100 twelfth-grade girls who had property stolen or deliberately damaged on school property, 128 boys had the same

experience.
http://nces.ed.gov/programs/digest/d10/tables/dt10_171.asp

For every 100 twelfth-grade girls who used alcohol on school property, 148 boys used alcohol.
http://nces.ed.gov/programs/digest/d10/tables/dt10_171.asp

For every 100 twelfth-grade girls who used marijuana on school property, 225 boys did.
http://nces.ed.gov/programs/digest/d10/tables/dt10_171.asp

For every 100 twelfth-grade girls who offered, sold or were given an illegal drug on school property, 134 boys did the same.
http://nces.ed.gov/programs/digest/d10/tables/

For every 100 girls suspended from public elementary and secondary schools, 215 boys are suspended.
http://nces.ed.gov/programs/digest/d10/tables/dt10_169.asp

For every 100 girls expelled from public elementary and secondary schools, 297 boys are expelled.
http://nces.ed.gov/programs/digest/d10/tables/dt10_169.asp

Higher Education

For every 100 women enrolled in college, there are 78 men enrolled.

http://www.census.gov/population/socdemo/school/cps2009/tab01
-01.xls

For every 100 American women who earn an associate's degree, 61
American men earn the same degree.
http://nces.ed.gov/programs/digest/d10/tables/dt10_281.asp

For every 100 American women who earn a bachelor's degree, 75
American men earn a bachelor's degree.
http://nces.ed.gov/programs/digest/d10/tables/

For every 100 American women who earn a master's degree, 66
American men earn the same degree.
http://nces.ed.gov/programs/digest/d10/tables/dt10_286.asp

For every 100 American women who earn a doctoral degree, 91
American men earn the same degree.
http://nces.ed.gov/programs/digest/d10/tables/dt10_291.asp

For every 100 women ages 25 to 29 years who have at least a professional degree, 84 men have at least a professional degree.
http://www.census.gov/hhes/socdemo/education/

For every 100 women ages 25 to 29 years who have a doctoral degree, 80 men have a doctorate.
http://www.census.gov/hhes/socdemo/education/data/cps/2009/T
able1-

These statistics are only the tip of the iceberg. For more statistics regarding boys and men, see *The Minds of Boys* and *A Fine
Young Man*. You can also read a literature review that was developed for the White House, in hopes that the White House would
start a Council on Boys and Men. The Proposal can be accessed at
www.whitehouseboystomen.com. Click the "Proposal" button.
The Proposal's data is quite current (2011).

The statistics above and in the other resources have been
repeatedly vetted by the nation's leading experts. They show an
increasingly dangerous failure rate among males in nearly all social
categories. Such failures don't negate issues girls and women face
in our culture, but the statistics don't get the attention in our psy-

chological, social services, and therapeutic professions that they need to get if we are to serve the other second sex.

I have never forgotten a meeting I had with a Department of Justice executive. He was a therapist who had moved up the government administration hierarchy to a position near the top. When I asked him why hundreds of millions of dollars were being spent on positive and preventative girls' and women's programming but little money on helping boys and men, he responded sheepishly, "Well, from the government's point of view, we already budget for boys and men—in our prison budgets." The irony and tragedy of the response continues to haunt me.

In our therapeutic professions, let's be brave. When it comes to boys and men, let's ask. "Are we as trained and informed as we are regarding girls and women?" Let's be brave and say, "Generally, no." People like Jeremy, Chris, and Tanya walk into our offices suspicious of our profession in some part because we seem somewhat out of touch regarding the plight of males today.

To whatever extent your own clinical dialogue is mainly about girls and women in your present environments, you may be involved in tacit distancing of male clients. You are not a malicious person, nor are others around you. But the inherent bias against boys and men, one of omission, freezes our profession's motivation to revolutionize therapy on behalf of everyone. Dads like Chris and moms like Tanya, who are sensitive and bright and have had negative or lackluster experiences with therapists regarding males, know the danger of our systemic lack of sympathy for the complexity of male crises. Males leave therapy, and then where shall they go?

Moving Forward Bravely

As we continue working together in this book, I hope you'll consider this idea: the old days of "girls are suffering, boys are fine," or, "women are victims, men are villains" are gone. These were simplified frames that worked sixty years ago; they were needed rhetorically in order to help our culture battle on behalf of women and girls. They were a crucial part of first-wave feminism, and the female empowering work of all the waves of feminism will continue.

But this is the new millennium—boys and men are suffering as profoundly as girls and women, and girls and women are succeeding better than boys and men, in uncountable ways. People in our profession have the honor of working minute-by-minute, hour-by-hour, day-by-day with millions of the people who belong to "the other second sex: male." We can do something about updating our frames, and increasing our compassion and learning regarding boys and men.

I hope you will share contemporary statistics and stories in your dialogues throughout your therapeutic communities. If you do that, you will be taking a first step of what I believe are eight major steps we need to take to serve boys and men as well as we serve girls and women. Each of the next chapters will deal with a new and cumulative next step.

As we have taken a first step in this chapter of beginning to look at male reality, I hope we take a first step toward motivating ourselves and others around us to alter our profession. As change happens over the next decades, women like Tanya, men like Chris, and boys like Jeremy will no longer approach our offices with suspicion or resignation, or an eye, always, toward the door.

Chapter 2: Understanding the Minds of Boys and Men

"Roots like these keep their firmness—
it's possible they've lain here for centuries."
--Olav H. Hauge

"You're dangerous," Sarah called out.

I had just shown brain scans in a workshop. The scans revealed differences between the active and resting brains of males and females (see below). After looking at the scans, the whole group had entered a lively discussion regarding some of the challenges therapists face with males—and some possible neurobiological reasons for those challenges.

"What's the danger?" I asked Sarah.

"These are gender stereotypes. We're not all from Mars and Venus. And we're not even all males and females. There are transgender and other kinds of minds all around us."

"I agree that there are all kinds of minds," I responded. "And by the end of this workshop, I think you'll see that there is no gender stereotyping here. But let's not wait—let's talk about our therapy clients. Are the men and women who come into your office the same—same approach to emotions, same way of talking about themselves, same issues and same ideas?"

She nodded, "They can be. Yes. Absolutely. If we socialize them to be, they can be." This answer elicited some negative head shakes from the people around her, and some verbal, "No way," and "Nuh uh."

"There's disagreement here," I offered. "But your viewpoint is important. Most people who have ever raised families or related to the other gender feel, instinctively, that we are not the same, but politically or socially, 'gender sameness' is often assumed to be a beneficial ideology. We're kind of caught in a bind in our profession."

"I'm not saying there aren't differences," Sarah continued. "I'm just saying they come from the way gender roles and gender stereotypes act on children. I'm saying, it's mainly about nurture, not nature. When you use this kind of brain science, you're using junk science."

I countered, "Why do you call it junk science? We're all looking at the same brain scans. All over the world, male and female brains scan differently in different neural states."

"It's still gender stereotyping. Whether you've got a scan or not, you're still trying to say nature means more than nurture or culture, and males and females are so different we should treat them differently. This is just retro, patriarchal, and leads to girls and women getting the shaft."

"Not so," I countered. "In fifteen years of training institutions and collecting data from systemic change models, I've seen girls' and women's success *increase* when professionals, schools, and workplaces learn about male/female brain difference. Data contradicts what you're saying."

At that point, I shared data that has been vetted and published in *Boys and Girls Learn Differently!* and *Leadership and the Sexes*. In training more than 50,000 teachers in male/female brain difference, the Gurian institute staff and trainers have helped schools close achievement and gender gaps for *both* boys and girls. Similarly, corporations such as IBM and Deloitte & Touche significantly increased their retention and advancement of *female* talent when the women and men in the leadership teams learned about male/female difference.

As I shared this information, a group dialogue arose regarding the past and the present. Sarah's comments reflected a fear many therapeutic professionals have that is grounded in past abuses of gender and science. While the new neuroscience is not abusive or dangerous to girls and women from an evidence-based point of view, some people still believe it is. And not every scientist agrees as to what the new brain research means exactly. In fact, as with any matter of science, disagreement is part of the process of honing ideas and theories.

At the same time, everyone in the room, including Sarah, was fascinated by the brain scans. For me, that fascination is the beginning of a second step toward helping boys and men in therapy, one that involves understanding gender differences regarding males with as much definition and clarity as has been used in our culture to help girls and women learn and grow.

Equal and Different Minds

Professor of Psychology at University of California, Irvine, Richard Haier has provided a pithy comment that speaks volumes: "Human evolution has created two different types of brains, male and female, designed for equally intelligent behavior." Other scientists in the field of gender science include Tracey Shors at Rutgers, Ruben Gur at the University of Pennsylvania, Simon Baron-Cohen at Cambridge University, Sandra Witelson at McMaster University, Daniel Amen at the Amen Clinics, and Louann Brizendine at the University of California-San Francisco.

Using PET, fMRI, and SPECT scans on human brains, as well as laboratory research on animals, and combining that research with biochemical analysis of both animals and humans, these and other scientists are developing primary research on male/female brain and biochemical difference. When that data is united with psychological, anthropological, and sociological research, scientists and lay people can explore the psyches of males and females from the inside out.

Because many of the science-based findings on gender difference are similar, no matter the continent or culture, a powerful new asset has become available to therapeutic practitioners. We are able to develop innovations and strategies for working with each gender that can cross cultures, even while we hone our skills and vision to be culturally effective with each ethnicity, culture, and individual.

My role in gender science has been to study all the disparate data published by scientists in the field of gender, sift through it for what might be most useful to practitioners, and develop theory and practice for *application* of the science in our homes, families, schools, communities, businesses, and therapy practices. In developing applications, I have of necessity selected and concentrated on certain aspects of gender science, as you will see in this book. Many of the research points I have focused on come under the category of neuropsychology.

The Gender-Brain Spectrum: Where You Might Fit

Gender stereotyping is an approach to gender that assumes superiority and/or devaluing of either gender. Science-based approaches, such as the approach in this book, spend no time arguing that either brain is inferior or superior, or that one should be valued more highly than another. Most of us in the gender science field know that "male brain" and "female brain" are just code words for "3.5 billion ways to be male" and "3.5 billion ways to be female." There is not one male brain or female brain, but instead, a spectrum of seven billion brains in the world, approximately half of which are male and half of which are female, and among which some brains and bodies are transgender.

If you are curious to take a "test" to see where your own brain fits in the "maleness and femaleness" spectrum, try going to the following website, where you can take a "Brain Sex ID Survey." www.bbc.co.uk/science/humanbody/sex/add_user.shtml. Also, for a quicker, though less scientific test, refer to *Leadership and the Sexes*. Its appendices include a gender/brain quiz for both women and men.

Scientists have now learned that the human brain is prepared for its gender in three stages—where you fit, as an individual woman or man, on the gender/brain spectrum depends on combined elements of these three gender-forming stages of life.

Stage 1. Genetic markers on your X and Y chromosomes (XX if you are female, XY if you are male). These genetic markers control fetal development of female and male body and brain. This first stage of brain gendering arguably occurs at conception.

Stage 2. Between five to seven weeks and five to six months in utero. Your chromosome markers trigger hormonal surges in utero that guide your body and brain to grow as male and female body and brain, including homosexual and transgender.

Stage 3. After you are born, nurture, socialization, and culture add to the gender mix. Your parents and others nurture you as "boy" and "girl," depending on how they see these genders. As you grow, your body and brain (especially at puberty) continually guide your male and female development toward gender difference and similarity from within, while the family and society enhance (or neglect) various aspects of gender difference and similarity.

Jay Giedd, at the National Institute of Mental Health, has placed an array of gender-brain scans on the NIMH (www.nimh.org) website. If you go to the website and explore Dr. Giedd's work, you'll see scans of boys and girls that show significant differences between males and females. You'll then see such differences contract by full adulthood. It is a powerful experience to observe that the brains of males and females start out looking obviously different. It is also powerful to observe that at adulthood they still include significant differences, some of which are undoubtedly socialized and some of which are baseline natural gender tendencies. Gender in the brain is an important part of human life, and we are learning more about it every day.

Because we now understand gender to be both a matter of nature and nurture, we can add a brain-based gender approach to our therapeutic toolbox. By the time a male or female arrives in our office, gender is genetically, hormonally, and socially constructed in the psyche of that person. It is a powerful part of who the person is; thus, it can become a new basis for helping the boys and men, and girls and women, in our care.

Focusing on Gender Differences

As I lead you deeper into specific gender differences, you might find yourself smiling and thinking, "Aha! I always knew that about men (or women or myself), but I didn't really understand the science of it before." Hopefully, after this chapter's scientific information, you'll know even more about why your instincts were so often correct.

At other times in this chapter you might say, "Well, you know, some of what that piece of science argues does not apply to me or to this man (or woman) I know." This is also an important internal experience to honor. Brain science is not a complete field (nor perhaps will it ever be), nor do we know everything about the brain, and in talking about gender science, we can never make rules that don't have exceptions.

With that said, scientists generally study four areas of robust gender difference in male and female brains: Process, Chemistry, Structure, Activity.

Process Differences

In general, men have approximately six times the amount of gray matter related to cognition and intelligence than women, and women have nearly ten times the amount of white matter related to cognition and intelligence than men. Richard Heier is one of the scientists who has studied this. Others are Simon Baron-Cohen at Cambridge and Ruben Gur at Penn State.

In both sexes, "gray matter" represents information-processing centers in the brain, and "white matter" represents the networking of, or connections between, processing centers. If you have noticed that your female clients may tend to more quickly "connect more dots" in their brains, and "see" more sensory, memory, and emotive detail more quickly and richly than boys and men, gray and white matter differences may be one reason.

These differences may also be a reason that girls and women tend to more quickly connect internal memory information with empathic and verbal brain centers, i.e. girls and women are often more *verbal-emotive:* more able to attach more words to their feelings and memories than boys and men.

Chemistry

Male and female brains process different degrees and gradations of neurochemicals. These include *serotonin*, which, among other things, helps us sit still, *testosterone*, our sex and aggression chemical, and *oxytocin,* one of our primary bonding chemicals.

In part because of differences in all three of these chemicals, males tend to be less able to sit still for as long as girls and women, and tend to be more physically impulsive and aggressive than girls and women. They may also need to move up in social pecking orders in order to flourish (conversely, they may become more depressed when they are at the bottom of pecking orders). The fact that males process less oxytocin than females may also provide one of the reasons males often feel less of a need to "please" others, including therapists, than females.

Furthermore, the male brain under stress or in crisis (a state of mind that reflects the neural state of nearly every client who walks in your door) relies more on "fight or flight" and "action" for stress-release and stress-response than does the female brain in crisis. During crisis, girls and women tend to rely more on signaling from the female chemical base, which scientists call a "tend and be-friend" response. Shelley Taylor's *The Tending Instinct* is a powerful study of the female stress response.

For us as therapeutic professionals, this is important information—our male clients walk into our offices at a different biochemical and neural baseline than our female clients do. Our males may need some very different strategies and logic models for stress-release and stress-response than our females.

Structure

A number of structural elements in the human brain differ between males and females. The *hippocampus,* our human memory center, is one of these. Females tend to take in more sensorial and emotive information to their often larger hippocampus while they are involved in an experience than males do (larger = denser neural connections). They also tend to be better able to access, later, that greater quantity of sensorial and emotive memory, i.e. when they sit in our offices. And they tend to be better able to attach the remembered information more quickly and fully to words than males do.

In this way, structural differences in the hippocampus connect with structural differences in the right and left hemispheres of the male/female brains. Females tend to have verbal centers on both sides of the brain, while males tend to work with language mainly in the left hemisphere. Thus, males not only have less verbal centers in general, but also may have less connectivity of memory/emotion to word centers throughout both sides of the brain.

The importance of these differences for mental health professionals cannot be overstated. We often talk to males as if they 1) experienced as much sensation and emotion as females did when an incident in their lives occurred, 2) stored as much emotional information in their memory centers as females during that event, and 3) are able to affix as many words to those emotions, senses, and memories as females are.

In fact, in most cases, the males in our office are not as adept at these things as we think they are—parts of their brains are structured differently than those same parts of the female brain.

Activity/Blood Flow in the Brain

Brain activity patterns differ between boys and girls, and women and men. Male brains, no matter how young or old, do not necessarily "rest" or deactivate (zone out, take a break from stress) the way female brains do. In the following SPECT scans, provided by neuro-psychiatrist Daniel Amen, you can see how "inactive" the male brain is when a boy or man is zoning out (bored and staring out the window, becoming glaze-eyed in front of the TV while channel checking, staring at a computer screen but not really doing much work, sitting in your office and not fully engaged in therapy with you).

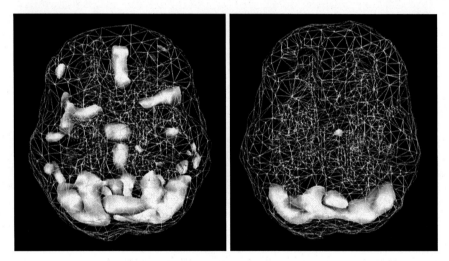

Scans Provided by Daniel Amen, M.D.

Male brains, when bored, look like the brain on the right. The brains of girls and women when they are bored, zoning out, or trying to rest and recharge, look like the brain on the left. Notice how, when girls are sitting bored in our offices, their brains may still be active, tracking what we are saying, remembering, emoting, processing words. When boys are sitting bored in our offices, they may not be hearing us, "feeling" us, concentrating on emotive material, or otherwise be as engaged as we think they should be. Their brains are more "blank."

This rest-state difference is only one male/female difference in blood flow that affects our clients as they sit in our offices with us. Another profound difference lies in quantity of brain activity at any given time—not just in a rest state but even when highly active. The female brains generally have more blood flow throughout the brain at any given time than do male brains, including while they are sitting in the chair across from us and engaged in emotive conversation. Hence, the girl or woman you are talking to can have more brain activity at any given time and in any state of mind for you to tap into with your words/feelings conversation than does the boy or man with whom you are conversing in that "sit down and talk" environment.

Bridge Brains

The gender differences I've noted for you constitute "a tip of the iceberg." Scientists have discovered approximately one hundred gender differences in the brain that can affect your clients. And as we said above, and as you'll notice in the scientific dialogue regarding gender around the world, there are always exceptions to every "gender rule." Fifteen years ago, I coined the term "bridge brains" in order to help clients and professionals look at boys and girls and women and men who "seem more like" the other gender, i.e. "bridge" genders, from a neural point of view.

The *bridge brain* client may be your male client who is quite verbal-emotive, connects lots of dots constantly, connects feelings to words quickly, and uses many words to accurately detail memories of emotional, sensorial, and relational experiences. This bridge brain male may also dislike pecking orders, may avoid male aggression, and may dislike large groups of males.

If you have a client like this or know a man like this, you might find (should you be able to do the brain and biochemical testing) that he has more oxytocin in his bloodstream than a typical male and lower testosterone than many other males. You might find that his brain structure and neural processing might scan more like a woman's than another man's might.

Two scientists who have explored this area of study with brain scans are Daniel Amen and Simon Baron-Cohen. Amen has been able to show brain scan differences between typical males and bridge brain males. Baron-Cohen has gathered evidence that allows him to estimate approximately one in seven men and one in five women's brains may appear at or near the middle of the gender/brain spectrum.

We will focus on how to work strategically with bridge brains in Chapter 8 of this book.

News We Can Use

The tip of the iceberg information on gender difference, and the constant caveat that there are exceptions to every "rule," I hope will lead us toward seeing whether we can draw some conclusions that we can immediately use. Here are some, and I will also continue to utilize this brain information with you throughout the chapters of this book.

Emotional Intelligence Differences

In general, boys and men may bring to our offices a different way of dealing with stress and emotions than do girls and women. These are important differences to keep in mind as we move forward strategically and practically.

*Boys and men tend to avoid vulnerability and weakness when in verbal/emotive situations, such as when talking with a therapist. In their past years or decades of life, boys and men have generally been less innately successful at verbalizing complex emotions as have been their mothers, sisters, female teachers, girlfriends, wives, and female co-workers. To walk into a therapist's office, where their success goal will be to become facile at verbal/emotive strategies is, for them, tantamount to failing before they begin therapy. Thus, boys and men enter the traditional therapy format either knowing they will fail at it or just feeling somewhat "yucky/vulnerable/weak," a feeling that is often frightening to them. In short, from a neural point of view, boys and men often bring a primal *fear of failure* to our offices, and we, without realizing it, set them up to fail, because we try to reach them, activate them, talk to them as we would girls or women.

*Boys and men often tend to look for a way *out* of a crisis immediately, a way to *fix* a crisis, or a way to avoid a crisis *quickly*. This may be part of a fight/flight response that males in all cultures tend toward. Whereas females tend toward increasing their number of bonding relationships in order to work through crisis, many males try to decrease their number of bonding relationships. Where females may want more emotive input and more time to verbally process feelings, males may want to expel the feelings quickly. Our quiet therapy office is set up better for the female brain in crisis than the male—it is a small, sit-and-talk environment in which a patient is supposed to want to talk his/her way through a crisis "for as long as it takes."

*Boys and men often enter a *rest state* (boredom/zone out state) far more quickly than we realize. Their brains can "go blank" within minutes of listening to us asking questions or speaking softly to them. Once in a rest state, males' brains lose focus on memories, feelings, and words. If you have never before seen the Amen brain scans, you might not believe it. But as you consider those scans, I hope you will contemplate just how blank the male brain can become when that male body is sitting in a chair without stimulation.

*The female brain, in part thanks to more natural blood flow through the brain, and perhaps especially because of a higher degree of blood flow in a "concentration" part of the brain called the *cingulate gyrus*, will often ruminate on and revisit more emotional memories more constantly than the male. Males, on the other hand, tend to complete their rumination of an emotive memory quickly, having analyzed it and "finished with it" in order to focus on some other "task" than a feeling state they were unable to analyze.

*Throughout all this, when girls and women walk into our offices in crisis, their *oxytocin* level may rise, which in turn can increase activity in emotive and verbal centers of the brain. When boys walk into our office in crisis, their *testosterone* may rise, which can mitigate oxytocin (bonding) cells, decrease verbal-emotive activity in the male brain, and increase the need for physical movement, aggression, and hierarchical intervention.

At a natural baseline, then, girls and women specifically bring to our office a physiological need and desire to sit with us and bond with us verbally in order for them to get emotional help. On the other hand, at their own natural baseline, many boys and men bring to our offices a psycho-physiological need to bond with us only if we can get through their aggression-defenses, deal with their fight-or-flight mechanisms, meet their hierarchical needs, and satisfy their movement/physical activity motivations.

Culture Matters

In providing these details of male/female difference, I am providing a nature-base to a great deal of what we have been told is "all cultural," or "about socialization," or "nurture not nature." I hope that you will move forward in this book with your nature/nurture scales a little more evenly tilted now than perhaps they have been, or were when you got your academic training.

At the same time, culture, nurture, socialization matter immensely. Sarah's objection to brain research at the workshop was a powerful reminder that no matter how we view brain research and gender—whether we love it or hate it, use it or do not use it—we must see culture in its proper context. How each of our innate gender differences will manifest in the world around us as we grow and mature is directly linked to how we are nurtured, acculturated, and socialized. Nature and nurture are intricately connected.

For instance, while nature impacts gender development of the brain in utero, culture has also directly impacted the cell growth of brain development in utero. Studies comparing the parts of the brain in which Chinese and Americans do math show *different areas of the brain used by individuals in the different cultures.* This finding demonstrates the probability that generation upon generation of language use in a certain culture in certain areas of the brain (in Chinese, symbol-using centers of the brain; in American, word-producing centers) alter the genetic development of the brains produced in that culture.

Culture also, quite obviously, affects gender and the brain in the quality of opportunity each boy or girl is given during their childhoods. Studies consistently show that when girls are told by their nurturers and socializers that they are bad at math, they believe they are bad at math. Even though test scores across the globe indicate that girls and boys test out similarly in numerical calculation ability, girls still feel inferior to boys, on average, in overall math ability.

One of the most profound ways culture matters worldwide manifests in our therapy, counseling, and social work offices. Our psychological culture has developed a sit-and-talk therapeutic model that is better for girls than for boys, in general, and better for women than for men. If we change our psychological culture to accommodate and nurture male/female differences, we will increase our success with all children and all adults.

I hope we will move forward in this book with some agreement that both nature and nurture build human beings and both build gender. As I reveal and explore gender innovations with you throughout the rest of this book, I will often "tag" the innovation to a brain difference I have studied and worked to apply in the real world. Most of my innovations and strategies grow from my comparing brain scans and biochemical information with psychological and sociological studies, then sifting that material to match best practices with observation and experience.

Which Innovations Should I Try?

The strategies that follow in this book are one colleagues and I have used with success, but not all will fit your practice. You may read these strategies and applications and say about one or more, "This is too idealistic." For instance, you might measure a particular strategy against how you do your insurance billing and think, "That can't fit my practice." Or you might not be able to put some of these strategies in place because of rules in your institution or parent company. Or a particular client's personality disorder or psychotic state will mitigate any new effectiveness from one of the innovations in this book. Thus, even if the practices might feel theoretically or instinctively realistic to you, you might say, "This is too idealistic for my practice, or a particular client."

Please know that I have factored that issue into this book. I hope that when you come to an innovation or strategy you don't feel you can use, you will still keep reading. On the next page or the next, there will be a strategy you can use wherever you are. I am presenting all options—even the ideal—in hopes of providing both a menu of useful strategies and a possible overall vision, for greater dialogue, about the future of our profession.

Ultimately, I will be asking you to think, one client or patient at a time, about how to change certain traditional and inculcated aspects of our profession that do not serve boys and men as well as they serve girls and women. I believe that both the micro-vision and the macro-vision need to be put on the table in our books, conferences, academic studies, and thought processes, if we are to fully serve all clients and patients, female and male.

Deepening our understanding of brain and gender science is a second major step we can take to increase our effectiveness with the whole gender spectrum of boys and girls, and women and men. I hope you leave this chapter intrigued enough to keep deepening your exploration of gender science.

If you are a person who, like Sarah, worries about gender stereotyping, I hope you will remain vigilant about that, while also opening your practice to important elements of gender science itself. Once we take gender beyond stereotyping and into deep science, whole new pathways for growth and effective practice open up. One of those appears in the next chapter—a rethinking of our therapeutic role with some of our male clients.

Chapter 3: Therapists as Mentors to Boys and Men

"Boys and men are absolutely starved for mentors."

--Pastor Tim Wright, Community of Grace Church

In the sixteenth century, a man who would later be named St. John of the Cross wandered around Spain in search of his soul. Born the son of Jews in the small town of Fontiveros, he had been named Juan de Yepes y Alvarez by his parents. When Juan was still a boy, his family converted to Christianity, and soon after, Juan's father died. This death hurt the son deeply, but with his mother and family left impoverished, Juan did not stop to grieve— he worked with his brothers and mother to support the family in any way he could.

When Juan was a teenager, the single-parent family moved to a larger city, Medina del Campo, where there was more work. There, the Jesuits began to mentor Juan into full adulthood. Juan entered seminary and prepared for the priesthood. In his early twenties, Juan met Teresa of Avila and felt changed by the grace of her calling to God. Juan made a decision to give himself to "the life of the soul." He devoted himself to others and the church, becoming a confessor for Teresa's order of nuns.

By then, Juan's boyhood of hardship had turned into a youthful, then adult, time of constant mentoring by both men and women. In his life were loving people to turn to when times were difficult. As a priest of the church, he in turn devoted his life to mentoring others. This foundation for self-development turned out to be important, as Juan's adult psyche was tested with extended time in prison and torture by betrayers and psychopaths. Political and religious camps and sects battled constantly in Europe during Juan's priesthood, and he found himself on the wrong end of the power struggle. In prison, he was beaten by other "priests" so severely that he became permanently crippled.

In this same prison—housed in the basement of a holy monastery—Juan had a number of visions. He saw himself with God and he heard God's call to his soul. In a state of abject suffering and pain, he realized there was still much learning and growth needed of him if he were to fulfill his destiny. Mentoring was still needed for him and of him. He deepened his understanding of "soul life," "God's love," and "mission and purpose" through direct mentoring—at least so he envisioned—by God himself.

Juan left prison to become St. John of the Cross, whose poetry and essays have lived on as some of the most impressive in Western literature. Among his works is a poem, translated by Daniel Ladinsky, "'Dig Here,' the Angel Said." In this poem, an angel appears to a man who kneels in prayer. She asks if she has met him before, even as a boy. He isn't sure. So she tells him a story of a hard-working man who worries constantly that he can't feed his family.

"Are you this man?" She asks.

"Yes, that's me," he says.

She mentors him to go out behind the monastery, into the forest. "Now, dig here," she says, "in your soul, in your soul."

John gets down on his knees and digs with his bare hands. Gradually, "he feels strength in his limbs that he had not known," and he finds the treasure he has been seeking. Finding it, "his relationship with the world changed." St. John concludes: "finding our soul's beauty does that—gives us tremendous freedom from worry."

The Role of the Mentor

Among the primal fears boys and men face throughout life is the fear of failure. Every boy and every man knows he is being and will be defined by what he accomplishes—with his body, his mind, his sexual energy, his work, his devotion to family and friends, his moral and spiritual *performance*. Boys and men are defined and define themselves by success or lack of success. They find success, love, and depth of purpose beyond their fear of failure with the help of developmental and lifelong mentors.

St. John of the Cross was always on the edge of failing, but succeeded in some of the deepest ways possible for a human being. He sought out and found constant mentoring toward increasingly difficult goals of compassion, care-giving, love, and character. Throughout his life, this man sought freedom to be himself—to pursue and discover the treasure of his destiny as a man—while equally focusing on devoting himself to mentoring others toward their own inner emotional and spiritual freedom.

The previous two chapters have been, I hope, useful in their own right, but also, good foundation for this chapter. I believe that a third step in helping boys and men involves understanding that, for both biological and social reasons, boys are hungry for mentoring from therapists.

Boys and men are beautiful combinations of impulsiveness and moral clarity, directedness and aimlessness, self-denial and hedonism. As their brains and bodies are evolving along male trajectories, they live in search of clear moral principles and a purpose in life, only to discover that "morality" and "purpose" are far more complex than even their own parents let on. They suffer pain and even tragedy, as Juan did. In our era, boys are more likely to lose fathers to divorce than death, but even divorce can attack the boy's psyche with pain that can seem, unless the boy gets help, to surpass understanding.

As anthropological data constantly shows, throughout history and across all cultures, male biology and socialization have been understood to require constant mentoring of males by elders. Without mentors, boys were seen as going astray or not finding their talents and gifts. Without mentors, they could become immoral, lost, undirected, unmotivated, and destructive. With mentors, they learned to serve family and society, develop moral and spiritual depth, and succeed in life.

In our era, as in St. John's, mentors are still essential (we often call them "role models" now), and they are immanently available to males, if we in our profession will re-frame, somewhat, our self-image. St. John's mentors were priests and nuns; our sons' mentors can be, quite often, therapists and social workers. I will argue in this chapter that they need to be—we in our profession need to *mentor* boys and men. Such mentoring will require a reframe of some of our therapeutic theories and practice, for "mentoring" is more goal-oriented than traditional therapy is often practiced to be.

I believe that when our sons (and their families) experience pain, family difficulty, addiction, loss of a parent, loss of male role models, failure in school, rejection by a girlfriend, or any number of other traumas, they turn to the psychology profession for help, not only because we are institutionally present in our era as "therapists," but also, subconsciously and at a very "male" and "primal" level, because we are seen by them as potentially the "priests and nuns" or "mentors" of our era. Though boys and men call us "counselors," "therapists," "psychologists" (because they respect the names we have given ourselves), these males hope we will be their mentors. Males have always been starved for mentors and, in our present era, they are more starved than ever before.

Boys and Men Need Mentors

In this chapter, I hope we will take a third step toward helping boys and men more effectively by adding the face of the mentor to the many faces we must and can wear as counselors, therapists, and mental health professionals. In becoming the kind of mentor I will discuss in this chapter, we will remain loyal to the psychological diagnosis we give the boy or man, but also we add the diagnosis of "mentor hunger" to whatever other diagnosis we have given.

After more than twenty years of counseling boys and men, I feel confident in saying that when most boys come to us, they need from us the kind of *spiritual depth* (care of psyche or soul) a mentor gave young Juan, for they are living in the wake of family or community tragedy or abandonment, and thus, are hungry for insight, attention, action, direction, goal-setting, and love from people who know what the life of the male soul is and can be. When they are teenagers, males hunger for mentoring toward correct ways to utilize the significant inner energy and impulses that flood through them during puberty and adolescence—energy that makes adolescent males feel as though they are both repulsive and radiant.

When they become adult males ("men"), males feel hunger for mentoring in even more subtle ways—whatever fear of failure remains unresolved in their first twenty-five years of life becomes a haunting presence in their adulthood, creating destruction in some aspect (or, ultimately, all aspects) of their adult male life. Since boys and men, in general, come to us when they are in crisis—in their dark night of the soul—they come to us immersed in fear of failure and inadequacy. Their sacred work has been torn away from them by recession, or some other cause of unemployment; their children have been taken from them; their marriages or other relationships are broken; their bodies and minds are betraying them toward self-destructive addictions or other negative patterns.

In their dark night of the soul, these males hunger for the kind of help they have always hungered for, since the beginning of time: for new mentors, both external ones such as therapists, and the internal mentors we in the therapy profession can help them discover. They need us to be visionaries who will help them face the primal elements against which males constantly measure their own life-success.

A key point in all this is that, as males, they come to us differently than females. Given their biology and socialization, boys and men develop their sense of identity first by their performance, second by their quantity of relationships, and third, by their cognizance of their feelings and emotions. Females develop their identity with less hierarchy of performance, relationship, and emotion, i.e. with more balance of the three. While girls and women need mentoring just as much as boys and men, girls and women tend to seek out more intimate relationships in general than do males, and they stay with them, quite often, longer than males; thus they don't necessarily approach therapy with the same hunger to find a singular, goal-oriented, task-focused, and wise mentor who will help them perform better: they often approach therapy in need of a friend and confidant.

But for boys and men, there is less need for "someone to talk to" and more need for goal-oriented mentoring. As males, these boys, adolescents, pre-adults, or adults are somewhat like St. John of the Cross, though generally not as verbal or poetic as he was. They come to us because they have been told that we carry some kind of *mastery*. It is this mastery they want us to share with them. Mastery implies goals to be accomplished and talents for mentoring other people in how to accomplish the goals. When they come to us, males come because they have been told that we know something elemental about the male mind. When they come to us, they come wanting us to teach them where to dig for the treasure of their future devotion to others and personal success in the hierarchies of performance.

If this makes sense to you, then I hope it will make sense that if you and I don't see each boy and man who comes to our profession with this truth in mind, we may miss the hope with which boys and men enter our office. Not understanding or realizing the male hunger for therapist to be also a "master," we may create the circumstance in which the boy or man or family or couple comes to us for the brief period of time it takes to see that we don't have the power of the mentor. Understanding this lack, he or they may leave us quickly behind.

Important Questions

To look at this more closely, please ask some questions with me, and see where your answers take you.

Right now, do we in the psychology profession see ourselves as visionary and wise mentors of the male soul? Do we see ourselves as "priests and nuns" to tragic, beautiful, confused, desperate boys and men? Or do we tend to limit our vision of ourselves to "counselor," "therapist," "psychologist," "social worker"?

Do we begin our assessment of the male in our care by seeing him as a "male" on a very "male" biological, social, and spiritual journey, or do we insist to ourselves that he is not male or female, but merely or mainly a "person" who needs "psychological assistance?"

Do we understand that the male in our care is not female, not a girl, not a woman (though he may share many qualities with females), and therefore he may need a different relational approach from us than many of our female clients may need? Or do we just hope that what we do with girls and women will work with boys and men?

Do we understand that this male enters our office searching for character development regarding how to access and achieve his life purpose? Do we understand that his life is very much about battling both demons and angels as he tries to ascend and descend hierarchies of failure and success? Are we willing to become mentors of those battles?

Do we realize that when a boy or man enters our room, he often believes that he has failed already at being a man, being free, being devoted, being real? Do we know that it is his failure that brought him to us? Do we see how completely his believes he has failed, even as he presents myriad defenses to us? Are we willing to do battle with his defenses as a mentor would battle the defenses of a traumatized boy who will need a little bit of coddling and a lot of challenge toward the good?

In short, do we see ourselves as "therapists," "counselors," "psychologists," and "social workers," who want to get people to talk to us from within our own guiding theoretical base, or can we also see ourselves as mentors and guides to boys and men who are on a male journey of success and life of the soul?

As you contemplate these questions, where do they take you? Does the St. John example make sense? Can you feel how he faced so much strife and trauma (and joy and grace) that he needed goal-oriented and role-oriented mentors to help him dig into holistic self-understanding in order to heal his response to trauma?

As you ponder these thoughts and questions, I hope you'll bring to bear the brain research we explored in Chapter 2; in that light, I hope it will make some sense that boys and men might be desperate from mentors in ways that fit their biology. Male biology is a higher-risk, less-emotive, less-verbal biology than female biology often is. Males need mentors at a baseline biological level, especially in adolescence and adulthood, because their high-risk and less verbal/emotive biology needs the structure and content of mentoring in order to acculturate and socialize fully into social and familial success. Males need mentors and role models from very young ages in order to learn how to contain and direct their substantial energies.

Mentoring in the First Session

When a client, male or female, walks into my office, I constantly remind myself of the reason I entered my profession: because I felt that I was called to *psychology*, a discipline in which I would help care for the *"psyches" (souls)* of other people. When a male client walks into my office, I know that males are "cut-to-the-chase" challengers to me and, I believe, all of us—and helpfully so—asking us to get right to the work, in the first session, on the goal of caring for the male psyche.

To go deeper into this, I mean: talk is cheap, to most boys and men. If the "talk-therapy" is not authoritative mentoring regarding something(s) the boy or man feels as relevant, he will more likely drift away. If the talk is not, at least initially, quite surgical in its usefulness, he will not return to us. If the talk is not focused on specific outcomes in the first session, he will suspect he is wasting his money and time in our offices. Talk is cheap.

Mentoring is priceless to males, and they know it. Boys and men silently say to us: "A mentor teaches me how to succeed in life and love. A mentor listens carefully, demands respect, allows for push-pull debates, has authority, is wise and willing to speak wisdom, sees the rest of the road, leads the mentee to a good place, teaches useful knowledge, teaches a boy how to become a man." When a male client walks into my door, I try to "hear" his speech to me. I hear: "If you don't become my mentor, I may feel lost, but if you will show me your mastery and mentor me, right living is possible for me, and right living is what I desperately want, even when I lose my battles with my demons for a time."

Because I believe boys and men enter our offices looking for mastery and mentors, I try to meet this immediate need by personally clarifying my role with them in the first session, i.e. making sure they know I am hopeful that they will see me as a mentor, as they need to. In pursuing this course, I am tacitly saying that deep psychological work will be housed, at least to some extent, in the mentor role, though I am honest with them that mentoring is not a substitute for medications, hospitalizations, and other interventions taking place outside my office.

Here are some of my comments from first sessions with boys, men, families and couples.

*I see part of my job as being about mentoring you on issues you are having trouble with. I believe that you have come here hoping I will mentor you, and I take that hope very seriously.

*At the end of every session, you and I will discuss some "tasks" (homework) for next week. (For boys, I say, "It will be fun and important." For adolescent males, "It will be different than school work, I promise you." For men, "You won't hate doing this, believe me. But it will take character and focus.")

*At the end of most sessions, I'll ask you what the takeaways and take home value were for you from this session. We'll make sure you're getting something specific out of my mentoring.

*If you're in a very emotional place, I'll help you go deeper into those emotions, but if you're not, you're not. I will respect that. Mentoring is not just about feelings and emotions.

*The effects of your mother-son relationship and your father-son relationship are going to come up in our work together. Part of a mentor's job is to help you determine how your relationship (or lack of relationship) with these two people is still affecting your life.

*You're in control of your counseling, so I won't control you, but as your mentor I'll feel free to direct you toward things I think you're missing or resisting.

*I'm a spiritual person who won't impose a religion on you but will refer to your 'soul' as part of what we're focused on.

*I will be as concerned with your character as your feelings. Counseling is about character and moral mentoring as much as it is about emotional work, and these are all interwoven together, which is part of why mentors and counselors are needed.

*If I think your assessment of a situation is not functional, I'll tell you directly. For instance, if you tell me you're having sex twice a week and that's just not enough sex for your wife to prove she loves you, I'll tell you what the national average is, and you might have to reassess what's really happening in your relationship

*If you have come here looking for me to help you get a divorce, you need to know my bias: if you and your spouse have children in the house still, and you as a couple are not victimized by, nor perpetrating, abuse or other substantial trauma, I will try to help you stay married, rather than get divorced. When kids are involved, my bias is to first try to help parents stay married. In areas like this, I am very goal-oriented. You need to know this and make sure you are okay with that.

*If it becomes clear that you and your spouse need to get a divorce, I will support both of you in transitioning, with special emphasis on helping both of you work together for the good of your children.

*If you think something I'm saying sounds like psycho-babble, let me know. I'm pretty strong. I can take some confrontation.

At a workshop in a hospital setting, participants reacted to these comments. One said, "You sound pretty directive, but I as a therapist am not directive. From a theoretical standpoint, I am passive, for specific theoretical reasons."

I responded. "I understand what you're getting at, but I am pretty directive with males, especially in the first few sessions, because no matter the theory we use, if we lose the males within a few weeks of therapy, we need to rethink. I find that being directive with males is crucial to keeping them in counseling or therapy. Of course, this directive-ness needs to be accomplished without feeling controlling to the client or patient, so we have to walk a fine line as clinicians."

Another participant said, "I don't dialogue or give-and-take a lot. I prefer to listen and let the client direct the sessions."

I asked, "Does this work better for females or males? In other words, do you retain your male clients, with your method, for the time it takes for the client to break through or change?" The therapist promised to ponder this by looking at her data, but she said she suspected she retained female clients longer than male by practicing the quiet therapy she had become accustomed to.

Another participant said, "I'm not sure I could just flat out say, 'I will focus on helping you as a couple stay married.' That seems disrespectful of where the couple might be, and what they might need."

"Yes," I agreed, "it was definitely a weird feeling the first time I said it aloud to a couple, especially when the couple had come to me because both people had had affairs, and the marriage was in severe distress. But couples are generally so appreciative of my stating my bias up front, they react well to it. And I stand by my word: if it becomes clear that the marriage cannot be saved, I am equally focused on mentoring the couple toward an amicable divorce."

Another participant said, "You seem to want to establish a certain kind of intense intimacy with the client pretty quickly. I prefer to have it develop over time." I asked, "Would you agree, though, that guys are pretty cut-to-the-chase?" She agreed that they were. "Let's keep looking at this, then," I suggested. "You might be waiting too long to establish your bond with males."

Another said, "You're promising a lot in each session. I'm seeing six clients per day. I can't promise to always give homework, and talk about takeaways, and so on." I offered, "If you worked with men in any other work or business setting, wouldn't you be quite clear with them about expected outcomes? Wouldn't you review the man's accomplishments with him, then set new goals at the end of a meeting?" She agreed that she probably would. While therapy is not a business meeting, she got my point.

All these and many other questions led our dialogue to a deeper understanding of boys and men from a "male-mentoring" viewpoint. We talked about how some personality disorders or mental health issues do not fit this model, and that is important to note. At the same time, the participants agreed that many of their clients, especially their male youth, were hungry for mentoring. We talked about how a mentor—whether a cleric, athletic coach, teacher, family elder—provides wisdom and information, is directive toward task-success, and teaches the mentee a great deal about life and emotions through directionality and task-focus, thus we talked about how models of successful male mentors exist all around our profession for our study.

We agreed that males don't crave directive mentoring every minute—they are quite capable of and enjoy being present and silent with a mentor. But, too, they want direction. When they don't get enough direction from their fathers, mothers, clerics, coaches, or their therapists, they flounder. When they do get direction, they can better discover life-purpose, and fulfill goals of service and success. When a therapist moves his or her practice more toward the directionality of the mentor, more boys and men get the help they need.

The Need to Close the Intimacy Gap Quickly

The issue of establishing bonding with the male relatively quickly was discussed a great deal in this group. We discussed the possibility that many boys and men need to have hierarchical and relational connection established quickly so that their individual gravitation toward intimacy with the therapist is less scary for the male.

Let me explain. My sense is that if a boy comes into your office and you remain distant, he is torn between wanting intimacy with you and also deciding you're not worth spending his limited emotional energy on. So torn, he may choose to remain self-protectively distant for a few sessions, until he leaves therapy. In certain instances, of course, he may try to open himself up to you, but as he finds you distant from him (i.e. just sitting, listening, nodding, waiting, and, in his mind, "not engaging,") he may feel betrayed.

It is important to remember that a male's own vulnerability may be so frightening to his developing or established core self that he cannot commit to opening up that vulnerability repeatedly, without constantly having to battle an instinctual fear of his own weakness and failure. Given that he probably sees little immediate worth in sitting and talking to someone about feelings, anyway, he'll often choose to avoid dealing with the fear of intimacy and vulnerability by specifically withholding intimacy from you. If you are someone who also withholds intimacy, the male will probably leave you behind.

If, however, you establish strong and flexible boundaries for intimacy early on (which is something a teacher, coach, cleric, or other mentor does relatively quickly upon meeting a person and bringing that person into the structure of the class, game, or religion), you show the boy or man that you understand his vulnerability; you show him that you are part of a structured environment in which, when he needs you to, you will hold his heart and soul safely in your "engaged" hands.

In reading these words, you might say, "Okay, but what about a narcissist, for instance? You can't just start creating intimacy with him by setting goals and telling him what to do. He needs a rewarding object, not another alpha." Fascinatingly, while this would seem to argue against my point and counseling style, I have found that even narcissists are often hungry for mentoring. I have found that, with practice, it is possible to be both a rewarding object and a mentor to narcissists. We do not have to become a competitive alpha in order to create intense and immediate emotional intimacy with males.

It is always worth remembering that girls and women are more likely to come into your office unconsciously (or consciously) believing that they have relatively infinite access to emotions. No matter what culture you study, you notice that, in their everyday lives, girls' and women's minds may be constantly working on feelings. Tiny details of tone or facial expression in interactions with a friend or teacher can create hours, even days, of rumination in a 16-year-old girl. Some words spoken by a husband at dinner can create hours of rumination that obstruct a wife's sleep. Their own well of emotion and emotional language is deep for girls and women, and they know it. They sense in themselves, quite often, near infinitude of emotional focus.

Males, on the other hand, more often come into your office without the same sense of constant feeling and inward rumination. While males can certainly ruminate sleeplessly about a wife's comment, or ponder a girlfriend's motives incessantly, males also know themselves as people with *limited* stores of emotional energy; and they specifically enter your office ready to *not* reveal their emotional material. They especially guard this limited emotional material with someone who is emotionally distant.

Added to this is the fact that males often see themselves as emotional failures. If not before, then by the time they reach adolescence, they generally see how much more adept their girlfriends are regarding emotions. Once they enter an adult love-relationship, most men feel emotionally charged and awakened for the first year or two of attraction, but then the pheromones and hormones back off, and they enter the next stage of relationship or marriage, in which their lack of emotional resources appears again. Relatively quickly, they may be told by their spouses that they as men are not emotionally fulfilling. Later, when they enter couple therapy to stave off a divorce, they hear their wives say to the therapist, "He won't communicate his feelings to me." "He wants sex but not communication." "He loves me by giving me things but not by caring about my emotional life." "He doesn't know how to be emotionally intimate."

Some men access their emotions constantly—yes. But most do not access them as much as girls and women do. This is not a flaw in men, actually. It can be immensely functional. Sometimes, the constant, incessant accessing of feelings can be detrimental to functional life. For us as practitioners, the emotional difference needs to at least partially guide therapeutic practice. If we are to serve boys and men, we must think more than we do about how to intimately mentor boys and men from the first moment we meet them, rather than how to remain emotionally distant until they open up to us emotionally.

As you experiment with this, remember: most boys and men feel that the wait-him-out modalities constitute a flawed system of thinking about gender in clients: it grows from "gender" mainly being seen in our profession as "what works for females." Boys and men don't know how to say it to us in words, but they want to say: "Within your present thinking about therapy are flaws in 1) your understanding of the emotional resources men have, 2) your understanding of your role as therapists in caring for males."

Ultimately, my point is this: boys and men may not say it aloud to us, but they are trying to say, "I desperately need you to mentor me from our very first session onward. Please don't wait me out. Become my mentor immediately, so that I don't have to leave you in order to drift toward someone else who might or might not be out there for me."

Thus I do try to create emotional intimacy quickly with many of my male clients, in the ways I listed above—from setting up homework to being honest about my biases to inviting confrontation. This kind of emotional intimacy has helped me keep males in my counseling practice, and keep them moving forward in their psychological work.

Can Women Be Mentors to Boys and Men?

More specific ways to strategically expand the therapy profession to consciously include a mentor's role will continue to evolve as this book evolves. Before going further, however, let's look at the questions female therapists have asked.

"Can women be 'mentors' to men?"

"Can women be as good with boys and men as men are?"

"If we keep going in a male-centric direction, won't we end up saying women can't be as good with boys and men as men are?"

Women are amazing therapists for boys and men, and they become especially amazing the more they are willing to expand their role and strategies as women to include being and becoming effective mentors to males. If women will work toward being Teresa of Avila for Juan, they will be working toward being both therapist and mentor. Teresa of Avila took a position on things with Juan; she told him when she thought he was right and when she thought he was wrong. She leaned forward intimately towards Juan, rather than sitting back and watching him.

Practically speaking, how can a woman therapist expand her role into "being a mentor of boys and men?" Three particular ways appear in this story by a man, Ray McSoley, who found himself in the presence of a mentor, Gurumayi—a Hindu guru, a woman mentor, who knew how to reach males.

Ray was 49 at the time of this experience—in a difficult time in his life. A dog trainer by profession, he had been called to enter Gurumayi's ashram in Fallsburg, New York in order to help her with her dog. As he performed his daily job, he became involved in some of the psychological and spiritual practices of the ashram. In one group meeting, participants talked with Gurumayi after meditation; when she heard them say something that made good sense, she, in Ray's words, "bopped them on the head or shoulders with her peacock feathers."

On one of the days, Ray observed Gurumayi as she told a man (who had expressed regret about being a loner/hermit) that he was not a hermit at all. Gurumayi said, "A hermit loves people. You're not a hermit; you're an arrogant recluse." This direct critique of the other male affected Ray deeply—it was a critique of himself, by this woman mentor, a critique he had heard from others in other places, but never quite "heard" as he heard it in Gurumayi's voice.

After the group session, Ray walked up to Gurumayi to thank her for what she had said. "I thought I came here to train a dog," he quipped. "The joke's on me!" Gurumayi laughed in agreement, lifted her peacock feathers, and bopped Ray on the head with them. This gesture touched Ray deeply.

"I quickly left the meditation hall," he reported later, "and went directly to my room, where I cried tears of joy for a long, long, time."

Three clues to reaching males appear in this slight story.

Tasks can initially be the focus of the woman mentor's challenge to the male client—the mentor makes sure to contextualize at least some of therapy/change into actual work that needs to be done. In Ray's case, the "task" was to train the dog, and after that, to meditate, then to engage in other tasks of the retreat. If a woman therapist is going to challenge herself to mentor males in her practice, and especially if she is someone who bonds mainly through listening, she may well need to challenge herself to verbally suggest directive courses of action to her male clients. Her change toward task-focus will give her male clients a sense of "having a job to do," "getting help with objectives and goals" from a woman mentor. These jobs and tasks will not generally be exactly the jobs and tasks the boy's mother or man's wife gives him, which is very useful.

Direct discernment is used by the successful female mentor. Gurumayi does not avoid making yes/no, either/or, you're wrong/I'm right distinctions regarding the deepest illusions a man carries within himself. She practices insight-based therapy at its most piercing and truth-oriented. When an insight of truth pierces a man's armor, and in the right circumstances of task focus and environmental safety, he will generally feel the piercing as a crucial, joyful moment in his life. He may put up defenses (anyone can do that at any time), but also, his respect for the mentor will help him accept the critique.

"Don't hold back," is what a man often, unconsciously, wants to say to his mentor. When women therapists can 'hear' him thinking that thought, they succeed better. "Tell me the truth!" the man is crying inwardly. "Please!" Men and boys often feel that women coddle them or wait for them to "know what's going on inside me," or "guilt" them, when, in fact, the male wishes the woman therapist would hear the boy or man saying, "I need someone to tell me the truth about myself." If the woman uses the man's unconscious yearning as an opening to shame, guilt, or manipulate the male, she may very well lose him; if, however, she tells him a truth like Gurumayi did, he can be deeply moved.

Rituals of person, time, and place are important markers for male relationships with mentors. Gurumayi's mentoring ritual is to bop clients on the head with peacock feathers. Rarely if ever will you or I use this particular Indian ritual! But the concept of physical ritual is ancient with males, and useful to therapy.

Your physical rituals in your offices can be handshakes, high fives, a prod of the shoulder, a hug (when appropriate). Ritualized physical contact brings boys and men into trust of the mentor. Males are very physical creatures. It is a rare mentor of a male in any walk of life who does not develop some form of a high five/hand shake/shoulder bop or other *physical* congratulation when a psychological success-marker has been reached.

Sometimes a therapist will hear me talk about this and she will say: "My theory and process don't fit this. I do not touch a client." I ask: "Could you at least shake hands and make eye contact at the beginning of a session and at the end?" Except in the most severe cases of mental illness or sex addiction therapy, she agrees that she can.

Males respect people who ritually structure environments for them. The rituals make the environment and relationship more emotionally safe for them than an un-ritualized relationship or environment is. A therapy office is an unsafe environment for a male, at least at first—it is a potentially dangerous world of emotional vulnerability. Rituals are needed for safety.

And fortunately, not all rituals need to be physical. Rituals can be rituals of process or object. For instance, the client and the female (or male) therapist can play a verbal challenge game (this process works especially well with boys) before every session. The verbal game can involve trivia the boy likes (the therapist can study baseball on the Internet and ask questions of the boy about the 1976 World Series at the beginning of a session). Therapists can play musical instruments, briefly, at a session's beginning—thus using a ritual of object. If it fits the boy or man, a guided meditation can begin sessions; the meditation can occur while the man holds in his hand an object sacred to him. This combines ritual of process with ritual of object.

Mentors Challenge Males

As you look at options, and as you experiment with them in the male/gender context of this book, you may feel some ambivalence, i.e. you may gradually feel yourself moving into a "challenger" role with males, but this move may at first seem counterintuitive, especially to you as a woman. Female therapists often report to me that they want to make their therapeutic environment safer by making it *less* challenging, *more* safe. As I say things like, "You need a way in your practice to 'bop the man on the head,'" they may feel off-put.

Yet, for many boys and men, the *more challenging* the work is, the *safer* it feels. Mentors of males always provide challenges. Mentors of males take the risk of "bopping him on the head" when appropriate, because mentors of males know that these quick, definitive, challenging rituals reach boys and men at deep levels. If you are a woman therapist who feels ambivalent about this, I hope you will talk with other men and women in the profession about this until it resonates, at least somewhat.

There will be exceptions to everything, and challenge-rituals are not needed all the time, but they can be a threshold point for women who are working with and hoping to add mentoring of boys and men to their toolbox. When women succeed at adjusting their therapy practices to include more challenge and less "sitting back and listening," their clients can succeed more completely, and the therapists themselves can feel less burnout and failure in their professional life. Things will get easier with male clients, and those clients will stay in therapy as needed.

Female Therapist as Team Leader

A further way for a woman therapist to both provide therapy and mentoring to male clients is to become the leadership focal point of a boy's success in searching for male mentors. Gina Cuen, a therapist who lives just outside Mexico City, did exactly this. As a counselor, she had been working with a number of boys and families in her area and noticed a gradual and tragic loss of the connection of boys with their fathers.

After reading *The Wonder of Boys,* she wrote me the first of many powerful emails about her work. "Your idea of creating a 'male tribe' for boys within city environments gave me, as a woman counselor, the idea to help create the 'Batsi tribe.' Our Batsi tribe is now in our second successful year, with twenty boys and fathers and other men who meet monthly in 'tribe meetings' and do organized (and disorganized) events, retreats, trips together."

Gina saw that a part of her role as a woman professional/mentor working with males was to "organize the guys' lives," i.e. to help the "relationally disorganized" fathers/men/boys to build organized social/emotional connections between males. She realized that boys needed "therapy" from their fathers and other men just as much as they needed therapy from a therapist or counselor. Acting on that instinct, she became an organizing mentor to not just a few boys, but a whole "tribe."

To pursue specific strategies for the facilitation of these "tribes," please see *The Wonder of Boys*, which provides whole chapters on "tribes" and "three family system" models for contemporary families and communities. You might also look at *The Minds of Boys*; in that book, Kathy Stevens and I developed the "parenting team" for use by team leaders like yourself. That model provides women therapists with many specific ways to help males find male and other mentors.

In both these models, the therapist helps get siblings, in-laws, grandparents, and many others involved in the boy's (or man's) therapy. These people become an essential *support team* for the boy's or man's development. Sometimes, the counselor-mentor will attend family team meetings to help all members work with the boy (more about therapist visits to homes and other locations appears in Chapter 6 of this book).

This therapeutic/mentor role can be especially helpful to the therapist when she is "having no luck getting through to a particular male" in her office. She can back off the sit-and-talk therapy for a while, and move to the task focus of helping the male find his full range of mentors among coaches, teachers, clerics, neighbors, older siblings. As the therapist moves into this mentoring role for a time, pressure is taken off the male to have to "talk" to the female therapist "about my feelings." At the same time, the therapist is doing something just as valuable—team building that will last her patient a lifetime.

Regarding this organizational/mentoring role, a therapist wrote me: "When I saw myself as an integral part of the boy's three-family system, I found a better way into his life than the sitting-and-talking method I was trying."

A psychologist wrote regarding a divorced father of three girls she was working with: "With this man, just sitting down for therapy with me once a week felt ineffective or like blame and shame, but my efforts to mentor a family team around him felt positive to him."

Can women be as good with boys and men in therapeutic settings as men are? Yes, absolutely, in their own way. Not only have I observed female success anecdotally in the therapeutic world, but our Gurian Institute team has collected significant statistical data regarding the effectiveness of training female teachers and counselors in new boy-friendly methods.

Initially, many women have started our Institute's training with the question, "If this male/female brain stuff is true, can I as a woman teach/counsel boys as well as men might?" Women teachers and counselors come out of the training realizing that the skills boys need from teachers, counselors, and school systems are skills both women and men can use in their own ways. Boys and men need both women and men in all their learning and growing environments.

Getting Inspiration from Your Own Mentors

Whether you are woman or man, you may have noticed something very useful when you bonded with your mentors in the past: the man or woman who changed your life did so because he or she saw *who you were,* including your gender. The mentor, figuratively, grabbed hold of who you were, mirroring you, challenging you, admiring you, helping you transform who you were to its highest success potential. Along the way, you learned more than you knew before about love, compassion, care, and success.

No matter who you are, and no matter how intransigent is the male in your office right now, this boy or man is most prone to open up to you if you mentor who he is—including his maleness, his *male identity.* Whether you are a woman or a man, you can do this, and you know you can because no matter your gender, you most probably had cross-gender mentors as well as same-gender mentors during your first thirty years of life.

As I wrestle in my counseling practice with my own balancing of counseling/mentoring roles, I often sit back in a peaceful moment, close my eyes and do a meditative exercise of remembering my own mentors, past and present. It is almost always an inspiring exercise. I remember mentors, both male and female, without whom I would have been much more lost than I already was as a troubled boy and young man.

Take a moment to try this silent meditation. Remember back to your mentors when you were the age of the client giving you the most challenge right now.

Perhaps you were athletic kid. You bonded with your tennis coach, let's say—immediately upon meeting you, the tennis coach assessed your strengths and weaknesses. While encouraging you to improve against your weaknesses, he/she especially guided you to build your strengths to heights you had not imagined you could accomplish before. He/she became to you not just a "coach" but a mentor because this person saw into you, and figured out a crucial aspect of your skill-set in order to help you develop.

In college or graduate school, perhaps your mentor sat with you over coffee, talking about whatever you needed to talk about, and you loved him or her for it, and you felt understood—not just because you talked to a confidant, but also because you knew where you stood, you were challenged by him/her, you failed but were not condemned, you succeeded and were given precious admiration-through-action by someone who had made you earn your praise.

Each of these people changed your life because they saw who you were and could be. They pushed their own particular gifts toward you so that you had to either resist or engage your own gifts. They were people of action as well as words.

Boys and men need that kind of mentoring from both women and men. Boys and men are certainly a diverse group, but they are also, in general, hungry to be in the presence of peers or elders who do not apply a general emotional rule to them, but, instead, see what assets and liabilities hide in the male, and mentor those directly, precisely, compassionately, and actively.

And for the boys and men who especially fit my descriptions above, e.g. males who inherently lack the ability to do complex feeling conversations we as therapists have been told to assume every person can somehow manage, the role of the mentor becomes the absolute crucial role for the therapist. If the therapist does not move toward a mentoring role (always returning, when possible, to the emotional/psychological confidant role), she/he will lose the male client.

It is certainly true that some boys and men, especially those who we might call "bridge brains," or "therapy lovers," enjoy traditional sit-and-talk therapy just as it is. At the same time, many do not. For many of them, mentors are needed. If we look carefully at becoming both counselors *and* mentors to boys and men, troubled males may well find the mentoring they did not get from mom or dad or someone else in their lives who abandoned or hurt them, and we ourselves may very well become the person we initially entered this profession to be: a person who protects the souls (psyches) of all the people in our care—a person who does what it takes to save the lives of all human beings, including boys and men.

Part II

Specific Strategies for Working with Boys and Men

"This is how he grows: by being defeated
decisively by infinitely greater beings."

--Rainer Maria Rilke

Chapter 4: Using Male Core-Themes in Therapy

"What is important is to accept the challenge, to fight the battle. What is important is to choose an opponent more powerful than oneself."

--Elie Wiesel

When I was a boy, my family lived for a year in Laramie, Wyoming. I enjoyed the beauty of the high mountains in the distance and the barren snow-blinding plains nearby. Because we had moved from lush, tropical Honolulu to mountainous and "Western" Laramie, I as a boy could not have felt a more stark contrast in physical environment.

In social environment, too, I now lived in a different world, moving from an immensely diverse big-city population of Islanders, Asians, and every other possible social grouping, to a relatively homogeneous, white small town. Also, I joined a population in which some of the other kids were not accustomed to, or just did not like, Jews. Within a month of my appearance at school in Laramie, I was being bullied. One major incident involved a group of boys following me on my walk home after school, pulling me into a yard, holding me down, and pulling on my nostrils with pliers to "see if the Jew nose will grow."

Core Themes in the Male Mind

In both the epigraph to this second part of this book by the German poet, Rainer Maria Rilke, and in the epigraph to this chapter by the Jewish philosopher, Elie Wiesel, words mirror each other from two cultures, German and Jewish, cultures that became enemies just seventy years ago, and now are friends. Both quotations make the same point: boys and men learn and grow through confrontations and experiences that pit their sometimes meager resources against forces, beings, themes greater than themselves.

You can see this male trance of battle in literally anything males do. Males constantly measure and are constantly being measured. They engage in real battles or pretend battles, inventing myriad games in which to do battle. If you have sons, you see this urge in their video games or graphic novels. If you educate and help adolescent boys, you can listen to rap songs as a therapeutic primer: battle over territory is rampant in these songs, and in the harsh life of adolescent males. If you work with men in a corporation, you may notice men interrupt others in order to "make their point," and even when you see men who say or do nothing combative in their friendship group or workplace, you might notice them returning to their desks and "doing battle with the stock market until I'm number one."

The need to pit himself against what is larger is a prime motivator for male development everywhere on earth. Every culture has art forms and historical and evolutionary songs that reach out to males to engage in a warrior trance in service of and against large forces. While some boys are exceptions to this trance, even the most sensitive boys I have worked with—even the least apparent "warriors"—often deeply enjoy their online role play game in which they can become their own form of the male who battles others.

When I work with boys and men, I do so in the belief that "doing battle" is one of the *core-themes* the male mind brings into my office on day one. I want to work with this core theme, use it, exploit it, and help males *through the lens* of this core theme. By core-theme I mean something similar to an archetype, as I will explore in this chapter, however, these core themes are not the Jungian archetypes themselves. They are more like the songs the archetypes are singing.

I believe that no matter what psychological theory or theories you work from—cognitive-behavioral, constructivist, object-relations, and any other—your awareness of male core themes can help you tailor your guiding theory and therapeutic skills to greater effectiveness with boys and men.

Core Themes as a Practical Tool

In this chapter, I hope you'll take a fourth step toward working in deep sync with the male psyche. Our becoming informed advocates for accurate dialogue about male privation was our first step; opening our minds to the possibility of nature-based factors in male development constituted our second step; expanding our therapeutic role to fit the mentoring needs of boys and men was our third step. Now our fourth step will be to add knowledge to our practices of how a male sees and measures himself in the world—as a servant of his "core themes."

When those boys attacked me in Laramie, they had a core theme in mind, and banded around it. They saw me as a dangerous alien, an enemy. They were socialized toward that prejudice, and the socialization was inhuman and grotesque, as any hate crime or racism is, but it was also instructive. Memories of it help me realize how *thematic* boys and men are to begin with—they get a theme in their heads and band together to work through the script of that theme as motivator or director of battle. Even without any empirical evidence around them that a curly haired mouthy boy named Mike was of any danger to them, they banded around the core-theme of "protection of their own against an enemy," and "bravely" protected their way of life against the category of danger in which I belonged. I was as much a part of their theme-life as I was a human being; in fact, while they were hurting me, I was much more a theme of "Jew" than a particular human being.

Here I am using the example of a prejudice to look at core themes, but truly, any categorical apex or alliance fits my point. I spoke recently with neuro-psychiatrist Daniel Amen about how "categorical: and "thematic" boys and men often become in their thinking and actions. He has studied more than sixty thousand brain scans. His book *Sex on the Brain* has been especially helpful in looking at questions regarding males and females. When we discussed the ways in which males lateralize brain activity (concentrating a task or thought-process in one part of the brain), we wondered if this could perhaps account for some of the male reliance on categorization of others and self for personal motivation. Daniel posited that perhaps because males tend to exhibit no verbal functioning on the right side of the brain ("the side," as he notes, "that gives people the gestalt of a situation,") they may create a greater sense of safety for themselves by acting in categorical and thematic ways when confronted with nuance. Categorical and thematic thought process can often create a "sense of the gestalt" without actually creating a fully realized gestalt.

Amen's idea appears to be supported by neuro-psychologist Simon Baron-Cohen, of Cambridge University. Baron-Cohen has used gender/brain scan research to posit that males tend toward categorical thinking in order to organize their lives and growth. He makes a detailed case for his argument in *The Essential Difference*. From his research, which includes information from many cultures beyond his native England, Baron-Cohen concludes that males tend more greatly toward categorical-thematic motivations, while females are more likely to choose more situational empathy in response to life's challenges.

Whatever is the confluence of brain and social factors that sets up males and females somewhat differently, anecdotal information supports research of Amen, Baron-Cohen, and other scientists such as Louann Brizendine and Shelley Taylor, who have added biochemical analysis to their theories on male/female differences in relational categorization. Males and females handle threats, stimuli, and growth patterns somewhat differently, in general.

For me, as a therapeutic practitioner, the science translates to action this way: when boys and men walk into my office, I assume they bring certain universal *male* core themes through the door with them—male "songs," male-centric needs, male categorizations. I assume that each male has in mind a set of core themes he uses as a lens by which to find himself in the world. I assume that if I lead with, "What are you feeling?" he might go blank, or make up something that is not a lie but is a shard, a sliver of what he really means, so I meet him prepared to look at core themes with him. This "core theme approach" has provided me with myriad ways to enter the inner world of the boy or man relatively quickly.

In making the core theme assumption, I am not thinking, "This man has lots of categories and themes in his mind, but few feelings." Rather, I am working under the assumption that he may not be able to access much of worth at all in counseling if his core themes are not foremost in my mind as his counselor. Experience has taught me that if we, as practitioners, keep in mind particular core themes (gradually discovering and mentoring those that are crucial to the particular boy or man in our care), a male may have more success, over time, at accessing the emotions and feelings that we hope to see him access.

Finding Core Themes through Primal Questions

Core themes can sometimes be discovered through primal questions about what I call CORE male identity. CORE stands for Compassion, Honor, Responsibility, Enterprise. As quickly as possible in the chronology of our counseling, I move toward questions that try to delve directly into areas where compassion, honor, responsibility or enterprise are thematic.

> What are you most ashamed of about yourself?
> What are you most afraid of in your life?
> Who are you most afraid of?
> What worries you about your children?
> What do you love about being a dad?
> What do you hate about being a dad?
> What will you sacrifice to do better?
> What do you like about your work?
> What are your hobbies?
> What were your most physically painful experiences?
> What are your most emotionally painful experiences?
> Who did you hurt this week? How?
> Have you been forgiven by _____?
> Have you forgiven _____?
> What do you regret the most about your past?
> What do you love the most about your past?
> Who has hurt you the most in this last year?
> Who have you hurt the most this week?
> What are your best qualities?
> What are your worst qualities?
> Are you a man?

This last question provides a further doorway into each adult man who walks into my door.

Core Theme: Manhood

Nearly any journey into a boy or man's emotional structure should include "manhood" as a core theme. *Manhood* is a theme every man and every boy cares about constantly. Compassion, Honor, Responsibility, and Enterprise are all, in some ways, subthemes of manhood. If you say to your patient, "What is a man, for you?" The patient's response is almost always useful. If the patient can't answer, you might say, "What is a real man, for you?" Probing questions regarding the boy's or man's understanding of manhood help him bring to the surface the wisdom he needs in order to deal with many other issues, including mother-son, father-son, parenting, relationship, and personality issues.

In asking questions about manhood throughout the time of therapy (over the weeks and months), a therapist shows the male patient—whether a boy or man—an understanding of one of his most important core themes. And through this revelation, we become both counselor/therapist and mentor. By making manhood a core theme in your dialogue and therapy, you show a male that you understand how precarious manhood is; that you know manhood shares many qualities with womanhood, but is also quite different from womanhood; that it needs to be earned (we are not born men, we must perform against strong odds to become men); that "being a man" is one of the most important subjects in a man's life, the unconscious thematic filter for many of a male's most powerful feelings and emotions, including compassion, honor, responsibility and enterprise.

Andrew

Andrew, 25, was a low performing African-American male who worked a clerical job, earning $28,000 a year, in Miami, where that kind of money buys nearly nothing. He had to lie to his mother to get her to pay his bills. He went to his brother's house whenever he could and raided the refrigerator. He seemed "self-centered" to his mother and "disturbed" to his father (who only talked to Andrew once a year). The parents had divorced when Andrew was ten. Andrew drank heavily (there were alcoholism genetics on his father's side); he smoked marijuana, he was underweight, and he had a strong body odor.

When I first met him in my office, I said, "Dude, you stink." That was a very "un-therapeutic" thing to say, but it worked. He laughed, smelled both his underarms, and said, "Yeah, I guess I don't shower enough."

"You're a good looking guy, and you've got water in your apartment, right?"

"Sure."

"Please, shower next time you come."

He dropped down into the chair. "Whatever. I won't stay in therapy anyway, but my mom insisted I come this first time. She's paying for this."

From this first interaction, I learned what Andrew's inner world as a man looked like. He was a pre-adult boy/man who presented to the world as a failure because he felt like a failure as a man. His slovenly "I suck" mask was not a cover up of the person he felt he was—it was a flagrant display of who he had come to know himself to be: the slovenly, "disturbed," "uncaring," "young man" whom everyone, including himself, had given up on. He had a low sense of responsibility, low self-esteem in his world of "enterprise" (work), little sense of honor, and little compassion for himself.

In fact, from the first moment I met him, I could see that Andrew had unconsciously decided to avoid becoming a man. Like many "pre-adult" males in our culture, most in their twenties or early thirties, he was a "guy" raised without father or enough male mentors, and/or in a position of poverty or wealthy entitlement that impeded his development into a mature man. He knew himself as a second or third rate male, not a man possessing what I would later discuss with him as a strong *core*-self.

Quickly it became clear that Andrew needed one or more mentors to help him become a man. That was not all he needed—he needed a psychologist to prescribe medication for depression, as well—but he needed the counselor who worked with him weekly to counsel and mentor him through the theme of manhood. He needed someone who would try to hear exactly what song Andrew was singing about himself as a boy/man.

Andrew is an example of a male for whom keeping the theme of "manhood" in mind led to successful growth and life-change for the client. The "Dude, you stink" opener was risky, but it succeeded in his case in part because I did not avoid his obvious and encrusted immaturity as a male but, instead, established my knowledge of it immediately. He respected me as a mentor who could "call him on his shit," as he later put it. This set up a relationship with him in which, when he lied to me (as he often did), I could simply say, "Andrew, you're lying. Why?"

"You busted me," he would frown, not too worried in our first weeks, but then, as the sessions progressed, he didn't like getting "busted" as much. He told the truth more. One thing that I believe helped move this forward was that I continually contextualized his lying as a way of "avoiding becoming a man." Together, we created a plan for approaching his mother (whom he clearly loved but was trying to individuate from) when he was in need, rather than lying to her. He also developed a plan for reaching out to his father.

Helping Andrew deal with and see himself through the core theme of "becoming a man" helped him do what a young man needs to do in counseling and therapy: grow up in the areas that are crucial to maturation of men no matter their culture: Compassion, Honor, Responsibility, and Enterprise.

Throughout this process, Andrew and I talked about feelings and emotions, but usually *after* we talked about manhood, honor, work ethic, grandparents, ancestors, compassion, ancestral culture, what he got out of smoking weed, why he was afraid of girls and sex, the father-son relationship, the mother-son relationship. I helped him break his life up into themes so he could look at his relationships and life with a lens easier to see, for him, than what he was feeling—the lens of manhood through which he could measure progress. Here is dialogue from a session regarding honor.

Gurian: "This lying that you do—do you, as a man, really think it's honorable?"

"I don't know."

"What does honor mean, to you?"

"I don't know. Doing the right thing, I guess."

"You talked about your grandfather Paul, who was such a success in business, but you talked about how he lied to get there. You said you hated that part of him. Right?"

"Yeah."

"And now you're becoming him somewhat, right? You're a liar, but without all the business success."

Silence. Thought process. Finally: "Okay, yeah. I'm like him, but not like him."

"You talked about how hard it was for you when he died. You cried at his coffin. You were close to him, right?"

"Yeah, I guess."

"So, three years ago, when you started this whole lying thing, did you decide to lie so you could be like this man you were once close to?"

"No. I'm not thinking about him when I lie. Anyway, I'm not really 'lying'—I'm just trying to get my bills paid and survive. My parents hate me and they won't help out. I have to lie."

"Does your dad lie like his dad Paul did?"

"Yeah, some. He's good in business. He's got a new family now. He lied to my mom and cheated on her. He thinks I'm a fuck up and won't help me. Yeah, he lies."

"So you're becoming like both your grandfather and your father in becoming a dishonorable man, but you're not becoming a financial success like either of them."

"I guess."

"Why not become a success like them? You're a smart guy, right? Your grades were great until your junior year. You are clearly a smart guy."

"Yeah."

"So, what are you getting from becoming the bad part of your dad and grandfather but not the good part?"

Silence, then: "I don't want to become like them, but I do want to become like them. It sucks. I can't figure it out."

Silence. Thought process. Behind his eyes, he is really pondering this. He remains silent, so I continue, "So, do you just give up? Is that what's happening: you just make your life worse and worse until you don't have to really think you're in their ballpark anymore—either the good or the bad part of them?"

"I don't know."

"You're kind of making sure you never grow up, right? You keep being the 'kid' part of the men in your family, but make sure you never have to become like them in the good, adult, man ways?"

"I guess so." Silence. Then: "You're right, okay? You're right. I'm a fuck-up, even in all that."

"Actually, I disagree. I think this tack you've taken, of not becoming a man, is pretty smart, in a way. You decided you just didn't want to become the bad parts of being a man, so you didn't become a man at all. That was a smart way to avoid becoming the immoral or problematic men in your family that you didn't want to become. You were ashamed of your dad and granddad and you wanted to avoid becoming that shameful man yourself."

"Yeah. I guess."

"Were you protecting anyone from those men, do you think?"

"I don't know." Further silence.

(In a later session we talk about how he has been trying to protect his mother, even though he was protecting her awkwardly and unsuccessfully).

75

"So the thing is, now you're moving toward thirty—what was smart for you as a boy growing up to become a man five years ago may not be as smart now."

"What do you mean?"

"What do you think I mean?"

"I guess I get it." Silence. He tries to articulate, then finally says, "Man, I don't know. Tell me." This "Tell me" is not avoidance—from his face I can see that it is really "Please help me understand."

"Well, you've become both the bad you wanted to avoid and a new kind of bad—a social failure."

Silence, then: "It fucking sucks. The whole thing sucks."

"Do you hate yourself, do you think?"

"Hate myself?"

"Yeah. A guy doesn't want to hate his father or his grandfather so he just decides to hate himself. Is that what you're doing? Hating yourself?"

Now he looks up at my face, making eye contact, emotion brimming. "What do you mean?"

He knows what I mean, so I remain silent now, sit back, concentrate.

He says, "Fuck. I hate myself. How lame is that, right? I really am a total fuck-up as a man. I'm a fucking weasel who hates himself."

Andrew's use of the word "man" in relation to himself was a break through. He had not used the word for himself before. Even though this particular session did not end with resolution, the constant contextualizing of Andrew's male experience through the lens of a theme, manhood, helped Andrew work on himself. The theme of manhood presented a constant refrain or leitmotif in our sessions. Andrew received mentoring that he as a male could feel at a visceral level. What he was going through got contextualized in the lives of other men from whom he came, and he never lost the thread of what we were working on because we broke the work up into repeated themes.

In this particular session, I led the conversation more than waiting for the client to lead. I led Andrew toward a conversational goal (that he had become the immature son/grandson who hated himself), rather than constantly waiting for the man to get to a goal that he couldn't put in words himself anyway. While I utilized silences as needed, I did not over-rely on them to the point at which Andrew lost the ability to make sense to himself, and so, gave up on the therapeutic process.

In the above session, you'll notice, "feelings" never came up in "words" but they were a constant nonverbal presence—and Andrew felt a great deal of emotion. But part of my job was specifically not to say, "Please tell me what you feel," which drives many males away from therapy, but to manage conversation, at least some of the time, toward clear thematic goals, which are attention-points for males.

In your own practice, this awareness of male categorization of experience can be used efficiently. You can organize some of your therapeutic work with males through the CORE model of Compassion, Honor, Responsibility, and Enterprise; or, you may have developed, in your research, a different sense of what is "core" or "essential" for the men you work with. Whatever direction you go, the theme of manhood is a category that can be utilized universally with boys and men. It provides a distinct advantage of therapeutic trust: by talking with a male about manhood as a core theme, you earn the respect of the man. Through that respect, the man feels more bonded with you. As long as "manhood" is not handled by you as a shaming/politicized theme, it should bear fruit in your practice.

If you are a woman therapist, it is worth remembering (and I am generalizing here, with apologies) many of the men who set up a first appointment with you will walk into your soft-lit office, sit down in one of its beautiful soft chairs, look at your well-groomed feminine appearance, and suspect that you are clueless about them. They will, in most cases, be respectful to you, sensitive to you, but just as suspicious of your office as you would be if you knew little about football, but you have suddenly been instructed to conduct therapy in an NFL locker room. As anxious as you might feel in that locker room, the man may feel similarly anxious in your very "female" office.

Thus, as quickly as possible, it can be useful to gain male trust by showing males that their anxiety in your office—their rise in stress hormones and fight-or-flight responses, including a proclivity to withdraw emotionally and then leave therapy—is not needed here, in your world, for you understand that boys and men are focused (whether unconsciously or consciously) on the core theme of manhood, and you want to be helpful in that regard. As the boy or man in your care sees that you understand *him* without patronizing and without judgment, but in sync with his core-themes, you gain his respect.

Core Theme: Respect

A second core-theme for males (and for boys and men in any setting anywhere), is *respect.* This is, thus, another bedrock theme for therapeutic process with males. Generally, boys and men need to first and foremost feel respected by us in order to go with us on the journey of emotion we want them to go on. To ask them to explore inner emotions and feeling without showing that we understand and respect them as *males* is like telling a girl or woman that she should become a man in order to succeed in life. No therapist would do this to a girl or woman, but without realizing it, we constantly do this to boys and men.

It is disrespectful. When we try to get them to talk about feelings like girls and women do, they feel disrespected by us, and they feel that we're setting them up to fail. They see us as wanting them to respect us from the out-set, and as wanting them to follow us into the heart of the matter, but they see that we are telling them that they are defective females, i.e. we are telling them to disrespect themselves as males and become a girl or woman, which they can't do. We ask them to follow us into human transformation, but show them we respect manhood and maleness too little to be trusted or taken seriously. They feel, without being able to express it, that we do not respect the client for who he is.

So if we show males a distinct respect for the journey of manhood, and if we respectfully challenge men and boys on the themes such as manhood, honor, or what-would-you-fight-for, we can get powerful results. This is even true for younger boys. As an example, here is dialogue with a 9-year-old, who had pushed another boy at school.

"Troy, was that the kind of thing a man does to get respect? Or was that little-boy stuff?"

"A man does it."

"Really?"

"You want me to say 'boy,' but Timmy made me push him."

"How?"

"He told them (he is referring to three other kids—one boy and two girls) I peed my pants."

"So you knocked him down."

"Yeah."

"He made you mad."

"Yeah."

"He dissed you in front of everyone."

"Yeah."

"You had to do something."

"Yeah."

Silence for a second, then: "I agree with you. In your place, I would have done something too. I'm proud of you for doing something."

Silence in which I let him take a moment to realize that I understand the reality of his situation, and respect him for doing battle in that reality.

"Thanks."

"You bet. And now the question is, was the thing you did the *right* thing to do? You had to do something, but was pushing him the right choice?"

"Yes."

"Really? Would your dad do that? (His father is serving with the Marines in Afghanistan). Let's say one of the guys on your father's team made fun of your dad, and I mean made fun of him with something silly like 'peed his pants,' would your dad push the person over and risk assault charges?"

"I guess not."

"Probably not. Especially not if the guy was one of his team. If he was the enemy, your dad would act differently, right? But Timmy is not someone trying to kill you. He's just another boy you kind of like sometimes and kind of don't like other times, right?"

"Yeah."

"So what would your dad do if he were you?"

"I don't know."

"Wouldn't he stand up straight, get right in front of Timmy, and say something strong and true, but not try to hit or push Timmy?"

"Yeah. Daddy would know what to say to a guy like Timmy."

"Yes. He would. And you're his son, remember. His strength is inside you."

Silence. He absorbs this.

Then: "So the next time Timmy or another kid like that disses you, what should you do?"

"Stand up straight and say something back to him?"

"Yes. And it will be scary to do that. I know that. It's actually less scary to just impulsively push Timmy, right? The more scary thing will be to stand strong and tall against the dissing, like your dad would."

He ponders this distinction regarding 'scary,' and waits in silence for me to say more.

"A 'man' acts like your dad would act to get respect; a man doesn't do what you did. A man doesn't over-react and take the less scary way out. He actually takes the harder way—he goes through the feeling of being scared but stands tall anyway, and uses words when he can."

Now our dialogue moves into more conversation regarding Daddy, what Daddy would do, what a man does. This leads away from Timmy and school and into feelings of grief regarding Daddy's absence, which lead, toward the end of the session, to tears and catharsis for this boy.

By starting with (or placing very early in discussions) challenges to the boy on how to regain his respect in the face of adversity, I am helping this boy ascertain possible gifts by working with a core-theme, respect, through which he can measure himself in his father's image.

Core Theme: Character

Character is also a crucial core theme for therapy with males. Males are very moral creatures, even when they stray from common morality in their impulsiveness and personality disorders. They parse morality and ethics in categories, and place themselves in those categories. When I work with boys and men, I make an internal "brain switch" from "emotion first" to "character first." If my client in the previous hour was a girl or woman, the "emotion first" self-direction generally works well. My female client needed and wanted (generally) to talk about what has happened, how she has felt, what she needs, where things are going. She needs to feel better, first; then I can help her feel stronger. Indeed, by expressing her feelings about the week's events, she often feels stronger by feeling better—the process-expression of her feelings is palpable in the room, and her words carry immense gifts of emotion for her.

When we end our session and I start transitioning to the next client, I review the gender of the client. If the next client is a boy or man, I know that, in general, being a male of high character will be more important to him than will be the accessing of his own feelings. While I as the counselor and mentor know that character and feeling and emotion and personality and personality disorders are all interconnected, I have committed to maximum effectiveness with both females and males, so I need to meet this boy or man where he is, at the outset. "Where he is" involves understanding his own character development at the most penetrating levels I can.

In comparing my male and female clients observationally, I have developed a comparative list of male/female psychological characteristics that apply directly to the reason I make a "brain switch" when I approach males. I hope this gender differentiation model is useful to you in your exploration of both male and female clients. It is based in the brain information that we looked at in Chapter 2.

Males tend to:

* *bond with others in shorter quick-bursts than girls and women do
* *seek to learn order, pattern thinking, ritualized action in order to feel safe
* *like to up-play performance, especially competition-earned achievement
* *promote and seek risk-taking opportunities, especially physical risk-taking
* *expect discipline and character development as much as they seek contests of skill
* *generally try to protect themselves against emotional vulnerability
* *guide others to defer to trustworthy authorities for direction and motivation
* *seek action and tasks as paths to self-worth
* *try to help vulnerable people "become stronger" rather than "feel better"

Females tend to:

>*bond with others in a larger variety of ways, especially including more emotion-talk
>*seek to receive and provide a wider variety of attachment interactions than males
>*emphasize complex development of emotional outcomes
>*avoid risks, if possible, especially those that physically harm others
>*search for and develop methods of direct empathy ("How is everyone doing? Is everyone okay?")
>*be more willing to become emotionally vulnerable, and see that vulnerability as a personal success marker
>*relinquish daily personal independence if required to meet others' perceived needs
>*use verbal encouragement, even if the praise has not been earned by performance
>*try to help others feel better as the best way of helping them feel stronger

These generalizations are based on constant assessment of gender/brain research in tandem with client observation. If you take a month to study your clients and check them against these two grids, you should find some logic to the generalizations. As you filter this logic through the lens of the word "character," some interesting revelations may occur regarding male and female clients.

Where girls and women want to "*feel* better" and help others *feel* better, boys and men more often want to "*do* better" and help others *do* better. When, for instance, boys and men are constantly verbally praised ("You're awesome!" "Great job!"), even or especially when they've actually not done a good job and/or not been awesome, they begin to distrust the parent or mentor. Girls, on the other hand, often feel greater immediate satisfaction with someone who praises them just to praise them, though girls, too, can become inured to excessive praise.

There is biochemistry and brain research behind these differences, and of course, these differences rise as part of socialization responses. For girls, the words of praise can stimulate bonding chemicals, such as oxytocin, and the parent's or mentor's or friend's verbal praise is often very useful in continuing long-term rapport with girls. Constant verbal praise of this kind can backfire, however, with boys more quickly than with girls. Boys and men often feel disrespected by and distrustful of constant, non-achievement-based or non-character-based praise.

To further explore this point, try an experiment: ask a group of boys and girls (an elementary school class, for instance) to write on a piece of paper their answer to this question—"What makes you do the right thing?" Girls are more likely to write more complex answers that involve their own feelings and intuitions about what is right in a certain situation. Boys are more likely to be cryptic in their association of right action with "following the rules" or "doing what's right because its right."

The association that Daniel Amen, Simon Baron-Cohen, Louann Brizendine, Shelley Taylor and others have made regarding categorical/systemic thinking among males—and the theory that there is less intrusion/use in the male brain of complex emotion-laden processing—is a brain-based explanation for the examples I've given, and for the conclusion I'm drawing. Whatever the ultimate reason for male predilections, those predilections are useful to absorb into therapeutic thinking.

For males, it is often essential that rules and rituals be laid out by a trusted authority, moral precepts be clarified by mentors, and boys and men be held to the highest standards possible for *action.* Words and feelings tend to be of less importance to males than action. This, indeed, is a more "character-based" self-understanding than "feeling-based." The male connects himself to a "system" and its authorities, and measures himself by how well he, by virtue of his character and actions, performs within the moral guidance of that system. He does not spend much time relating to how he feels. Metaphorically and archetypally, he is more like a warrior attached to a System than an empathizer empathizing with people in given situations.

The upside of a character-based rather than feeling-based gender approach is that, if healthy authorities (such as mothers, fathers, mentors, faith-communities, and therapists) are provided to boys and men, these males will tend to sacrifice nearly anything to be men of high character in the authority's world. The downside of the gender-specific approach of males is, however, two-fold: 1) if those caregivers and mentors are absent or (in the case of my enemies in Laramie, misguided), males can get lost in impulsivity, violence and self-destruction; and 2) when males get lost, they do not have as much immediate access to impulse control and empathy as females, so they will often do very bad things (of low character and high danger).

As you ponder this, watch males and females around you with a gender lens. Look at how they bond with one another. More than females, males will tend to bond in large group activities (larger than two or three) where there is high risk of danger. If you observe this, you will be in good company. This observation has been corroborated in research on humans by researchers David Buss and David Gilmore, as well as in research regarding chimpanzees and gorillas. Males often test themselves in large groups, and these large groups have less time to activate feelings and empathy responses than do female groupings. Females tend to form more dyadic or "small groups" in their bonding.

The large male group must of necessity adhere to a schema for success that breaks down and builds up character, and the large group must use that schema to battle through the multiple layers of challenge the group and its individuals will face in a rather dangerous and high-risk life. The smaller female groupings—dyads and triads—can certainly get involved in being warriors and stuffing back feelings (as well as becoming verbally aggressive with one another and socially ostracizing a girl in the group), but group challenge will not be as important to the smaller female group as verbal empathy (or verbal and social manipulation) will be.

Is this generalization true for every person? No. Some males despise large groups, and avoid them completely. Some females like large groups, not small groups. But even with all exceptions noted, we must remember that the males who despise large groups are not the ones leaving our dyadic-small-group therapy offices in droves. The males leaving our therapy offices are the ones who feel more comfortable in the large group *character* challenge than the one-on-one *empathy/feeling* conversation. These boys and men need us to fully understand character development first, and feelings-talk second. They know without words that our traditional therapy model, set up as a one-on-one "Let's talk about feelings" environment is "not male" and "anti-male" for a vast number of males in the world.

If, however, a boy or man walks into your office sensing that you are a mentor of character who understands and respects the male journey of success and character building, you will be accommodating a core theme he lives by. When I talked with Andrew, I was attacking issues of character with him, as I was when I worked with the bullied boy, Troy. In other sessions with both these males, I suggested they watch Ridley Scott's *Gladiator.* After they had done so, I talked with them about honor, responsibility, and character through the lens of that film. Both these males, one a boy, one an adult male, who were relatively silent during other counseling sessions, now had a great deal to say. In the film, they saw the core theme of character elucidated, and as I worked with that core-theme in session, they were able to explore their own emotions in depth.

When I have brought up this issue of "character building" in workshops and conferences, I have often been amazed at the honest dialogue that ensues. Our psychology profession has become so verbal-emotive, so sit-and-talk, so void of action, we have inadvertently removed the essential theme of *character* from our thinking and theorizing (and thus our delivery of services) as mental health professionals. When, however, therapists, counselors, and social workers reassess maleness as dependent on character building, every film, story, and interaction can become potentially illuminating, for there are literally millions of references in the male patient's life and in the society around us to the core theme of character.

Core Theme: Motivation

Either as text or subtext, when a mother brings a son into therapy in our era, "lack of male motivation" may be part of what she laments. In 2011, in the course of two days, I got phone calls and emails from:

*A mother of a 9-year-old who was unmotivated in school and, thus, failing.

*A mother and father of a 13-year-old boy who had become unmotivated in school.

*A father whose 17-year-old son quit the soccer team, had declining grades, played video games most of the time, and was unmotivated to "get up off his ass."

*A wife whose husband had lost his job and had "looked for a new one for six months but now just can't do anything, and we have three kids to feed."

The pain and depression experienced by these families was immense, not just because human failure gradually or suddenly overwhelmed the family life of each, but because the family members felt unable to change their situations. These families saw boys who once were energetic and feisty and free-spirited and full of vigor become lackluster, "lazy," "under-motivated." They saw boys who "fell behind" and, soon, "failed." They saw men who once ran the world become lost, without energy or hope, without motivation to run anything except the television.

If you are seeing boys, men, and families in situations like these, you are not alone. This "under-motivation of today's young males" is a kind of male epidemic that is growing, and there are many theories as to why it is growing. Here are some of the most promising theories. Your cognizance of all of them—even ones you might disagree with off-hand—can be useful in providing therapeutic solutions to issues that fall under the male core theme of *motivation*.

Theory 1: Something is going on chemically with Gen X and Gen Y males. The chemistry could have something to do with the wash of *estrogen receptors* in plastics, pesticides, or other chemicals. Estrogen receptors have been proven to lower male sperm counts throughout the industrial world. Some researchers believe certain parts of the male brain that are wired for testosterone receptors, such as the basal ganglia and caudate nucleus, are not receiving the chemical balance they need—which ends up lowering male motivation. If possible, suggest to client families that they look closely at plastics, pesticides, and other chemicals near them.

Theory 2: Something related to chemical toxins could be affecting DNA to RNA transfer *in utero*, i.e. pregnant mothers are ingesting *toxins* without knowing it and those toxins are affecting the fetuses of boys and girls. With boys, specifically, researchers posit that we are seeing higher incidents of genetics-based disorders in Gen X and Y than before--disorders such as autism, ADHD, depression, violence, and, among some boys, lack of motivation—"male lethargy." While there is little we can do about this possible area of causation for already born clients, we must keep encouraging study of this theory. American rates of these diseases and disorders are higher, on average, than any other country's rates, thus, something is going on that must be understood, especially in the United States, as soon as possible.

Theory 3: The lack of *father influence and male mentors* (role models) among many males is affecting male development to the detriment of male social ambition and male motivation to learn, grow, mature, and succeed. Researchers argue that without father-influence and modeling from motivated, driven, directed fathers and other male mentors, boys grow up seeing no distinct and important male future, and become lethargic as males in a world that does not seem, from a socio-psychological point of view, to need boys and men very much. This theory is one we can act on immediately with our male clients. Chapter 5 of this book focuses on fathering specifically.

Theory 4: Concomitant with studying the lack of adult males raising sons, researchers study the fact that *rites of passage into manhood* have become largely divided into three inadequate categories: nonexistent, meager, or anti-social. In some boys' lives there are no significant rites of passage at all. In some boys' lives there are only the psychologically meager rites of passage, such as having sex for the first time. For other boys, (i.e. gang members, for instance), the rites of passage involve violent behavior that may temporarily initiate the "man" into a tribal and homogenous group, such as gang or fraternity, but does not help the male integrate himself into the larger, diverse society. In the Notes and References of this book, you will find notation regarding rites-of-passage programs you can help your clients use, should you see a lack of rite-of-passage as a factor in the lack of motivation in the boys you are seeing.

To these four theories and bases of male motivation research, I can add two that our Gurian Institute team and I have been studying in our work around the country.

Theory 5: K-12 schools may be contributing to under motivation of males through the lack of understanding of *male learning styles.* Schools are run and classes are taught in verbal-emotive modalities most suited to more female than male learners. Males find much of what they learn irrelevant, and they rebel against school. They are not able to learn as well as we wish in the present-day classroom and they act out their failure in ways that further erode their ability to learn and be motivated to succeed.

Theory 6: Parents are *doing-for* their children in ways that may be harming healthy male development of motivation-to-mature. When parents don't demand work from children, children are more likely to delay maturation. With boys, lack of work and lack of high character expectations can become especially detrimental, because boys' developmental arcs are, biologically and socially, less internally defined than those of girls. What do we mean?

While girls have a number of options for maturation (menstruation, social care-giving, emotional verbalization, and cultural opportunity) boys physically lack the first one and generally lack the second and third. Boys have no female-commensurate biological maturation (getting pubic hair and growing larger bodies, bones, and sex organs do not compare to the girl's ability to bear children); and boys do not gravitate toward, nor are they generally compelled to, baby-sit, etc. in order to learn care-giving of children (in fact, most parents would specifically rather a boy *not* be the babysitter of their children). Furthermore, boys are not able, in general, to verbalize their internal maturation journey with as much self-awareness and motivational energy as a girl. Thus, boys often need to be raised *toward* maturity from early on, through parental, extended family, and community attention to tasks, work, expectations, and motivation.

These, then, are just some of the possible reasons unmotivated boys and men come into our offices for help. In all but the second theory, your efforts to deal directly with the cause of the lack of motivation can bear fruit. You can coach parents and teachers on how to better raise and educate males. You can help with rites-of-passage, increased father or father-figure involvement, and environmental changes around the boy.

A seventh reason for lack of male motivation, one woven through all these others, and especially clear in under-motivated boys is clinical and/or situational *depression* or *dysthymia*. The boy who is not doing homework and may have been bullied at school may have experienced depression triggers; parents or teachers may not realize the clinical condition because males sometimes do not manifest depression or dysthymia as females do. Terrence Real, William Pollock, Michael Thompson, and many others have noted: depression is felt deeply by males, but we may not notice it because males try to cover it through acting out, rebelling against teachers and school, battling parents, or withdrawing into the "excitement" of video games and television.

Helping Under-Motivated Boys and Men

A core theme for males is motivation, and for us as counselors and therapists, it can be life-saving to help client-families and individual boys and men develop a deep understanding of the seven possible reasons for the under-motivation a particular male is feeling. Assuming, then, that we have looked at the possibility of depression (or other disorders) very early on in our sessions with the boy and family or the adult male, here are other suggestions for weekly work with under-motivated male clients. I have employed all of these solution areas in helping under-motivated males and their families. These touch points constitute a menu of possible opportunities rather than a single success point. They are tools to use in "motivation recovery" in males, and many of them (if remolded toward girls and women) can help with female clients, as well.

*Help the client and family refocus themselves on the particular male's *internal values and goals.* As we work with males on motivation issues, we might realize that our therapeutic default position, taught to us very well in our training, is often to try to see what is happening in the client's emotional structure; while this can be helpful, it is also crucial to remember that human motivation also grows from attention to values and goal-setting regarding how to pursue those character values. The passion with which human beings motivate themselves is a matter of emotion, of course, but if we do not first help under-motivated males to set new goals and regain their internal values, our success with them can be lackluster, at best.

*To motivate males, help their authority-figures and loved ones use leverage to refocus the male's family and care-giving system on tasks, jobs, and performance expectations. Quite often, you must coach parents to take away TV and/or videogames and/or laptop in order to use the taking-away as leverage for helping under-motivated boys regain performance objectives in school and athletics. We as practitioners can help families work out areas of *leverage and reward-consequence systems* that utilize the few areas of focus the under-motivated male still succeeds at—e.g. video games.

*Help explore values, goals, and emotional structure through *family-of-origin issues,* both past and present, which contribute to this boy's lack of motivation. Divorce trauma is often a contributor to male lack of motivation—it is a family issue that can provide a place to start therapy. Loss of father (or mother) is another place to start. The mother-son and father-son wounds often create motivational obstruction for boys and men. Boys and men often respond very well to mother-son and father-son memory review and psychological exploration.

*When working to get *fathers and other men* involved or re-involved in the boy's (or man's) life, look for areas of interest that can help with motivation-recovery. For instance, it can be helpful to look for males who do/perform/teach something the boy specifically enjoys, including computers, video games, other technological skills, athletics, or anything at all that the boy presently excels in or once excelled in. Even with attempting to re-engage estranged fathers, areas of common action-interest are useful tools for involvement of men in boys' lives.

*Work to help the *mother* (especially if she is a single mother) to alter her parenting style to include more hard-expectations and clear-consequences. The boy may "hate her" for a time, but if she does not help him grow up right now, he will hate her in other ways later. Helping a single mother see this can often help her become a parent of less "doing for the boy" and more "making the boy do for himself."

*Believe boys, to whatever appropriate extent, when they complain about school as "the problem." Many schools really do not understand how to teach many of our boys. As practitioners in psychology professions, our *advocacy with the school* is often very important. We need to help parents and schools receive training in how to make schools boy-friendly, i.e. better set up for the way boys think, work, learn, and motivate themselves to success.

Forward Progress

Manhood, Respect, Character, and Motivation are just four themes you can use to focus your energies on the males in your care. In the Notes and Resources section of this book I have listed books that can help you further use the CORE themes of honor, compassion, success, and responsibility. Exploration and use of a core-theme approach constitutes, I believe, an important fourth step in moving toward more successful practice with males.

Ultimately, focusing on thematic therapy with males is a methodology by which to help males peer inside themselves toward the core assets and vulnerabilities they are experiencing. The inner male world is embattled between primitive urges and the highest ideals of a civilization. No matter how tough a male seems, he is constantly fragile because he is constantly measuring himself against the larger themes of manhood. This fact is actually useful for us as practitioners; it is good that he brings both his fragility and his thematic battle with fragility to our offices. These give us a chance to understand male fragility through themes that background it.

For boys and men, therapy in the context of core themes provides a male-friendly approach to better fathering, husbanding, living, and gender equality. And if the male in your care is "straying" from therapy as you now practice it, focus on core themes can give you a strategy for engagement of males. Most males want to talk about bravery, battle, honor, character, manhood, fatherhood, protection of others.

If you will decide to try the "brain switch" in order to add core-themes to your work with males, you will add a powerful tool to your toolbox, and enhance your already organized use of nearly any psychological theory. If the male presently in your care is the kind of man who enters therapy thinking, "Therapy isn't for me," you will answer his suspicion by immediately showing him you can cast therapy as being about mentoring the core issues men care about.

If the man walking into your office is the kind of man who comes into therapy thinking, "She won't understand me," or "I'm only doing therapy for my wife anyway," or "I'll fail at this," you can use your engagement in core themes and thematic therapy to immediately show the man that therapy is more than a feeling— therapy will help him become a better and more successful man. Males will tend to enter and remain in therapy that promises not failure, but success.

Chapter 5: Helping Males Adapt to Changing Male Roles

"Changes in gender roles are everywhere, and those changes
are mainly being led by girls and women. Pretty soon, boys
and men will have to also lead those changes."
--Judith Kleinfeld, National Director, the Boys Project

Louie and Mary came to me for couple counseling. Among
the number of issues they faced, one was what our cultural conversation calls "the changing male role." This issue evidenced itself
within a few minutes of our meeting via the mention by both people
of two things: shared housework issues, and Louie's unemployment.

Mary said, "I've got four kids, three of them boys, and their
socks and other stuff are all over the house. No matter what, I can't
get them to clean up around them. I work all day, then come home
to a mess. Louie works out of our home, and he's basically unem-
ployed right now, so he really does have time to take care of the
house, but he doesn't do it. I'm always the bad guy on home clean-
up. Louie just doesn't care about the house."

As Mary continued to describe her frustration, I watched
Louie's face go blank, then quietly and slowly develop a nod and a
smile. He had much practice, I could see, with preparing a glaze-
eyed smiling face with which to meet his wife's frustrations regarding his behavior or lack of action.

When Mary completed her story, I acknowledged her frustration, then asked Louie what he thought. "Oh she's right about
everything," he chuckled. I waited for him to say more, but he
didn't. He just kept smiling, waiting me out.

"About everything?" I asked. "Which parts of everything?"
I hoped to gauge the accuracy of the statement regarding his hands-
off attitude toward household chores, but also, I wanted to see
what, if anything, his facial cues and body language, voice-tone and
pitch, would reveal in response to his wife revealing his unemployment—that unemployment would feel more shameful to him than
his neglect of housework.

Louie chuckled again, rolled his eyes slightly, and nodded. "Well, you name it."

"The housework issue? Is she right about that? Or the good guy/bad guy? What?"

"Definitely that she's the bad guy and I'm the good guy."

Mary added, "Of course I'm right!" She was frustrated not only by her memories but by her husband's mask and reticence, both of which she had obviously witnessed many times before. "He lets the boys listen to songs like the Beastie Boys *Girls*. All that hip hop stuff where girls are hos and housework is what they should do and all that. It's repulsive. And I end up doing everything."

"Is that right?" I asked Louie.

He shrugged, smiling. "Yeah, I guess. I mean, a song is a song. Kids are smart, they know it's just entertainment, but Mary doesn't like that stuff, that's for sure."

Our dialogue continued along this line for about five more minutes. Mary's frustration grew, but Louie's defenses were very strong. Louie was able to deflect (and even somewhat disrespect) Mary through keeping things self-deprecatingly funny in his own mind. It appeared to me that he felt like such a failure in his role as a man, and felt so shamed by Mary's constant verbal rage, that he needed his defenses to stay very strong in order to keep his marriage going.

This seemed especially true as more information was shared by Mary: as a couple, she and her husband faced battles with banks and foreclosure, a disabled child who needed more resources than the couple had, Louie's unemployment, and the normal stresses of marriage and raising four children. The stress level of the couple, after fifteen years of marriage, was as high right now as could be.

At the end of the first session, we set up logistics for further counseling, and I asked Mary, "If there's one thing you want Louie to do to help with the housework issue, what would it be? Pick just one thing—one part of the house, for instance, that you absolutely need to be cleaned up when you come home from work."

She responded immediately. "The clothes, backpacks, books and everything else in the hallways—if Louie could just make sure, every day, that the kids take these things out of the hallway by the time I get home at 6:00 o'clock, that would be huge."

I asked Louie, "Can you do that one thing starting today?"

"Sure," he said immediately, smiling.

I pressed, "You love this woman, don't you?"

He nodded.

"I can tell you do. You clearly want this marriage to work. And you can see what the messy house is doing to her, right?"

"Yeah, of course, I see."

"So can you help her with this one thing right now—out of love and compassion for her?"

He nodded seriously, his smile gone. "Sure. It does drive her insane, all that stuff everywhere. I can help out with that one thing, sure."

"Okay, so, to be clear: will you make a pact with her to get each kid to pick this stuff up?"

He smiled again, interested in the pressure I was placing. "Sure. I'll make a pact."

"She's the woman you love, right? When she becomes your servant or the kids' servant, the love is destroyed by anger and frustration. You see that, right?"

I saw his eyes tracking me carefully. Now he was gauging whether I was part of the shaming he experienced from Mary (and probably assumed he would receive from counseling), or whether I was trying to fraternally inspire him toward change. In speaking as I had, I chose to be directive, show authority, make a concrete suggestion. I also chose to leverage this man's love for his wife rather than presenting a role change regarding housework as the most important therapeutic issue.

Simultaneously, he and I both knew that I was saying, "Your role as a man is not what your grandfather's might have been, and Mary's role is not what her grandmother's might have been; this conversation in this office is about loving one another differently now. You need to fit the needs of this marriage, now, and do something 'micro' like getting the kids to clean up the hallway, as a show of your great love for your wife."

In all this, I was looking for alternative ways to work with this man regarding gender role changes than the recently traditional approach of shaming men for not doing things around the house that seem relatively trivial to them. The shaming tack that Mary had been using for a long time was simply making her husband defensive, and obstinate. Mary saw housework as a moral issue; Louie did not. Mary cared about it; Louie did not. Louie needed leverage and an appeal to love, I hoped, rather than shame.

Awareness of the Gender Politics

Helping couples understand changing gender roles can help marriages survive. It is a fifth step in the process of becoming more effective with boys and men. It is also a step rife with gender politics throughout our culture, and especially in the field of psychology. Our male clients know this, even if subconsciously, when they walk into our offices.

"Changing gender roles" is mainly an issue that women have brought to the forefront of culture. Most males are not as concerned with many of the aspects of changing gender roles that many women are concerned with. Many men are suspicious of therapy because of the sense they have, as one client told me, "Our previous therapist was a woman who just basically supported what Diane said; I was always wrong, Diane was always right. The whole marriage depended on me changing to become who Diane wanted." This man was living out a male truth regarding gender role dialogue in psychology—one that afflicts our profession, and causes the loss of many male clients. It is the false "truth" in our profession that males are generally wrong, and females are generally right.

When working with boys and men on this issue, it can be immensely useful to have contemplated fully our own gender politics each time a client walks in our door. In order to work successfully with boys and men (which ultimately leads to success for the girls and women they are relating to), I have spent a great deal of time adapting my approach. Early in my career, I tried contextualizing housework and other gender role issues as "men's issues" to men. This was the politically correct way to work with these issues, and it seemed only fair: why should gender roles be a "women's issue" and not a "men's issue?" Fairness dictated that men should care about all these issues of changing gender roles as much as women.

Indeed, in various ways, men do. But I quickly saw that men don't generally care about them with the same intensity as many women (and many of our politicized approaches) do. I discovered that if I say to men in a session (whether in exact words or as subtext), "You should care about changing gender roles as a men's issue," many men's eyes glazed over. Men often see through this approach relatively quickly, even though they are polite about it for a session or two, especially if their wives or significant others are in the room.

I believe males see through "changing gender roles are a men's issue" because our culture wears its gender politics on its sleeve, and on that sleeve is the idea that men are considered defective, and the "male role" is considered defective. Men don't like this constant attack on their historical and personal character as males, and they tend to avoid therapeutic environments that dictate, "What women want regarding gender roles is what men should care about." Underneath the cultural language regarding "what women want" and "changing gender roles," men hear "men are more defective than women." All of this gets muddled in our present gender politics in therapeutic settings, and while many men keep smiling, they remain distant from therapy.

To help further focus this discussion, let's look at four experiences boys and men have in relation to gender politics. Please see if these fit some of the males in your care. (I am articulating these as if a male is confronting us in the therapy professoin with these points, for I believe this is what males are saying, even though they would perhaps not articulate these things this way in a given session).

1. You folks in psychology put "gender politics" and "gender stereotypes" higher on your priority list than "manhood," "respect," "character," and "motivation." That's a mistake. If you want to teach us guys about "gender roles," you really need to contextualize changing gender roles in core themes and concerns that are immediately present and most psychologically pressing for me as I try to survive as a male in this world.

2. Boys and men know that, for the most part, the deep issues we face—depression, anxiety, fear, failure, abandonment—do not grow mainly from gender stereotypes. As a boy or man, I am usually dealing with other major life issues, such as violent or absent parents, broken marriages, addictions, or failure at work, that have little to do with the fact that I don't like housework or don't talk about feelings a lot, or still want to provide for my family.

3. The girls and women we love are not as good at understand-
    ing and being empathic toward males as you psychology
    professionals would like to think. We, as boys and men, ex-
    perience a lot of girls and women as highly judgmental and
    destructive and shaming. As a therapist, you need to al-
    ways remember this. If you try to help me as a male "to
    adapt to changing gender roles" by telling me that women
    know what's what better than I do, you'll lose me.

4. When statements are made, such as, "Boys and men have
    more social privilege than girls and women," or "Life in
    America is better for boys and men than girls and women,"
    or "Girls are behind, boys are ahead," or "Men get the
    breaks, women don't," or "Girls are behind, boys succeed,"
    we as boys and men know these statements are "politics,"
    not objective truth. Boys and men in therapy are generally
    not having a better life than girls or women, nor are we gen-
    erally ahead of girls or women; we have not had a lot of
    breaks, and we have not succeeded in many areas of life, in-
    cluding school.

With a man such as Louie, who was already relatively gender equal in his thinking (but blind to and defensive against a number of the changes happening in his role as a man), I kept gender
politics in mind but made sure to contextualize those politics in
matters of love of wife and family, and high character. As I worked
with him over the months to help him sort through his own anguish
about losing his job and letting his family down, I asked him to explore new ways of "providing and protecting," including becoming
a stay-at-home dad for a time.

Gradually, Louie moved more greatly toward enjoying his
role as a stay-at-home dad—but his attention did not waver from
trying to return to the workplace of prowess and achievement
again. As we met together, I asked Louie to write e-mails to each of
his children and also to Mary—e-mails detailing the kind of father
and husband he wanted to be. He did not end up sending any of
the e-mails to his children, but he did send a number of e-mails to
Mary. These became emotionally powerful parts of their couple
therapy. As we moved more holistically into the couple work, I
helped Louie and Mary create new divisions of labor so that Mary

was not overwhelmed by both the housework and the children after her work day.

Simultaneously, I helped Mary understand that she would only get a smiling face from her husband, not the depth of love she wanted, if she forgot that he, as a person and a man, needed to be *needed*. Mary needed to erase from her mind the idea that she was right and Louie was wrong. Throughout the process of counseling this family, I helped Mary back off her shaming, and I helped her look deeper into her husband's psyche.

Especially from the male point of view, I suggested to her, if males don't feel needed, they will not function successfully and lovingly, no matter how much we want them to "adapt to changing gender roles." Though Louie was willing to keep improving himself related to household issues with Mary, doing housework the way Mary wanted it done, or loading the dishwasher the way she wanted it loaded, did not constitute, for Louie, ways of being needed. This couple had to go deeper.

Boys and Men Need to Be Needed

With boys and men in my practice, and especially with boys and men in distress, I have found "Am I needed?" to be three of the most powerful words in family and couple counseling. Mothers of sons immediately understand this language, especially as regards their under-motivated boys. These boys don't feel needed. Many wives and girlfriends can see, if we just help them to do so, that males will make nearly any sacrifice for their loved ones if they see that their sacrifice is *needed*.

Louie was like many conflicted men in my practice and also perhaps in yours—in large part, he felt worthless because he couldn't work, but he also respected Mary for earning good money, and being the breadwinner. He felt conflicted about this not mainly because he was grieving "that the traditional male role was dead," but mainly because he was trying constantly, internally, to determine how he was needed as a man, now. It was this determination on which his successful future hinged.

When Mary saw this clearly, there was a release of tension for the couple. Mary realized that even this very "modern" man, who was open to all sorts of alternatives to traditional male roles, still needed to be needed. She realized that when he felt needed, he felt comfortable with Mary's workplace ascendancy and economic prowess. When he felt unneeded (internally useless and externally shamed by Mary), he projected his fear and anxiety onto Mary, and withdrew from holding authority in his family, and withdrew from fully loving his wife.

And Mary saw that for Louie, "being needed" could involve Louie doing more around the house, but that was not going to be enough—he needed to find other ways to be needed, too. It was this understanding that led to work between the couple about providing and protecting. During one session, Mary said, "Wow, I didn't realize it, but I've been thinking about Louie like he didn't exist as a man. I really need to understand what a man is. I'm sorry for taking him for granted." Mary had come from what she called "a hard-charging family of five girls raised by a single mom." She confessed, "Our father abandoned us, and so we just didn't take men too seriously."

Males Still Need to Provide and Protect

A crucial thing to remember when working with males is a truth boys and men know instinctively, for they have experienced it in their culture and in their homes: psychological dialogue regarding "the changing male role" is laden with minefields regarding how males must become more "sensitive about feelings" and "do what women want" and in that minefield are signs well displayed everywhere, signs that read something like: "Men no longer need to provide and protect. That's traditional male role stuff. Men are needed for something else—though we're not sure what it is. It definitely involves being sensitive and nice, though."

In our gender politics and gender political debates, we often lose males because 1) they know it is inaccurate to say "males are no longer needed for providing and protecting," 2) "we're not sure what else males are supposed to be needed for" is dangerously confusing, and 3) being nice and sensitive is not necessarily functional all the time.

Boys and men look around at the dangers and challenges of the world and know that, in some ways, gender politics today open up important topics for debate, but also, in some ways, they are out of touch with reality. Boys and men look around and see that males must still protect others. They also know that sometimes you can't survive or protect others and yourself if you don't fight back against bullies, because in the future, you may need to take up arms against oppressors and terrorists and protect your family from them. Sometimes you need to develop hard emotional shells; without those hard shells, some families and nations can't survive. Males know they need to see through, at least some of the time, the rhetoric about nice guys finishing first because if you are always the nice guy, you can get mentally or physically destroyed.

And even in situations like Louie's and Mary's, wherein males are open to new ways of thinking, males still know that a man had better learn how to provide for his family, even when public dialogue seems to say women now want to be the providers, because at a certain point, a wife or significant other may say, "I want to have children now, so I want to work part-time or work only at home for the next five years." Males sense from early boyhood that one day they will have to provide for a family. They don't necessarily see this as "the traditional male role." They see it as part and parcel of the sacrifice they will make to be a man.

The factual corroboration of what males know and bring into our offices does not often appear in the media, but sometimes it does, and the statistics become echoes of what males have intuited. Dr. Karen Sibert, writing for the *New York Times* in June of 2011, revealed what is happening in just one field, Medicine.

"I'm a doctor and a mother of four, and I've always practiced medicine full time. When I took my boards in Texas in 1987, female doctors were still uncommon, and we were determined to work as hard as any of the men.   Today, however, increasing numbers of doctors — mostly women — decide to work part time or leave the profession. Since 2005 the part-time physician workforce has expanded by 62 percent, according to recent survey data from the American Medical Group Association, with nearly four in ten female doctors between the ages of 35 and 44 reporting in 2010 that they worked part time.

"About 30 percent of doctors in the United States are female, and women received 48 percent of the medical degrees awarded in 2010. But their productivity doesn't match that of men. In a 2006 survey by the American Medical Association and the Association of American Medical Colleges, even full-time female doctors reported working on average 4.5 fewer hours each week and seeing fewer patients than their male colleagues. The American Academy of Pediatrics estimates that 71 percent of female pediatricians take extended leave at some point — five times higher than the percentage for male pediatricians."

Dr. Sibert's analysis is, as she notes elsewhere in the article, "not politically correct." But most important to our subject in this book, it is what boys and men live with—they bring this knowledge to the counseling office, and their bile rises up and their defenses harden (and they figure out how to leave our offices for good) when we tell them that "providing and protecting" is somehow not needed from males. They know that at some point they may not only need to protect, but also be the main provider.

And most of them today do not see "providing and protecting" as a way of competing with or disempowering women. While some males are narcissistic, violent, abusive, misogynist or otherwise pathological, most of the male clients I work with have no problem with women working. Most men are men of our post-feminist age—they defer to their wives in important ways. With some clear and useful mentoring, most men will bend over backward to help the people they love, including their wives, to facilitate a wife's success at work.

But all through these adaptations to changing roles, males also know that more than one-half of women will ask to stay at home with children or diminish their non-child workload to part-time at some point in their lives. So, males know that gender politics, or the "politically correct" view that males should now "evolve beyond providing and protecting," is not the correct frame for them—it is not "real." Most men know that while "providing and protecting" is indeed changing, it is also not changing, for many families, when kids come.

All of this enters our offices when males enter it. To better serve boys and men in our care, we need to openly talk about the contradiction between what various social frames are teaching in academic and popular culture regarding gender roles and what boys and men are experiencing.

One model I have found helpful in piercing political correctness is that of political scientist Warren Farrell. He discusses "the multi-option woman and the one option man." He is pointing out something you may have seen in your clients. From the primal viewpoint of most men, "male power" is different from "female power." It is not necessarily better or worse, superior or inferior, but it is different. Most men know, despite what they've read in gender political arguments in the media or professional journals, that a woman has a lot of power and a lot of options a man does not have:

*A woman decides whether she will or will not have a man's child.

*A woman decides whether she will or will not work outside the home during the early to middle child-care years of the man's marriage.

*A woman decides, from the beginning of new romance, what mate to select, and whether the man is worthy.

*If there is a divorce, the woman will most likely get the most access to the children.

While various pathologies and personality disorders, as well as any given set of personal circumstances, can curtail these female biological and social powers, still, this is the power-reality for many men. To work more effectively with these men, our profession must evolve, I believe, in dealing with men and women around changing gender roles. Advancing our thinking and our gender politics beyond old frames does not lead to unfairness for women—with men like Louie, I constantly check in on whether he is fulfilling his agreements regarding shared household tasks. Simultaneously, evolving our political frames avoids unfairness to men, and male exodus from therapy. We must remember: men who feel they are being treated unfairly by therapeutic culture—whether by our academic political correctness and/or our female-centric in-office strategies—generally leave therapy unchanged.

My role is to keep men working on themselves so they can adapt to the world. If they leave my office after one or two sessions, I do them, their families, and the larger society little good.

Helping Families Understand the Role of the Father

In few areas of counseling is our profession and culture losing more males to depression, withdrawal, and negative, even violent reprisal than in our approaches to fathering. One of the reasons Warren Farrell formed the Commission to Propose a White House Council on Boys to Men (featured in Chapter 1) was to help the federal government grapple with how to understand the importance of the role of the father in a way that would no longer be "male vs. female" or "mothering vs. fathering." The research available on both mother-bonds and father-bonds has become so vast and cross-cultural, there is no longer any reason to see one bond as more important than the other.

Dr. Farrell and our commission gathered the following data in 2011. For the sources and references on each piece of data or analysis, please see the notes and references section for this chapter.

Did You Know?

*One out of every three children in America (over 24 million children) live in father-absent homes. Among African-American children, 64 percent live in father-absent homes.

*Almost 40 percent of American children have little or no father involvement.

Simultaneously:

*The amount of time a father spends with a child is one of the strongest predictors of empathy in adulthood.

*The more the father is involved in a child's life, the more easily the child makes open, receptive, and trusting contact with new people in his or her life.

*A June 2010 study of more than a million Swedish children aged 6 to 19 found that both boys and girls were 54 percent more likely to be on ADHD medication if they were raised by a single parent. Fewer than half the cases could be explained by socioeconomic factors.

*The National Center for Health Statistics reports that a child of unwed or divorced parents who lives with only her or his mother is 375 percent more likely to need professional treatment for emotional or behavioral problems. The child is also more likely to suffer from frequent headaches, and/or bed-wetting, develop a stammer or speech defect, suffer from anxiety or depression, and be diagnosed as hyperactive.

*Elementary school children without fathers were likely to have greater anxiety and more nightmares. They were more likely to be dependent and inattentive.

*When fathers are not involved, girls showed greater signs of being hyperactive and anti-social. Both boys and girls showed signs of over-dependency on the mother.

*The most important factor in preventing drug use is a close relationship with the father.

*Living in homes without fathers is more correlated with suicide among children and teenagers than any other factor—for both sexes.

*Eighty percent of preschool children admitted as psychiatric patients in two New Orleans hospitals came from homes without fathers. Similar percentages emerge among fatherless children in Canada, South Africa, and Finland, at ages from preschool through teenage.

Crucial Questions

Like the statistics collected by Tom Mortenson and published in Chapter 1, these statistics from Dr. Farrell and our commission team are just the tip of the iceberg. The National Fatherhood Initiative and many other groups can be accessed via Google, and each site provides further statistics and studies. I hope you will go to all these sites for more information, including the site: www.whitehouseboystomen.com.

Essential to us in therapeutic settings are, I believe, are individual answers to these questions:

*Do I know as much about helping fathers be effective fathers as I do about mother-attachment and helping mothers be good mothers?

*Do I have as much sympathy for fathers as I do for mothers?

*Do I help families protect the role of the father as much as I do the role of the mother?

*Do I know how to mentor families in dealing with unfairness in the family court system that affects both mothers and fathers?

Here is a stark example of what one couple faced regarding our cultural and psychological confusion about the father's role. This story involves the father's son from a previous marriage. I always keep this case in mind when I contemplate issues regarding males, and I have thanked this couple for letting me help them through this. This case seems emblematic to me of how far away our psychology-based professions are (and thus the courts are) from fully understanding boys, men, and the role of fathers.

Paul and Elaine took in Paul's son, Johnny, from his first marriage. Johnny, at eleven, had begun to become belligerent to his birth mother, Leslie. Elaine, his stepmother, loved Johnny and considered him "one of the boys" (she and Paul had two other sons, nine and seven). Leslie agreed to the new family arrangement for her son.

After about a year of blended family life, Johnny began to become belligerent toward Elaine in the way he had become with Leslie previously. Paul and Elaine were both active and engaged parents; they worked with Johnny to help him navigate through his anger. On one occasion, Johnny shoved Elaine and shouted, "You're a fucking whore." On this occasion, Paul grabbed Johnny by his left arm, pulled him to his room, pushed him onto his bed, and told him that behavior would not be allowed. "When you've calmed down, you will come downstairs and apologize to Elaine," he commanded in a loud voice.

Johnny began to cry, and took time to regain equanimity. Ten minutes later, he came downstairs and apologized to his stepmother and his father. Things returned to normal in the family. The family ate dinner together and later settled in for homework, TV, and other activities. A moment of father-discipline had succeeded in the family—at least so it seemed.

A week later, Paul was served with a Restraining Order. A CPS investigation was begun, and Johnny was moved out of the house and sent back across country to his mother's house. Paul was accused of child abuse for grabbing his son's arm and pulling him upstairs. Johnny did not accuse his father of abuse. In fact, Johnny protested to CPS and later, the court, that he had been treated fairly by his father. But the whole cascade of events followed Johnny's phone call to his mother the day after the incident actually occurred. In that call, he reported to her that he'd been "bad," and got punished by being physically grabbed by his father. The phone call set things in motion for Leslie, who reported "abuse," then the social work system got involved, then the courts.

Six months later, in court, Johnny talked about how he appreciated the discipline and saw the moment with his father as fair, not wrong. The court, however, deemed that the child abuse laws were clear regarding the kind of "physical assault" Paul perpetrated on Johnny. Paul's Restraining Order was ordered to remain in effect.

Over the course of the next months, then into the next few years, legal fees climbed into the many thousands of dollars, and Paul was ordered to pay both his own and Leslie's fees. The financial stress took a toll on the family, but even more destructive to everyone involved was Johnny's change in behavior. Without his father's influence, Johnny moved from being belligerent toward his mother to acting out in school to stealing from a neighbor to drug and alcohol use. Paul was never allowed to have custody of his son again. Just after his sixteenth birthday, Johnny was arrested for the second time, this time for felony burglary, and sentenced to two years in juvenile prison.

The cascade of tragedies in this case grew from many factors, as every tragedy does; among those, one causal element was the destructive approach taken by the social workers, the CPS system, and the courts to good fathering. Paul, Elaine, Johnny, and the other two sons who loved Johnny—indeed a whole family and social system that cared about family stability—lost stability, richness, attachment, and healthy emotional life because a father did for a son what even the son himself knew he needed. Rather than see this case on an individual basis, the legal system, adhered to the idea that any significant angry, physical touch by a parent on a child is actionable.

In a particularly moving counseling session, Paul cried as he said to me and Elaine, "I'm so sorry. If I had known what would have happened, I wouldn't touch my son. But how can it be wrong to be a father? A boy needs a father."

With tears in her eyes, Elaine comforted her husband. "Paul, you did the right thing and your sons know you're a great father. It's the system that's screwed up. You can't blame yourself."

What else could be said? Paul, Elaine, and most of all, Johnny, were victims of a system that misunderstands and devalues the role of the father to the point of tragedy.

Advocating for Fathers

If our profession is to be more effective in helping boys and men adapt to changing gender roles, we will have to take up all sides of those gender changes. We will have to be courageous in looking carefully at how we in the psychology and social work professions help the legal system understand issues from male points of view. While you and I cannot solve all the difficulties in legal systems, I hope we will join together in the next decade to rethink how to use our psychological knowledge and talents to fully advocate for families by advocating for fathers as well as mothers.

Simultaneous to helping our legal system protect women and children against violence and abuse, we as a profession are called now to advance our thinking about boys and men from the viewpoint of the father's role. In many cases, the father's point of view is also, actually, the mother's or stepmother's point of view (mothers such as Elaine are very supportive of their husbands). Even when it is not, as in Leslie's case, it is our job to look after the best interests of the child, and, in the case of Johnny and his father, the best interests of the child were best served by letting this father be a father. The system failed Johnny because it failed to advocate for the father.

Aggression and Violence

In providing the story of Paul, Leslie, Elaine, and Johnny, I hope, among other things, to set the stage for dialogue about something so important to working with boys and men, its power cannot be overstated. Perhaps the most common mistake we make today is to unconsciously combine *aggression* and *violence* into one behavior, which mitigates our ability to work with males (and thus, their families). The social workers, psychologists, and judges who worked on Johnny's case confused aggression and violence—they did not see that Paul practiced healthy aggression, not child abuse or unhealthy violence.

If our profession is to help our clients, patients, and the larger culture assist women and men with gender equality, we must look closely at how each of us feels about aggression and violence. This is a crucial part of therapy and social work because most men and boys do not operate in the real world as though aggression and violence are the same thing. In fact, to be even more accurate: most boys and men see aggression as ultimately *useful*. For them, aggression is *constructive* of the self. Violence is, in most cases, destructive, but aggression is just the opposite.

To see this distinction empirically, observe the children and adults around you. Start with boys in preschools who build up high towers out of building blocks then concentrate, with both laughter and wonder, on aggressively knocking the towers down. Aggression, for them, is a learning experience.

Now, move onto the playground outside the school. Watch boys come to the aid of another boy or girl who is being incessantly teased or bullied—the boys will, if brave enough, aggressively gather around the hurt party, in order to stand up against the offending party.

Move into the backyard of a house down the street from the school you were just in. Notice the boys at play. If you can, pick a home in which the parents have specifically raised their boys never to play with guns or swords, or any similar "aggression-toy." Even at this home, you will most likely still notice the boy bend down to the ground, pick up a twig, and make it into a gun or sword, concentrating on his aggressive battle with unseen forces.

Keep moving. Go into another house in this neighborhood. See what kinds of video games the boys are playing. Notice the aggression (and violence) in these games. Ask the boys what they get out of playing the games. In your dialogue, notice how clearly the aggressive games feed the development of male self-confidence.

Move to a quieter place in the house. Find the boy who doesn't like the video games and the noise. See what he is drawing. Notice the science fiction storyboard he is drawing. Notice aliens and humans negotiating and fighting; notice how, through pictures of aggressive action, the boy doing the drawing is trying to learn how to become cooperative, too, through aggression.

Move anywhere in your neighborhood, institution or culture and you will see patterns of male play and relationship that involve useful, constructive, and natural competition and aggression. As you do, you may at first group all this aggressive play into some form of "violence." I hope you will let me challenge you to look at it differently. One of the keys to working more effectively with boys and men is to see that aggression and violence are not the same thing, whether in the natural world, or in the human social world.

Aggression is the attempt of an individual or system to manipulate, exploit, or control another individual or system. The person being aggressive expects, even hopes, that his or her interlocutor or "other" will fight back, i.e. will debate him, challenge him, compete with him, discipline him, and thus help guide him to grow and learn *via and within* the aggression activity.

Violence is the attempt of an individual or system to destroy another individual or system (this includes the self). Violence can destroy individuals, systems, and selves through repeated psychological control over the developing core self of the other individual or other system, and/or through physical attacks that lead to physiological harm or death. Those who are violent do not wish for debate, challenge, competition, or discipline from their interlocutor. They want to destroy.

In the case of Johnny and Paul, healthy aggression was practiced. The father was not violent. He made no attempt to destroy Johnny's core self or body through violent attacks on Johnny. Johnny deserved an aggressive response to his own violent response to Elaine's mothering. Johnny knew that the name he called Elaine was destructive of her core self. Johnny got an aggressive response from his father to the verbal violence, and Johnny respected the aggressive fathering Paul practiced.

In some kind of ideal world, perhaps, fathers (or mothers) would never have to physically grab and carry a child into another room so that he cried. But in the world of human nature and nurture—in the necessities of natural growth and psychological maturation—physical touch is useful, when practiced as healthy aggression, not violence. Loud voices, commanding tones, angry outbursts are all useful when they help build the self of the child or adult.

When I work with families, especially with families desperate for fathering, I teach the "aggression/violence" distinction. In my trainings with professionals, I spend a good deal of time looking, from various points of view, at how to help families and communities study aggression/violence distinctions. The issue of spanking inevitably comes up, and I give my bias: I have never spanked my children, but I have carried them to other rooms and scared them with my loud voice. Given that most American parents do spank their children, I make the aggression/violence distinction: to swat a child on a clothed behind once in a while can fall under the aggression category; to do more than that, i.e. to pull pants down and use belts or anything else, is violence.

Even in the very controversial area of spanking, the aggression/violence distinction can help our profession work realistically with clientele. We will most likely not stop all parents from spanking, but we may be able to help parents set rules for healthy *aggression* that help keep the spanking from becoming *violence*.

If all of us in the psychology field would be willing to study situations around us through an aggression/violence lens (or through your own adaptation of that lens to your own viewpoint and guiding psychological theory), I believe we would see a sea-change, a veritable revolution, in family law and in social work. While we would not forgive violence nor diminish our vigilance against it, we would understand our clients better, especially our male clients. By understanding the fact that aggressive and violent behavior beg for healthy aggressive response, we would understand much better than we do how to help children and adults develop useful impulse control; and very importantly, we would better understand and respect the healthy aggressiveness of many fathers.

In saying these things, we are not saying that girls, women, or mothers are not aggressive (or violent). In fact, just the opposite: we can learn a lot about female clients by factoring in aggression/violence distinctions. While females don't tend to be as physically aggressive as males, they can be far more psychologically and emotionally aggressive. So, too, with violence: girls and women can be very destructive to the core self of another person. The aggression/violence distinction is a human distinction, not just one that pertains to males.

Ultimately, if we can better understand both male and female aggression and violence in our modern world, we will also better understand changing gender roles from all safe and useful points of view. We will help boys and men by advocating for fathers, and we will further help improve the lives of girls and women by keeping more males in therapy, by helping more mothers and fathers and children work effectively together, and by creating a gender balanced world in which all of us can move into a new millennium of changing gender roles with mutual respect.

Moving Forward

Boys and men feel so misunderstood by our profession that when they find a counselor or other mental health professional who does understand males, they are more willing to enter into deep psycho-therapy; and they are better able to accept our mentoring of them into new, dynamic gender roles. The traditional male gender role has indeed changed already. Fortunately, you and I can be mentors who help males make further changes they need to make, in productive and important ways.

At the same time, if our profession does not advocate for fathers and for male points of view in gender role changes, we will not inspire or foment cohesion between women and men. We will continue to face a divorce rate of one-in-two marriages, and all of the crisis and trauma that ensues from that divorce rate. Some divorces will always be necessary, but many are not. Many marriages and families can be saved by our profession if we expand beyond seeing the new gender role as mainly about emotional fulfillment of and economic opportunity for women. While the new gender roles include those needs as foundational, we have only barely scratched the surface of what the male foundation for adaptations and changes are.

Without doing that other important work, our profession will continue to tacitly support more tragedies in families and courts than we realize we are doing. If, however, we do this new work, a fifth step toward male-friendly counseling and health care will help our profession into the new millennium, for we will see males and the male role from all sides, including some sides we have not yet fully explored.

Chapter 6: Using Peripatetic Counseling and Other Alternatives

"Human beings, like other animals, have a genetic predisposition to seek out for their habitats those landscapes that are most conducive to their well-being and survival."

--Michael Pollan

The word "peripatetic" means "of or related to walking" in Greek, and is associated with Aristotle's teaching and mentoring style—Aristotle took students on walks during instruction.

I began using this counseling technique early in my practice (much more with boys and men than with girls and women) because of my interpretations of what I saw in brain research and brain scans regarding male brains. In the traditional sit-and-talk approach, I saw the "rest state" occurring just behind the glazed eyes of the boys and men. I felt a sense of failure on my part—I was failing to activate the minds of my clients toward healing and change by just practicing sit-and-talk.

Stepping outside the box of traditional therapy, I decided to begin the practice of walking with some clients around the neighborhood. This worked—not for all but for many (and some girls and women wanted to try it, too, although most did not feel they needed it). When I say it "worked," I didn't have data or any double blind studies to show that a specific outcome grew in groups of boys and men who walked versus groups that did not. Admittedly, all I had was the sense that a lot was happening in the minds of the boys and men with whom I walked, and confirmation in my client charting.

As I reviewed charting and notes in August, which is my down time for looking at the year's progress, I saw that male clients stayed in counseling longer, and I saw, in my subjective opinion, more progress for the clients during my peripatetic year of providing counseling than during the previous year, in which I practiced no consistent male-friendly innovations. By then, my peripatetic counseling had expanded farther than the sidewalks near my office: I was also meeting and talking with some clients in their own worlds and habitats.

In this chapter, I will ask you to look at peripatetic counseling strategies that allow your client, quite literally, to "move" beyond traditional sit-and-talk therapy. We will look at the advantages of venturing therapy into the client's habitat and everyday world. I will also look with you at other strategies that allow clients to safely bring their own worlds into your office. Each of these strategies can be added to your toolbox as and when they fit with the environment of your own therapy practice or the demands of your psychological theory. Your experimentation with these strategies can constitute a sixth step in working more effectively with boys and men.

Peripatetic Counseling

The most obvious form of peripatetic counseling occurs when you take your client on a walk rather than sit with him in your office. This can be practiced anywhere, in any scenario, in any city or town. If the weather outside is uncomfortable, it can still be practiced. If the weather is dangerous or severe, it should not be practiced. With some client disabilities, it cannot be practiced either, but with many disabilities it still can be used. You can push your client's wheelchair as you "walk and talk." Even this change from traditional in-office sit-and-talk can lead to different parts of the client's brain being activated in ways different than might happen indoors or while sitting still.

From a nature-based point of view, the effectiveness of peripatetic counseling lies in the fact that physical movement stimulates the brain to activate word and feeling centers of the brain that do not get activated if the brain tries to sit for long periods of time in a chair. For girls and women who sit in chairs in your office, speaking while sitting is easier than for boys and men. We've explored some reasons for that already in this book. Primary reasons include:

1. Female oxytocin (bonding chemical) levels rise when females sit and talk with you about crisis and difficulty; on the other hand, male testosterone levels rise in crisis, and that chemical may inspire fight-or-flight chemistry, which can specifically shut down the brain-functioning that therapy needs in order to succeed.

2. Females have more access to words and word-feeling linkages in the brain in nearly any environment, including and especially in a sit-and-talk environment. Females may not need an alternative modality by which to increase their access to words and word-feeling linkages in the brain. Males may very well need an alternative modality, such as physical movement, by which to access words and feelings.

3. The male brain goes to a rest state in a way that the female brain does not. A male sitting in your office can easily become glaze-eyed and zone out, his brain nearly blank (his blood flow in the brain nearly effaced). In this state of mind, his brain is relatively useless to the therapeutic process, for it cannot remember, connect dots, see emotive clues, or follow your verbal guidance in the way you might think it should do. That male brain may need physical movement by which to reactivate out of the rest state.

These are just some of the brain-based reasons I use peripatetic counseling. It is more difficult for a client's eyes to glaze over and his brain to shut down when he is walking. A great deal of bonding between males can go on when we are shoulder to shoulder, moving and talking. A great deal of conversation and neural activation can occur when we are "doing" something together, such as walking together. The simple act of physically moving around while we interact can keep the client in counseling and therapy for many more than two of three frustrating visits.

If your client is physically dangerous, peripatetic counseling may be obviously be too risky. But in most cases—including most personality disorders and clinical theories utilized for personality disorders—peripatetic counseling can bear fruit. Fortunately, it is the kind of clinical strategy you can try a few times without harm, and disuse if it does not fit the particular client.

Habitat Visits

If walking with your client near your office is the most obvious form of peripatetic counseling, the next obvious form involves going to the house, apartment, neighborhood, or playground of the male you are working with. It might take you a few false starts to get yourself to do this. You might think of a hundred reasons why you can't. But once you do, you may feel a sense of effectiveness with males that you have not felt before. By visiting your client's habitat, you and the client make progress in one session that might not happen in your office for weeks or months. Your client feels respected and understood by you in ways he might not in your office.

In this modality, you can spend time watching your client moving around in his life and habitat. You can observe interactions you would not have seen before, and you can see environments that form the male. Thus, you gain the neural advantages of physical movement we just described above, and you gain further advantages in understanding the client's issues, an understanding that transcends the meager words your client has brought into your office thus far.

If, for instance, you go to the "cave" the 10-year-old boy has made for his depression—his dark room in the basement of his house—your trained instincts as a therapist will reveal a great deal from observation of this surrounding. You will hear his music playing there, talk to him from within his habitat and home turf regarding his pain and sadness, discover assets and roots of difficulty and even some solutions you would not have seen before.

Similarly with adults: you can go to the house of a couple that is having troubles in their marriage. As you meet them in the habitat of their troubles (and their intermittent joys), you can walk around the yard and garage and admire the man's cars or tools that form part of his expression of identity. You can sit and talk on the porch that is so well kept by the woman and her family—the porch and home that form a part of her identity (and, of course, these identity markers can be switched between genders). The personality disorders you may have diagnosed in these clients, about which you may have guessed in your office, may clarify now, in this habitat (or your diagnosis may change).

With boys who are often quite inarticulate in a sit-and-talk modality of the counseling office, your visit to their active habitat might be as informative as your visit to their home. You can go to the skateboard park in which the boy "works out," and encourage him to show you "his world." You can go on a walk after a soccer game in order to talk with a boy who sits like a lump in your office but who, when you catch him after soccer, opens up emotionally. You can watch as the boy, nine, comes off the soccer field and interacts with his peers, his mother and/or father, his stepparents, girls (or another boy).

Gopal, age nine, greets me, and I begin to walk with him. We realize he has no bottle of water with him. I suggest: "Why don't you go back, before your parents leave, and get your bottle." He gets his bottle, comes back to where I'm waiting. "You need something to eat?" He goes back to a bag of goodies to grab a protein bar or orange or some other snack brought by the "snack parent" that day. Now he comes back to me to walk toward the sidewalk.

A lot has already happened. I have seen who he is in his own setting (*his* habitat). This is, of course, only one environment, one "moment" in his life, but it's still revealing of more of him than his sullenness in my office last week as he plopped down in *my* environment and territory (an environment and territory set up for therapeutic talking) rather than *his* environment and territory, which are set up for action and talking-through-action. By coming to his habitat and territory, I've signaled, "I want to know who you are, in *your* place, I want to pay you that respect."

The respect and rapport building in this one session are worth many sessions of failure. And this is not just about a feeling-state—this is also about the physicality of this boy's environment and territory. To continue the brain-based reasoning we just discussed above: if as you read this you put yourself in my position with Gopal, you will almost literally see in his eyes and body the neural chemistry of successful counseling.

Gopal's dopamine, adrenalin, testosterone are primed because of the physical exercise and the "action" of soccer practice that pumped his brain full of chemicals and activity. He is now potentially in much better shape for talking, listening, thinking, and feeling than he would be in a sit-down-in-the-chair-and-stare hour in an office. It is now nearly impossible for his brain to go to a rest state/boredom state here, on this walk, after the stimulation of soccer practice. In an office, it's not only possible, but likely, that he could drift into inner drowsiness, then feel frustrated, then go home and say to his parents, "this counseling is stupid."

So, too, with a grown man who is your client: for similar reasons, peripatetic counseling and habitat visits work well. You can decide to take a walk with the man after the man's day at the office. This five o'clock time might be his normal therapy hour, anyway. You can meet him downstairs as he comes out of his office building. You can get a hot dog from a hot dog stand with him, sit on the steps of a building with him, watch people go by.

A conversation like this ensued between myself and a client on the steps of a library near his office building.

Gurian: Check that guy out: he's walking that dog, checking his Iphone, a little bit drunk. Yeah?

Tony: I guess. He's still got his bedroom slippers on.

Are those bedroom slippers or clogs?

I don't know.

Now what's he doing?

He's checking out that woman.

He seems pretty lonely to me. What do you think?

I guess. I think he's waiting for a call. He's not putting the phone in his pocket. He's just holding it.

And he chews on it once in a while. I wonder if he just quit smoking, or needs a cigarette.

Yeah. Good catch. Maybe.

(Silence. Both Tony and I eat more of our hot dogs.)

Tony: You guided me to that guy, right? You're doing your counseling   thing?

I guess. Why do you think I did that?

You think I'm lonely.

You hate the word "depressed," but you seem lonely, yeah. Your psychiatrist prescribes meds for you, but you don't take them. Every day you get more sad. Sitting in my office or your psychiatrist's office doesn't get through to you. But loneliness is part of why things are getting worse for you at home. When I see that slovenly, troubled, confused guy over there, I see you. You've got your work-suit and work-face working today, but your insides are messed up like that guy.

Tony frowns, eats more, thinks about this silently. Because Tony and I are out in the moving, changing world, I can use his projections to help him. Because we are staring at a lonely man "in the real world," not just thinking about loneliness in my office, Tony can project himself onto that man experientially; thus, we can make his counseling three dimensional. We can give his psyche (and feelings) an object on which to objectify themselves.

In my office, talking about his issues, he can be more resistant, because he has no experiential, projective, objective fodder for "seeing" what's going on right now. With Tony, who would initially not take medication for depression but desperately needed it, an experiential and peripatetic process was well worth trying. Fortunately, Tony did finally commit to his medication, and he and I were able to work together well.

The Peripatetic Logic Model

Whether going to a boy's soccer game and then talking with the boy after the game, or meeting a man after his shift, I am using male brain information to gain more success with my clients. Because I gain success, the client feels successful and wants to work harder to heal pain and distress. I am keeping the boy's and man's brains active, fed, projective, thinking, reasoning, "doing," present.

Rather than fighting against brain science, or wishing it didn't exist, or pretending it means nothing, I am committing to it in clinical strategy with these males. Sometimes, the soccer game elicits no new growth. Sometimes, taking the time to meet a man after work just leads to his venting about how everybody is trying to "fuck me over," including that "bitch in HR." Certainly, there is no hundred-percent success rate for peripatetic counseling.

But the success rate for this modality is higher than if all I do is meet boys and men in my office. Meeting them in their own habitats, territories, and environments makes counseling three dimensional, and leads to greater access to the outcomes a counselor, therapist, and psychologist hopes for.

Logistically speaking, because of travel, I may have to bill the client for one and a half hours rather than one contact hour, but in the end the client may also succeed in breaking through his obstacles more quickly and with more solidity than if we spent many hours sitting in my office; thus, the financial aspects of the peripatetic counseling even out.

If you decide to try this innovation, you could pick just one patient to practice this new approach with. You can disclose what you are doing and why. You can show the patient the brain scans in Chapter 2 of this book. Some male clients will not want to leave the safety of your office, but some will jump at the chance to take a walk or engage in some other form of peripatetic counseling. And some girls and women will, too.

Not only for the client, but for you as a practitioner, there can be powerful growth here. I have learned a great deal about how to improve my verbal counseling skills by engaging in the multifarious nonverbal stimuli that arise from peripatetic counseling.

When this modality goes well, I Gopal's eyes light up with emotion and insight after our session; we high five and he waves at me as I watch him walk up to his front door, and I know that something good is going to happen for him this next week, and for his family.

And when Tony "gets" the projection, and even "forgives" me for setting it up with him over hot dogs, he opens a part of himself to his sadness, and we travel down the road of shame and sorrow he is so afraid of, and I learn, the next week, that after our last session, he called his daughter at college, said he apologized to her for having an affair with her mother's best friend. Even though his daughter hung up on him, Tony says, "I'm gonna keep trying. I did wrong. I know it. I can't wallow in it forever. I'm gonna keep trying."

Drawing, Writing, Music, Gaming

Along with peripatetic counseling, the expressive arts can be highly effective tools for working with males. Four "arts" I'll look at strategically with you in this chapter can help boys and men move past psychological defenses and toward emotional expression. As with all innovations I use with boys and men, my use of these innovations grows in part from my connecting them to parts of brain science through the gender lens. These nature-based practices can work with girls and women as well. Each and all can be adapted to nearly any office and nearly any psychological theory.

Music

I first used Dave Matthews' music in sessions just over ten years ago with an adolescent boy I was counseling. He played "Crash into Me" on my office CD player, and we had a powerful discussion about his sexual fears, masturbation, shame, Catholic upbringing. He then played "Proudest Monkey" for me, and this brought up intense dialogue about pride, "stupid pride," and loneliness.

From another client—a girl—I learned about Coldplay's song "Fix You." This song moved her, and helped me work with her. As I worked with a 40-year-old man on a different day, I played "Fix You" for him. He wept. We talked about whether he was fixable, how it could happen, how much he tried to fix and save others, and failed. He brought in other songs by other artists, some of them hip hop artists, explaining songs to me, teaching me, learning about himself.

Music opens up emotional pathways like few other life-experiences can. New studies come out nearly every day regarding music's power to affect the brain's performance. Scientists at Emory University recently learned that certain songs and melodies "stick" in the memory of teenagers because of neural cell activation in the nucleus accumbus, a reward/pleasure center in the brain that stimulates the release of dopamine. This is news we can use in our practices.

Music can be used as content for a session, and it can also be a good way to ritualize the beginning of a session. As the song plays on your iPod or CD player, therapist and patient(s) can listen, feel, breathe deeply, and then get into the session. Sometimes, one opening song can dominate the whole session through repetition of certain musical passages, and dialogue about certain lyrics.

Music can also become "homework" for counseling. Males will often do homework if it is relevant and "fun." As homework, a client can burn a CD of his favorite songs off iTunes for his therapist. You can then listen to the songs during your commute during the week, picking ones to play in your office in your next sessions with the client.

Boys and men who would often go into a zoned-out rest state during a session may not go into a rest state when they listen to and analyze music. Boys and men who may often not have access to feelings and emotions through "talk" may feel and emote a great deal more when music affects emotive and sensorial centers of the brain, and thus helps the brain produce more powerful words, sentences, and inner discoveries.

Visual-Graphics

Pictures are crucial tools for therapy with males. As we have learned, boys and men tend to process words in the left hemisphere, whereas, females tend to process words on both sides of the brain. What do males do on the right side, instead of language? To a great extent, they create and process spatial, visual, and graphic stimuli: pictures, graphics, moving images, physical movement.

If we want to be effective with males, we have to accept and utilize their brain formatting rather than going against it by only using words. When we rely mainly or only on words in working with clients, we are saying to the females, "Let's use both sides of your brain," but to the males we are saying, "Let's only use the left side of yours." When we use more graphics/visuals in therapy, we are saying to males, "We will use both sides of your brains, too." The more "male" your patient is on the gender brain spectrum, the higher quantity of graphic stimulants he might need for accessing emotional life. His self-assessment abilities may very well hinge on the pictures he sees in his head more than the words he can use to understand himself.

Some ways to use graphics include:

*Photographs. Ask your client to bring to your office various pictures of people or locations he loves, family members, schools friends; ask him to bring yearbooks or scrapbooks. As he leads you through his life in pictures, his family-of-origin work, his father-son and mother-son work, his cognitive-behavioral work, his attachment and object-relations work—all can work better because he is seeing his life in pictures and attaching words to pictures.

*Celluloid. In this era of You Tube and mobile devices, you can also give your client "homework" in a celluloid therapy context, such as:

"Go find a movie clip off You Tube that shows a boy lying to his parents."

"Go find a clip that shows the kind of father you wish you had."

"Go find a clip of a boy who is misunderstood by his teachers."

"Go find a clip that shows the way you got bullied."

"Make a short video of your life."

If you try celluloid therapy but your client does not have the skills to accomplish these homework tasks, you can yourself suggest specific movies and movie clips to use for discussion. Here are movies I have used recently to help men and boys in their counseling:

> *In a Better World*
> *Love Actually*
> *My Bodyguard*
> *The History Boys.*

Sometimes I use clips from these, other times I ask the client to watch the movie at home, still other times I have watched the movie with a client in two or three installments over a period of weeks. Celluloid therapy of this kind can be very effective with males (and, of course, with females). For further resources, you can google anything like "bullying" and "boys" and see how many movies come up. Also, you can get *What Stories Does My Son Need?*, a book that lists one hundred books and movies that help engage males in developmental dialogue. The book includes discussion starter questions with each book and movie.

It can be a powerful feeling for a practitioner to use these visual strategies and watch the normally stolid male start to cry, or the sullen male quickly laugh; it is powerful to feel the scene unfold with the patient and see insights behind his eyes. Most importantly, a male can often more deeply discuss his own feelings through the use of movie clips than just a verbal prompt from you as you sit in a chair. His brain has been stimulated toward emotion by the enhanced emotion of the TV or film clip.

Some very powerful moments with clients have come in my practice from using the last ten minutes of *Saving Private Ryan.* Most males, including myself, tear up as we watch the end of that movie. Though I do not lose my therapeutic distance with the client, my own modeling of tears is liberating for him, and his tears help him open himself to deeper work.

As you experiment with visual-graphic tools, be ready for a man (or even an adolescent boy) to bring porn into your office. If a man brings in a porn clip to shock you or simply because he needs to talk about it, your response can be measured, not shaming. This is true whether you are a male or female therapist. Many boys who don't have fathers need female therapists to be ever more helpful to them in helping them understand their own sexuality, and/or help them find assets who can help them understand.

One 16-year-old discussed his feelings with me about penis size, puberty, bullying, girls, even his feelings of despair—if I had overreacted to the porn he brought in, this work would not have occurred. I told him he had to turn it off (he brought it in on his mobile device), but I engaged with him in dialogue. He had no father and no coach he was close to. He needed help with what his own expectations of himself and others should be. Simple questions of penis size plagued and scared him, and our session was helpful to him in ways it would not have been if he hadn't begged for help by "shocking" me with the visual porn.

Drawing a Life

Movies, DVD clips, YouTube, other uploads—these are "new school." Drawing is old school, and never gets old. You may already know the therapeutic gifts that come from asking a boy to draw pictures. You might not have tried it with men. It can work quite well with certain men. I hope you'll ponder the use of it with any male (and any female who would benefit). As with photographs and movies, encouraging a person to draw can say to the male, "I do want to help you use your whole brain, not just the parts of your brain that make words."

"Drawing" can come in many forms. You can make sure your office has a sand tray in it, as well as blank sheets of paper and some small canvases. You can make sure you have crayons, colored pencils, and other accoutrements for drawing. If you meet a boy or man who reveals to you (or who you discover to be) graphically talented, use that talent. Once you set him up with questions to draw answers to, a great deal more of his emotional structure and trauma will be revealed. And even if the male in your care is not graphically talented, he can still draw stick figures to help him emotionally and verbally process.

The use of archetypal psychology can blend well with drawing and other visual-graphics. The Jungian and archetypal iconography of king, warrior, magician, lover, explorer, hero, villain, as well as many other types, can become subject matter for drawing. The video game industry is almost completely based in archetypal psychology. It is a highly visual-graphic medium that therapists can learn from. Jungian and archetypal psychology stimulates males in therapy. It has been successful in helping tens of thousands of boys and men through the mythopoetic men's movement and the workshops of poet Robert Bly, storyteller Michael Meade, psychologist James Hillman, and others. Michael Meade has specifically focused his archetypal work on helping hard-core boys and men in prison environments. Archetypal psychology is primal to males, and that primal quality can give an internal language to males who have difficulty finding a visual or spoken language for emotion.

If you decide to utilize drawing in your practice, and if you have not already done so, you might gain a great deal of helpful insight from books like *Iron John* by Robert Bly, *The Power of Myth* and *The Hero with a Thousand Faces* by Joseph Campbell, and *King, Warrior, Magician, Lover*, by Robert Moore and Douglas Gillette.

For an experiential approach to male mythology, you might enjoy my books, *The Prince and the King* and *The Invisible Presence*. These two books are used by therapists to help boys and men interpret their own words, drawings, art, and dreams as regards father-son and mother-son relationships. These latter two books also provide guided meditations and other experiential and peripatetic work that can be done with you and your male clients through use of the archetypal/gender lens.

Writing as Therapy

Many boys and men are intimidated by writing words on blank sheets of paper. They do not feel naturally gifted at the practice, and/or they have had bad experiences with the way writing was taught to them, and/or they are functionally illiterate. That said, writing is still something to consider trying with any boy or man (or girl or woman). Narrative therapy and simple free-writing can be effective. I have seen relatively illiterate males write very emotional letters to their dead mothers or fathers. These letters brought up emotional content for many weeks of counseling. I have seen recovering addicts write letters to their drugs of choice. "Dear Booze, I'm done with you…" "Dear Coke, you've taken my best years…" "Dear Oxy, I want to feel pain now, I don't want to hide behind you.…"

Parents and children in family therapy can use letters and e-mails as writing tools. Each person involved in a family's therapy can keep journals, even on their computers, and you can teach them how. Every month or so, in a somewhat ritualized way, each patient can write a short letter/e-mail to the other, which is brought into therapy for reading aloud by the patients, and for therapeutic material.

One thing I nearly always suggest to couples is for each member to write one continual free-written letter that says *everything*, even the things he or she would never show anyone, including the lover or spouse. I then suggest that a second letter (e-mail) be edited from the free-written letter, or written while doing the first. In the second more carefully crafted document, there is greater concentration on what can be shared. From these documents, many feelings and thoughts emerge.

Some males enjoy poetry and will write poetry as a "homework assignment" between sessions. For these males, analyzing the

poetry of the masters can be helpful. I keep copies of poems that
are powerful for males in my office, reading a poem aloud to the
client, then having the client read the same poem aloud to me. We
go through the poem to seek wisdom. We do this with pieces of essays, as well.

The anthology, *Rag and Bone Shop of the Heart*, is a powerful
volume to have available in your office for poetry about men's lives.
The anthology, *What Is a Man?*, is helpful for reading pieces of essays from such men as Sophocles, Teddy Roosevelt, Martin Luther
King. Sometimes boys and men become so inspired by the written
words that they try to write their own manifestos. When this is the
case, I help them break their manifestos into themes:

*Boyhood
*Manhood
*Risk-taking
*Fathering
*Loving
*Sexuality
*Compassion
*Honor
*Education
*Work
*Success
*Failure

As the boys and men write what they believe in each category, in a blending of the categories, or in any other category they
choose, we discuss the boy's or the man's core-values, needs, and
flaws. This approach echoes the "core theme" model of Chapter 4,
in which we are enhancing male verbalization abilities by tasking
his words around themes that are relevant and crucial to the male's
perspective and personality.

If you want to try more writing tasks with your clients, it
can be useful to enhance the ability of males to write more words
and feelings on paper by playing music in the background, and by
suggesting that the boy or man draw a storyboard of what he wants
to write before he starts writing. Many males will stare at blank
sheets of paper with few words forming in their brains, but when
they draw the outline or action of what they want to say *before* they
write, they can refer to the drawings they've made and write words

based on a visual graphic stimulant of their own creation. This practice generally leads to greater word/emotion production than the blank sheet of paper does.

Gaming in Therapy

A boy of eight came into my practice with what his parents called a "video game addiction." That he was so obsessed with video games raised clinical questions of addiction, which we looked at carefully. Simultaneously, his "addiction" indicated that he was a very visual-graphic boy. My assessment from speaking with him and his family was that he processed his internal and external world through visual-graphic-spatial thought process even more than might another boy. He was more "male" on the gender-brain spectrum than many other boys were.

Knowing this meant knowing that traditional sit-and-talk therapy was going to have to play second fiddle to visual-graphic-spatial tools. Furthermore, since the boy, Brandon, was already a young master at video games, I could use his gaming interest in my counseling. I had Brandon show me pieces of video games he found most inspiring and fun. We did a lot of work with that video game. He showed me the quest he was on, who his enemies were, how he had thus far succeeded and thus far failed. Since video games were his dreamscape and internal habitat, we analyzed this dream habitat. I got access to his internal emotional world and was better able to help the boy and his family because I entered the boy's inward "territory" through gaming.

You can utilize gaming by setting up a Wii or other play station in your office. You can also utilize gaming without setting up equipment—you can rely on the boy to bring in his own mobile device. With Brandon, a mobile device worked. He showed me the game, and it was easy for me to see the wash of dopamine in his eyes as he received visual and psychological rewards from playing the game.

Video games are only one kind of gaming that can help you reach boys. I have played chess with young males, as well as various card games, and specifically, poker. These games keep boys' brains active, competitive, rewarded internally, healthily "stressed." They also create multiple bonding opportunities.

Other Male-Friendly Innovations

Other male-friendly innovations include the following. All and each are brain-based: they try to increase therapeutic effectiveness by helping males feel neurally comfortable and mentally awake in ways that can mirror their comfort and enjoyment of their own "habitats."

*Give the boy/man a squeeze ball (small nerf ball) to squeeze while you talk with him in your office. This hand-squeezing motion keeps the brain stimulated—more able to process emotions/words. The squeezing of the nerf ball imitates the boy's tendency in his own habitat to twirl his own hair or tap a pencil or otherwise do something with his hands while talking about tough things.

*Ask boys to bring in their favorite action figures (or other objects) from home to your office; let them play with these figures as you talk with them. This hand-eye play keeps their brains activated and provides fodder for conversation via the male's experiential concentration—through his hands and eyes—on core-themes applicable to action figures, such as respect, character, heroism.

*Allow and encourage boys and men to doodle while they talk. Doodling is not generally disrespectful or necessarily distractive. It can be a safe and comfortable way for males to keep their brains awake and attentive to verbal/emotive tasks.

*Let males move around your office while you talk with them. Pacing (for adult and adolescent males), rolling on the floor (for boys) can be helpful in keeping male brains activated. When boys and men think about intense things at home or in another comfortable habitat, they often do something physical (pacing, playing a game in which they move around, or getting up and down in their chairs). You can replicate their safe habitat experientially by letting the male do the same kind of thing in your office.

*Bring a Stairmaster (or similar piece of equipment) into your office—let the male climb the Stairmaster while you talk with him; this activity keeps his brain more active, and provides him the "doing" that can help the "talking."

*Develop a habit for giving boys and men a lot of silence-and-think-time before you expect their answer to a new question, especially a new question that switches focus or concentration.

Some males will answer questions right away, transitioning well between thoughts, but quite often, in order to get the clear and truthful answers you want, you may have to wait longer for males to process emotional information than females. Males may need lots of silences in which to transition between thoughts and feelings in the brain, then attach those feeling transfers to appropriate words.

*Males often hear less well than females. They often need a louder voice from you than girls and women do, and they may tend to talk in louder voices when they are working on problems. Talk louder if needed, and don't worry too much about male loudness or male "loud tones."

*Boys in general tend to mature at a slower rate than girls, so make sure to study the boy you are working with in order to have clear and reasonable expectations for his verbal, emotive, and other abilities. The male/female maturity gap is most clear in the younger years, but it can apply just as well to adolescents and adults. Variety of words and depth of content attached to words may simply not be as developed in many males as early as in many females, so our expectations need to shift to accommodate the reality.

*Because of differences in the rods and cones of the eyes of males and females, boys and men often need bright (not blinding) light in the room in order to perform better in their thinking/talking tasks. When working with males, you might consider avoiding soft candles and dim lights, unless your meditation or hypnotherapy technique calls for that environment.

*Humor is emotional currency for boys and men. Ask your male client to bring jokes into therapy (even "dirty" ones that are not dangerous or demeaning). What jokes the male brings into your office will reveal a lot to you. Furthermore, jokes build rapport and open emotional pathways. Tell jokes of your own, though beware of becoming "cheesy," i.e. trying too hard by telling jokes that patronize or just don't go anywhere. Remember: if you are unable to joke around with some males, you may lose them as clients. Males test other people through jokes.

*Because boys and men do not tend to read emotional cues on faces and in words as well as girls and women do, be very clear with the male on what you are feeling or thinking. Don't assume he knows where you are emotionally or intellectually. Repeat yourself as needed. And make sure he tells you exactly what he believes his wife, girlfriend, mother or other person is feeling. For males, who very often do not know what others are feelings (but are expected to know), it can be powerful to make sure you confirm reality.

*When you feel therapy straying, come back to a boy's interest areas as topics of conversation. A useful way to work this into therapy is to constantly "test" the male on the trivia in his interest area. Ask him to tell you some obscure fact you could not know but can admire him for knowing—concerning football, basketball, gaming, literature trivia, spelling, music. Any interest area has its trivia, and you can find all trivia quickly through the Internet.

*Become the therapist/mentor who is known for "working with boys and men." Generally, clients and patients will know you are that therapist if you show education in two areas that males may need your help in dealing with outside your office:

--for boys, the difficulties boys face in today's schools

--for men, the gender differences that affect marriages.

In both school and home, males today often find themselves in environments that do not feel like their own "habitat." As we've noted, their school classrooms are often not set up for the way their brains work, and so they have trouble feeling "at home" at school. Similarly, marital and other relationship expectations are mainly set up around more "female" sit-and-talk, or talk-about-feelings modalities, and many males do not feel at home in that kind of constancy of emotion-talk. We must remember: for males, just sitting and talking does not often feel "real." Action is real for boys and men. Harvard psychologist William Pollack uses the powerful phrase "action love" to denote the way males see feelings through action.

Thus, moving our own clinical practices beyond sit-and-talk, and helping clients move toward greater innovation will bring more *action* into therapy and couple communication. Through more action, we help connect therapeutic process and inner work to the real world of boys and men.

The Minds of Boys can help you become briefed on what is happening to boys in school who feel a lack of reality, resonance, action, and relevance in school. *What Could He Be Thinking?* can help you provide information on gender differences to adult women and men. These books, and others like them, can help you become an advocate for males—an advocate for more action and innovation in therapeutic settings. The more you delve into the male "real world," the more you become the innovative mentor boys and families, and adult men and couples want to work with. And word of mouth spreads quickly. You will get and hold more clients and patients.

*Use phone or Skype when needed. Some of the things we've discussed here can be done innovatively through telephone or Skype. For instance, a phone client, a boy, in another city can draw pictures and his mother can take a photo of the picture and send it via iPhone. Similarly, with DVD clips and video games, a phone line and Internet connection allows a therapist to use visual-graphics with faraway clients. I have talked with men who were working out on their Stairmasters/treadmills; I was on a land line, they were on their Bluetooth. With a boy and his family with whom you speak via Skype, you can suggest the boy squeeze a squeeze ball while you all talk.

Thus, many innovations and strategies used in your office can be set up in long-distance therapy. Given the global nature of our world in the new millennium, I think it is possible that more and more of us will be called to expand our counseling and coaching practices, via technologies, to other parts of the country and the world. Fortunately, the tools for engaging clients, both male and female, already exist, though perhaps in ways we may not yet have tried.

Next Steps

By using peripatetic counseling as well as musical, visual-graphic, expressive arts, and other stimulants for brain activity in males, you are taking a sixth step toward re-aligning your practice to be more effective with boys and men. If you approach all of this from a historical and anthropological viewpoint—recalling, for instance, the Greeks— you might find inspiration to try these innovations.

All of our ancestors used hands-on work, peripatetic instruction, the arts, and physical movement to counsel boys wherever and whenever they needed help. At about the same time historically that our human cultures started to negate these practices from our schools (about a hundred years ago), our profession also set up counseling practices to operate relatively devoid of boy-friendly strategies, as well.

Michael Gurian

In this new millennium, armed with brain research, we now have a chance to re-assess the usefulness of good counseling and mentoring practices for boys and men. It is a chance most of the males in our counseling practices would be very grateful for. They desperately want us to innovate. They want to change their own lives for the better through therapy and counseling, but very often, they can't discover or inculcate those life-changes unless we meet them in their own "habitat," and their own male nature.

Chapter 7: Working with
Male Anger and Aggression

"The efforts he makes to save himself can bring him to ruin."
--Paul Tournier

Adie Goldberg, ACSW, M.Ed., has been a mentor to my daughters, and a therapist to many women and men, and boys and girls. She is gifted at working with both male and female patients. She also specializes in early attachment, and is the co-author of two books in that field, *It's a Baby Boy*! (2008) and *It's a Baby Girl!* (2008), with Ob-Gyn Stacey Bering, M.D., and the Gurian Institute.

In the late 1990s, Adie read *The Wonder of Boys* and became interested in the research on the male brain. She began to apply some of its material to her practice, and we enjoyed many discussions about how different it was for her, as a woman, to treat girls than boys, and women than men.

"Male aggression is especially complex for me," she said. "Except for the most sensitive boys I work with, most boys and men need me to understand their aggression better than I do. And they need me to not overreact to their anger. For me, as a woman, there's a different chemistry working when I try to bond with them. I'm trying to bond *without aggression* so that we can talk about and deal with the man's issues, some of which may have been that he is too aggressive with his spouse, for instance, or his kids. But in many cases, the male I'm working with is trying to bond *through his aggression*. He wants me to confront him or he wants to confront me aggressively.

"This is not the case with every male, of course, nor with a confrontational male all the time, but the more I see males through the gender science lens, the more obvious this becomes to me. I as a woman have different chemical and neurological approaches to therapy, and I've been socialized to rely on a different way of bonding than have many of the boys and men I work with."

In pointing out this personal experience, Adie is, I believe, speaking also for the therapy profession as a whole. To "get at the deep issues" our clients need help with, and to help the client's work be immanently possible in a small, closed office that sits next to other small closed offices with thin walls between them, we unconsciously ask (even beg) our clients to sit down in their chairs and leave their loudness and aggressiveness outside. Ironically, we are asking many of the males to strip themselves of a great deal of their power once they enter our room. And this is one of the reasons males leave our offices unchanged.

In fact, to take this even farther, we don't just ask males to leave their internal power behind—we also moralize that power as inherently defective. We signal to males that there is a "right" way to be in therapy and a "wrong" way. We contemplate only the downside of aggression and anger (unconsciously feeling that aggressive, angry actions by the man previously brought him or his wife or children to the edge of ruin), and thus *a priori* we moralize feelings and emotions linked with aggressiveness and anger, inadvertently signaling to males that whole parts of their way of being are inherently defective or "wrong." The "right" and effective way to be, at least in this therapy room, is quiet, sitting down, contemplative, "nurturing." The wrong way is angry, aggressive, one-upping, and confrontational.

The consequence of this moralization: many males walk into our offices knowing that their most accessible feeling—anger—and most accessible tool for growth—aggression—are part of the "wrong" way of being in therapy. The wisdom of William Blake, that sometimes "the tigers of wrath" can be "wiser than the horses of instruction," does not appear in our offices (at least from the male point of view), and so, as Adie was intuiting, we lose many boys and men. These boys and men need for us to expand our practice toward the wisdom of the poet, and the fuller, wider wisdom of human psychology.

Aggression Nurturance

A seventh step we can take toward working more effectively with males is to confront in our profession (and then reframe and re-strategize) the way we deal with male aggression and anger. Though many therapists may unconsciously feel frightened of male aggression and anger, actually, most male anger and aggression is an effort by the male to save himself and others, and while some aggression and anger can ultimately lead to his ruin, most is helpful.

In this chapter, I will go even more deeply into this subject than I did in Chapter 5. I will also provide a number of suggestions and tools for theory and practice regarding male aggression and anger. As we work together with this material, it is crucial to say that some suggestions are risky and "outside the box" and some can, if applied at the wrong times, be counterproductive. You as a practitioner must choose what works and when, and if you feel you are in any danger from a client or patient, that feeling trumps anything I say here.

At the same time, it is important to say that if you are not presently succeeding with male clients as much as you wish, and if you suspect your own feelings about male aggression and anger have anything to do with that, you may be transferring more unnecessary fear than you realize to your patient load.

Adie continued her analysis this way: "Then there's the personal experience of many women who are therapists. Many of us have felt hurt in our families, marriages, or relationships by male anger and aggressiveness—whether from our fathers, our boyfriends/husbands, or other men at work—so, that stuff scares us. We don't want to spend our work day as therapists potentially hurt by more male anger and aggression. Without realizing it, as a form of self-protection, we do what we can to minimize male aggression and anger."

Adie's wisdom extends beyond the female gender, too. I have spoken with male therapists who have been hurt in relationships with their fathers (which hurt was one of the reasons they got into the therapy profession). These and other men can fear male aggression and anger in their offices and professions as much as their female colleague might.

To take a seventh step towards doing better by our boys and men, let's look through a lens of care-giving, empathy, and nurturing called "aggression nurturance." Anger and aggression are a lot of what males bring to therapy, for males know (unconsciously and in inchoate ways) that aggression, anger, and competition are useful, important, productive, and healing mechanisms for success. So let's explore this thoroughly.

Expanding What We Mean by "Nurturing"

In observing males and studying anthropological and neurobiological information regarding male behavior, I developed the term "aggression nurturance" in 1995 in order to try to help professionals and parents look at males more closely. My specific interest lay in hoping to accurately describe differences between the ways males and females nurture others and themselves toward self-confidence.

In both rural and urban environments in the United States, then in comparative research during two years in both rural and urban environments in Turkey, I observed that males (such as fathers) tended to nurture themselves and others through more direct aggression than females, with less emphasis on distended verbal nurturance, i.e. when they used words, they used them in quick bursts not long paragraphs. Females, in general, tended to nurture themselves and others through less direct aggression than males, substituting more direct empathic responses to particular situations, and utilizing more distended word groupings. Though my research goal was somewhat different than theirs, my ultimate outcome mirrors the work of Pepper Schwartz at the University of Washington and Deborah Tannen, in *You Just Don't Understand.*

By now, in 2011, everyone has perhaps observed this kind of difference anecdotally, in their own lives. But still, let's illustrate it. Here is a piece of dialogue I heard recently at a local park as two teenage boys walked off a basketball court. When they parted company to go to their separate cars, they said:

"Right, then. Later."

"Yeah. Love you, dude."

"Stop it, fucker!"

"Yeah. Peace, man."

"Peace."

Grinning, they both got into their cars.

Perhaps some part of why they grinned was from sheepishness at this intimate ritual being seen and heard by a gray-haired stranger, me, walking by. But no matter the reasons for nuance, this kind of basic male ritual occurs all over the world. It involves one-upping, masking-of-vulnerability, aggression, a mock show of anger, deep nurturance, and clear mutual love.

This kind of ritual is an example of what I call *aggression nurturance.* This nurturance style, one based in male brain functioning, male biochemistry, and male socialization differs from *direct empathy nurturance,* which favors female biology, chemistry, and socialization. Thus, while aggression nurturance can happen between two girls, it is more likely to go on between boys and men, for some very natural reasons.

Male/Female Differences in Emotion and Empathy Response

When an observer or spouse or even a clinician says, "Men keep their feelings bottled up," they usually mean men keep grief, sadness, fear, and pain bottled up. These same males may not keep their anger bottled up. It can seethe, ooze out, and can sometimes do physical harm to men, women and children. So, when people say, "Men should show more feelings and emotions," they do not usually want men to show more anger and aggressiveness.

When people say, "Women are constantly in touch with their feelings," they usually mean grief, sadness, pain—not anger or aggressiveness. The women who constantly feel their own sadness may often not show much of their anger. That unexpressed anger can do harm, just as male anger and aggression can, but generally the harm females cause is not as physical as it is adroitly psychological.

In saying this, we are not saying that these tables are never turned. Some women are obviously and constantly aggressive, some men repress all their anger and feel proud of saying, "I've been married thirty years and never raised my voice to my wife." Anger and aggression are human, not just "male" or "female." But even with that caveat, there is useful learning for us as mental health practitioners if we focus on male/female differences in emotion and empathy response.

Try an experiment. Find a game of volleyball on a beach or softball on a field or street hockey in the neighborhood—look for a game that has both boys and girls or women and men in it. For the sake of this observational experiment, stick with these games for as long as it takes for one of the children (or an adult) to get hurt. Watch how the males and females nurture the fallen person.

When I observed a basketball game between 13-and-14-year-olds (about one-third girls and two-thirds boys) in a local park, I saw a contrast of male/female nurturing styles. In the middle of a full-court press, a boy fell, injured. A girl teammate ran to him, bent down beside him, and said in a softened voice, "Are you okay? Are you hurt?" She tried to engage him in conversation about his affliction. A boy teammate did not break stride as he shouted, "Paul, get up! Come on! We need you!"

The girl's approach involved "direct empathy." In order to nurture the hurt boy, the girl relied on becoming intimate with the hurt person (via close proximity and words). She also utilized a soothing tone, and even if she felt perturbed that the boy fell and thereby negatively affected the competitive full-court press, she showed no anger or perturbation. Most important to her was to be verbal-emotive with the boy in a way that would *not continue* the boy's physical or psychological pain, but instead help him "feel better."

The boy teammate, on the other hand, practiced "aggression nurturance." He did not care much at all whether the fallen boy's physical pain continued or not. In fact, "no pain, no gain" was his unconscious edict. For the boy teammate, physical pain meant nothing compared to the potential humiliation his friend would feel if the fallen boy was the cause of failure (losing the game). So the boy teammate nurtured the fallen boy by motivating him through pointing out how the aggression-system (the competitive game) *needed* him; and thus, by re-accepting and re-valuing the fallen boy in the aggression system of the competitive game.

Both the girl and boy teammates cared about the fallen boy; they just cared, nurtured, and were empathic differently, with a different focal point for the empathy and nurturance. The girl nurtured the fallen boy's self-esteem through direct empathy; the boy nurtured it through hierarchical protections in aggression systems.

When Adie was analyzing male/female difference in the therapy office regarding aggression and anger, this is some of what she was analyzing. Women (and most male therapists, too) set up therapy offices in a traditional therapy model—the therapy office is to be a place of *direct empathy* not *aggression nurturance*. Therapy offices are not competition/aggression systems like a basketball game is. They are sit-and-talk environments that favor female styles of direct, verbal, empathy nurturance.

Baseline Strategies for Supporting Aggression Nurturance

In realizing this early on in my career, I began to look for ways to expand counseling and therapy toward some semblance of aggression nurturance. I developed baseline strategies and environment changes in order to become more male-friendly.

Here are some immediate suggestions you can try as you look carefully at your talking style, your posture while in conversation, your office iconography, and the subjects you bring up with boys and men. I hope my suggestions will help you alter your environments to accommodate boy's and men's aggression-nurturance proclivities. You might find this alteration to be especially important if your office-world is, right now, mainly or only suited for direct verbal-emotive empathy with girls and women. After we look at these strategies, we'll go more deeply into verbal styles that utilize more aggression nurturance.

*Take down one or more of the soft-colored pictures on the wall and replace it or them with pictures of sports heroes.

*Add books (biographies, etc.) of sports heroes and other male heroes to your book shelves.

*Place books like *A Dangerous Book for Boys* and other similar books on male development on your bookshelves.

*Place literature about Boy Scouts of America and boys' rites of passage programs on coffee tables.

*Keep comic books of action heroes in your office, and include graphic novels on your bookshelves.

*Place sports memorabilia, such as signed football caps or signed baseballs, on a shelf or table in your room.

*Place a video game console with screen in your office and don't hide the video games. Even if one of the games is *Grand Theft Auto* (a game which you, like me, may find morally repugnant and misogynistic), let it be of use to your office as a topic of discussion for guiding boys' character development.

*Use the video games you have—play one with the boy or man—not only to build rapport and stimulate the male brain as we discussed previously, but also to help you "get in the head" of the boy or man's particular aggression and anger patterns.

*Play aggressive/competitive games with the boy or man, including chess and poker, and if possible in the logistics of your practice, spend some time with the boy or man at a basketball court or another game field. If nothing else, you can also go outside to toss a baseball with a boy for a half hour of your session, talking while you throw the ball harder and laugh together.

These are small things you can do, but they are significant for the males in your care. They can act to inspire you and the males around you to expand your therapy practice toward male energies, and toward even finer and more complex approaches to male anger and aggression.

Risking Confrontation with Male Clients

In the final chapter of this book, we will look closely at the most sensitive boys and men in our practices, for whom direct empathy nurturance and verbal-emotive environments might work better than they would for males who are more "male" on the gender/brain spectrum. For such sensitive boys and men, aggression is somewhat anathema, and our traditional sit-and-talk therapy model may be fine. In fact, with these boys and men, traditional sit-and-talk therapy might work so well that we may think, "See, what I'm doing is fine for boys and men."

But then we must ask: which boys and men are staying in therapy with us? Psychologist JoAnn Deak, who has developed a number of brain-based models for therapy and counseling, calls sensitive boys and men, "the 20 percenters." As we'll note in the next chapter, there is a significant amount of brain-based research supporting the idea that just under a fifth of our males are the highly verbal-emotive males who do well in traditional therapy.

That leaves the other 80 percent of males who need therapy but may not fit our sit-and-talk, direct-empathy environments. Given the corroborative research on bridge brains that we discussed in Chapter 2 and given research we will look further explore in Chapter 8, it appears that most boys and men in our cities and towns, our neighborhoods and our prisons, are not highly verbal-emotive, at least and especially in the first few counseling sessions (the ones in which we lose them), so I am arguing that most males need more mirroring activity, from us, regarding aggression nurturance.

I believe these males want to test, from the beginning of our interactions with them, whether we are "strong enough" to handle their aggression and anger. They may not be conscious of this internal proclivity, but it is part of who they are as boys and men. Even if they never confront us (but just withdraw during therapy sessions or leave therapy within a few weeks), they are constantly judging whether we know how to handle their inborn (and socialized) aggression, and their constantly brewing internal anger regarding their own failures, the rejections they've experienced, their abandonments and enmeshments.

For these boys and men, confrontation skills are key skills we need in our therapy and helping professions. These boys and men need confrontation with us (safe confrontation, of course) by which to trust us, and by which to inspire their own aggression nurturance, problem-solving, self-confidence building, and moral and emotional growth.

"Trust" is a key word, here. It connects with a important clinical idea regarding males: *confrontation is often a best way to build trust with males.* That may seem anathema to our profession, especially given the calm, direct-empathy, sit-and-talk strategies we generally use, but actually, a clinical focus on how males build trust can be very useful to expanding our field and discipline to better include males.

The Gift of Confrontation

I was given the author's name, Lee Child, by a businesswoman sitting next to me on an airplane. She saw that I was reading a Joseph Finder thriller, *Paranoia,* and she said, "If you like Joe Finder, you'll love Lee Child's Jack Reacher series." She was right. I've read every one of Child's thrillers, almost always on long airplane rides, and each time, I see gender science at work, especially regarding how to reach boys and men. In my counseling practice, I've asked both male and female clients to read Lee Child books (and others in that thriller category) if they are clients whose aggression and anger occupies a great deal of their own psychological focus.

Lee Child's protagonist, Jack Reacher, is a former Army MP, 6'5", 250 pounds, highly skilled, very smart, and very strong, who wanders the United States solving crimes. In one particular novel, *Worth Dying For*, Jack Reacher gets into a confrontation with five men while trying to protect two women and a man. Here is a scene:

"The guy (in front of Reacher) reversed the gun. Right hand on the barrel, left hand on the stock.

"The guy behind Reacher moved. He wrapped his left forearm tight around Reacher's throat, and he clamped his right palm tight on Reacher's forehead.

"Immobile.

"The fourth guy raised the gun horizontal, butt first, two-handed, and cocked it back over his right shoulder, ready to go, lining it up like a spear, and then he rocked forward and took a step and aimed carefully and jabbed the butt straight at the center of Reacher's face and

"CRACK.

"BLACK."

Unconscious from this attack to his head, Reacher is tossed into a basement, where he wakes up to assess the damage.

"(Reacher) raised his hand to his face. Slowly. He knew it would be like shooting himself in the head. But he had to know. Because something was wrong. He touched his nose. He gasped, loud and sudden, like an explosive curse, pain and fury and disgust.

"The ridge of bone on the front of his nose was broken clean off. It had been driven around under the tight web of skin and cartilage to the side. It was pinned there, like a mountaintop sliced off and reattached to the lower slope.

"It hurt like hell."

I have shown these scenes to both boys and girls. There is no 100 percent rule on responses, but in the main, girls feel less affinity for the scenes than boys. For the boys who say, "Cool!" there is often a visceral affinity with graphic novels or other stories, like Lee Child's, that feature *aggression-heroes*. Given that boys spend more self-assessment time parsing through these sorts of affinities with these heroes than girls do, I believe these boys and men understand and assume three things at an inchoate level.

1. To be whole, boys/men must confront enemies; indeed, males/heroes must *seek out* confrontation that can do "good" for them as individuals, and/or make the world and their relationships more moral, right, or safer. (While some men and boys seek out violence for immoral ends—psychopathic or abusive males—most males do not seek out confrontation only to destroy).

2. Male/heroic confrontations and wounds are "cool," "badges of honor," not to be avoided but to be sought out, for to be confronted and wounded is to be willing to change, adapt, and grow. (This is often missed by observers of confronta-

tions—we often miss that for many males "growing" means getting wounded).

3. Male anger is "heroic" and good and useful when it is "right"—it's nothing to be afraid of, unless it does immoral things or hurts people unnecessarily. (Heroism and good and right are all interwoven in the male psyche, as we analyzed earlier in looking at male focus on character development—emotion is interwoven here, too, and often, through passionate anger).

These are three crucial, and mainly unconscious, resonances in males across cultures. As we noted in Chapter 5, when most boys and men read graphic novels or comic books or watch similar cartoons, movies, or TV shows, they do not moralize aggression as violence in the same way that they perceive many girls and women do, including mothers, wives, female teachers, and therapists. In their video games, graphic novels, novels, and TV and film, boys and men often applaud the heroic confrontations, inspired by the way each confrontation models for males how they should direct their own anger and aggression toward "the good" and "the successful."

Confronting Boys and Men

I hope that the analysis in Chapter 5, as well as this analysis in Chapter 7, resonates in some way with suspicions or intuitions you have had with your own sons, husbands, boyfriends, fathers, and male clients. If you do agree that there is something important to consider here, you may gradually find yourself becoming more effective with male clients. By doing simple things that we mentioned earlier, such as putting up sports heroes on the walls when you see a boy or man, you accommodate "maleness" just a bit more than before. By expanding the confrontational tools at your disposal, you will go even further and deeper into helping boys and men.

As we move into looking at these tools, and as with all the other points made in this book, two caveats must always be made:

1. Everything I am saying must go to the back burner if you feel in danger from a patient.

2. Some of what we are exploring regarding confrontation of males will be helpful in retaining and working with female patients and clients, as well.

With these caveats in mind, here are seven principles that can help you as a practitioner further adapt your practice toward more effective confrontation with males, thus, toward more aggression nurturance. I will illustrate how to practically exploit these principles through case studies shortly.

*Males often trust self-assessments developed through confrontation more than assessments developed through passive conversation. This may be a result of the fact that when the male is involved in the confrontation, it elicits anger, and males often trust anger more than we realize. If we help boys and men recall confrontations from the past, the males may get a great deal of immediate insight into themselves and others, for in past confrontations males may have invested their core selves in profound, revealing ways in which they may not have invested themselves in more passive experiences.

*As you have probably noticed, when boys and men enter intense confrontation with others, such as their spouses, children, parents, friends, or therapists, they often project onto the "other" the feelings they would otherwise be unable to access verbally themselves. This can be immensely helpful to an observant therapist—you can use that projection as a mirror for boys and men (I will present more on the understanding and practicalities of this in a moment). Because males are not as internally aware as females, they often move toward unconscious projection and transference very quickly.

*Because confrontational conversation is so emotionally intense, and if the therapist is willing to be confrontational, boys and men often trust the therapist's discernments more than if dialogue remains passive. Quite often, a boy or man will feel that your comments are much wiser after a confrontation has established trust between you, than when your comments just come as part of a dull sit-and-talk conversation, week after week.

*Often, in order to be effective in confrontation with boys and men, confrontational success requires the therapist to interrupt the patient. Practically speaking, if a male (or female) patient is droning, becoming tangential, or becoming repetitive, therapist interruptions can create powerful confrontations; if handled surgically, the interruption can gain the respect of the patient, especially the male patient. This may sound anathema to the ways in which we were trained as counselors or therapists, but it can often be crucial for building rapport and respect with certain males, even narcissists.

*Confrontations are not only frightening, at times, for the therapist, but also for the client. This can be a very good thing—a "good" stressor—for when you carry on a confrontation with an adolescent or adult male, the fear he feels can be useful to you and to him. Fear means vulnerability, and while vulnerability feels like flaw and weakness to a male, it can also be a defining moment in the therapist-client relationship. The way you handle the male's anger can show him how you will handle his fear and vulnerability. What he most wants to know is how you will handle his fear and vulnerability—his trust of you is very much based on how you handle his weaknesses.

*The art of apology is often needed in confrontations with males—there is rarely a loss of authority or therapeutic power in apologizing to a client after a confrontation. Perhaps you can apologize for your own raised voice—this is especially the case if the male has come to tears. Your frank (though not cloying) apology regarding something you said can act as a way for the male to regain his pride, and that regaining may be essential to retaining the male in therapy.

*During confrontations, words from boys and men such as, "I don't care," "I wasn't scared," "I hate my mom," or other quick-burst defense/aggression phrases, often show that you are getting close to the kinds of honest responses you are looking for in your confrontation of the male. These quick-burst responses often mean the opposite of the words themselves, i.e., "I care deeply," "I was very scared," and "I love my mom." Confrontation can bring these convex mirrors into conversation, and when the confrontation cools, you can sit back and analyze the boy or man's feelings and emotions "in his own words."

To go deeper into these observations regarding confrontation with males, let's look at four case studies. I hope that these case studies, presented in the present tense for maximum affect, not only illustrate the ideas and theory of this chapter, but also provide practicalities for putting the ideas to work in your practice or institution.

Aaron: Recalling Confrontations

Aaron, 42, is divorced, with three children. I have been working with him, along with his girlfriend, Carol, for two months. Carol is out of town this week, so he has come into my office alone. He has just said in the session that Carol exaggerates everything and he's been confronting her on her exaggerations. He says that her exaggeration "makes things bad in the relationship because she can't be trusted." I need to confront Aaron about his own lack of trust in Carol by helping him remember his confrontation with his girlfriend now.

Gurian: How did you get from A to B? I mean, everyone exaggerates. Do you think everyone is, therefore, untrustworthy?

Aaron: No. Not everyone exaggerates.

I disagree. Everyone makes things up sometimes. Everyone tells little lies. Why does it bug you so much?

It just does. Especially when Carol does it. It drives me crazy.

Why?

Because she's not talking about reality. She's making things up.

Give me an example.

(Pause.) This weekend, I fixed the back fence. It took me four hours. She said, "You've been doing that for three weeks. It's great you got it done, finally." Three weeks! Finally! Hell, I only measured it last week, which was about just getting a design in my head, then I did the job this week. This was not a three-week project.

And the exaggeration drove you nuts.

Yeah.

Why?

(Silence). I don't know the why or whatever. It just did.

Because?

I don't know. That's my point. I don't know.

You gotta do better than "I don't know."

(Silence).

Gurian: Let's think about it. When she exaggerates, is it always connected to some criticism by her against you?

What do you mean?

Like "it's great you got it done, finally." That was sarcastic, critical.

Yeah, she's sarcastic. That's how she is.

She was saying you should have done the fence a week or two ago. She's not satisfied with you.

I guess.

That sarcasm implies that you're inept. She wants you to move faster, be smarter, do better.

I don't know. I guess.

When she exaggerates, you think of it as her being out of touch with reality, but your ego feels her words as criticism by her, and failure by you. She's putting you up against impossible odds that you cannot win against.

You think so?

What do you think?

I don't know. I guess so.

You guess so.

I don't know. I gotta think about it. I mean, so you're saying…. (Silence)

What do you think? Think back to what happened inside you when she was sarcastic.

I got angry and told her she was exaggerating. Then we got in a fight.

Right. Then what happened.

I told her I was sick of her exaggerating. I told her she always exaggerates. I told her to do the damn fence herself.

Yes. So, do you trust Carol to love you?

Huh?

Do you trust her to love you?

I don't know. I guess so.

If you did, would the exaggerations and sarcasms bug you so much?

I don't know.

Think about it. Why do the exaggerations bug you so much? If you trusted her as your lover and friend, wouldn't you just slough off the exaggerations?

(Pause) Maybe.

It sure seems like neither of you trusts the other person. Your lack of trust comes out differently. Think about it: when she critiques you in her way, isn't she saying, "I have to be watchful of you all the time because you can't be trusted?"

Hmmm….yeah, I guess. I mean, slow down. Let me think about that.

And aren't you saying, "She always wants me to be different somehow—take less time to do a job, or do it differently? She can't just let me be—I have to always be watchful of her mood and her words."

Yeah. Okay.

And back when you started going out with her, what's the chicken and what's the egg? Who didn't trust whom first? Did you not trust her first, so now she doesn't trust you, or did she not trust you first, so now you don't trust her?

Fuck. I don't know. But you're right. Neither of us trusts the other person. We're always watchful. We're both always dissatisfied.

Yes.

Fuck.

In helping Aaron, who was difficult to help toward insight and break-through, I pressed relentlessly, and used language such as "You gotta do better than 'I don't know'" that challenged and confronted Aaron rather than waiting him out. If you were a fly on the wall in this session, you would see me leaning forward in my chair, my jaw set, my eyes looking directly at Aaron. As I took this stance, I filled in words and thoughts for him in the hope that he would become increasingly agitated and push toward active engagement.

From previous sessions, I knew that Aaron was abandoned by his father, thus Aaron had difficulty trusting himself and others in relationships. He constantly selected women whom he could confront concerning what he saw as their flaws (picking women who themselves had been abandoned, and lacked self-trust). He selected such women so that he could have marriages that were constant battles.

With men like Aaron, passivity on the part of the therapist had not worked. Aaron has been in and out of therapy for years. His conflicts and tensions with significant others were gold mines of opportunity for growth, for he wanted and needed a counselor to challenge and push against him as he was constantly pushing against lovers toward self-respect, but he had not received confrontational mentoring regarding how to mine his relational interactions for wiser results. In becoming surgically, tactically (and relatively noninvasively confrontational) with him, I was successful over a period of weeks in helping him recognize what was going on in his hypercritical relationships.

Tom: The Mirror and the Song

Eight men, including me, sit in a men's group circle in a carpeted room. We have just finished music and meditation, and are now ready to "check in." Because this meeting began after a long workday, at 7 p.m., music and meditation have been useful in helping the men transition from work life to team/group life.

Tom is one of the eight men, and with him, I felt I needed to be even more confrontational than with Aaron. Because this venue is a men's group, "verbal combat" has occurred in the past, and will occur again tonight.

Tom has begun talking about issues regarding how emotionally distant and uncommunicative his wife is. "She won't open up, she won't communicate. I just want to have some close conversation, but she just doesn't know how to be close. She's afraid of intimacy. I'm sick of it. I feel alone in my own house." He becomes angry as he speaks, and in listening to his rendition of his communications with his wife, it is clear that he becomes angry at her during their confrontations.

A key fact in this case is that Tom has sung this same "song of complaint" nearly every week. He repeats exact phraseology of analysis of his wife without realizing that this phraseology is not just accurate to the person he is complaining about, but also an accurate projection of himself in the mirror of his complaints. I decide that this evening is the time for a confrontation that will help Tom see himself in the mirror and listen to and actually hear his own song.

Gurian: Tom, you're singing your song again. Do you realize that?

You could say that, but why don't you help me fix it? Nothing I try works with Hilary.

Everyone in this group has been making suggestions and helping you out for months. Have you tried some of the things with Hillary we talked about previously?

Everything. I've tried everything.

Have you tried going one whole week without complaining about her?

I'm telling you, I'm not complaining. It's true. She's cold.

Complaining about someone who is not present in group does not lead anywhere. You know that.

I know. We don't complain in this space—we're here to do deeper work. But....

(I interrupt.) Is Hillary afraid of you?

What?

What is her body posture when you tell her you want her to be more intimate with you?

Her body posture?

Does she physically stand or sit away from you?

Well, I mean, you know, I'm kind of criticizing her, so she gets a little defensive.

Okay. And when she gets angry at you for something, do you feel defensive, too?

Sure. But I'm not angry at her, I just want her to communicate more.

How often do you get angry at her?

(Pause). I'm saying, I don't get angry—

(Interrupt). But how often, would you say, you get angry at her? Ball park it.

(Pause). Not often.

But you bring this up every week, so you must be getting upset with her about this at least every week. Is it every few days? Do you try to talk to her about this every few days?

No. I'm saying, I don't get angry.

But you must be—you bring this up every week. So she must be scared of you, wouldn't you say?

What do you mean? I just talk to her. Why would she be scared?

But she's got to feel ashamed, right? Like a failure? Think about it: She can't help you, she can't fill up your heart and soul, she can't satisfy you. She must feel some pretty powerful feelings when you come at her over and over again about not communicating correctly with you."

(Silence).

Gurian: And this happens every few days at least, right?

(Pause). I guess.

So, is she afraid of you? Does she feel fear?

(Pause). I mean...fear...well....

If I can sense how angry you are at her, what do you think she senses? Do you really think she doesn't sense and feel your anger?

It's not anger. I love her. I'm not angry. I'm just…okay…afraid, I guess. I've been in therapy for ages—I get it—I feel afraid when a woman doesn't love me and care about me intimately. I get all that family of origin stuff.

I know. You do. Very well. But do you realize how angry you are?

(Pause). I'm needy maybe, but not angry.

You're angry.

(Silence. He looks down at his feet, thinking.)

Gurian: Why wouldn't you be angry? You're so afraid of being close to someone you love, you don't know how to communicate how much you love your wife, and it eats you up, and so you get angry at *her,* not yourself.

What?

Is it possible the exact things you constantly complain about with her are actually the things in yourself you wish you could change?

Like what?

You constantly complain that she is not intimate enough, kind enough, generous enough with you. Are you being intimate, kind, and generous with her?

(He looks down at his hands folded on his lap, mind churning). I guess not. Hmmm. I guess…I mean…I'm just, like…complaining about her. (He looks up at me, looks around the room at the other men, then looks upward, away from us. He takes a deep breath, stands up, holds his head with his hands, starts to pace behind his chair, along the wall on his side of the room.) I'm a fucking asshole, is that what you're saying? It's all me, I'm a fuck-up. I'm projecting a bunch of shit onto her, but it's all really my shit?

(I take a deep, respectful breath, knowing that this 'I'm a fuck-up', is also one of Tom's songs.) Nope. Not a fuck up. Your song is real. It's just that it's not only about Hillary, it's also about you. Sometimes Hilary is cold, no doubt, but you get mad at Hillary a lot of other times, too, when really you're mad at yourself. You create confrontations with her so you can feel stronger, and she can be weak. You make her feel inadequate, when really it's you who's afraid of his own inadequacy. Could that be so?

Shit. And you're saying, now I'm doing with Hillary what I did with Gillian (his second wife). Shit, man. I'm glad you pointed this out. I'm scaring the shit out of Hillary. I'm pushing her away. I'm such a needy fuck, I get afraid and scared and throw my anger at her and just screw things up.

You get scared and so you feel like you have to make the people who love you scared, too.

Yeah. I'm so weak, I don't want to be scared, so I'd rather be strong and powerful and make my wife scared. That's the shit you're saying, right? (He comes back to his chair, sits down). Unbelievable. I think of myself as such an enlightened guy.

Ask Hillary if she's scared of you. Can you do that? Would you come back and let us know what she says, how it goes?

I guess. (He turns to the other men). What do you guys think?

Now some of the other men get involved, and the group dynamic takes over. Men share stories of their own fears and their own instances of making their spouses afraid of them. Tom is engaged, feels helped. The next week, Tom is careful not to "sing his song," jokes about it, but moves on. A week after that, Tom and Hillary call my office and I see them for four sessions to help with couple communication. Tom looks back at the evening in group almost sheepishly, saying, "It was so simple, what you were getting at, but I didn't get it until you confronted me on it. Thanks, man."

Quite often, boys and men can't understand their own internal fear/courage drama unless therapists challenge them with it. In working with boys and men, I have found that verbally pointing out fear-projection (the mirror and the song) can be useful, but helping them experience their own fear-projection through confrontation can be even more powerful. And following up that experiential awareness with action steps that show courage can be equally useful.

So, for instance, if a man's internal projection strategy is an unconscious, "I feel scared so I will make the person I love scared," I need to help him see this clearly, not just with insight, but, often, through verbal confrontation. Adolescent boys, too, can see their projections, and are often amazed by them when confronted. Upon confronting the male with his projections of fear—and thus creating opportunities for experiential self-awareness in the male—I need to help the boy or man create action steps (through couple counseling, in Tom's case), with which to confront their fears.

The fears do not disappear, but relationships can be assisted in profound ways, and male psyche and maturity development can proceed functionally. A male can get "unstuck" through verbal confrontation. This "unstuckness," and the transformations for self and relationships that may ensue, might not happen if the therapist remains relationally and verbally passive throughout the therapeutic process, i.e. avoids providing aggression nurturance.

Torry: I'm Gone

Nothing works all the time, of course. The failures teach us. Here is one verbal confrontation regarding the client's fear that ended up in the client, a 17-year-old new father, abandoning counseling with me.

Gurian: You're the one who's scared, you know.

Torry: No way. I'm not scared.

You're scared to death, so you make everyone else scared.

What am I scared of?

You tell me.

I ain't scared.

You want to take care of La Toya and Lionel (three month old baby), but you're scared you can't do it; you're scared you can't be a good father, so you give up, abandon your baby; you're scared you can't get decent grades in school, so you drop out. You give up on basically everything that could be important because you're so scared.

Fuck that shit. I ain't scared. No one messes with me.

They don't need to. You mess with yourself. You're on track for prison by the time you're twenty and death by the time you're twenty-five. All because you're scared to do anything important. Selling Oxycodone to rich kids isn't important. It's something a guy does who's scared to do the real stuff.

(He is angry, frowning, fuming, but thinking).

Can you look at me, Torry? Why won't you look at me? Huh?

(I wait for eye contact, then, upon receiving it, continue.) You know what a real man does? He protects his woman and his child. He does that bravely, and everything else comes from that. If you're not doing that, you're not a man. Are you a man?

Fuck you!

(He jumps up, balls his fists, stares me down. I stand up, too, fold my hands across my chest.) He yells, "Fuck you, asshole!" turns, opens my door, walks through, slams it, is gone.

I took a risk with Torry—told him the truth he won't face— but I overdid the end of the confrontation, and made a crucial mistake regarding eye contact. First, Torry was not resilient enough to handle "you're not a man." I misread his fragility. Second, the eye contact I forced on him created a severe fight or flight response in which the flight modality won. Also in Torry's case, my being a middle-aged white man and he being an inner city African-American boy must certainly have affected our relationship at inchoate levels.

Torry's case is one of those experiences early in my career, and early in my use of tactical confrontation as aggression nurturance, that taught me to better utilize eye contact, timing of critique, and racial/cultural factors. But it did not negate the efficacy of verbal confrontation in breaking through fear/courage barriers with males of any race or circumstance. I believe Torry still needed some form of measured, intensive, and motivational confrontation in order to help nurture him toward maturity. I simply did not provide it well.

Sylvan: I Miss My Dad

Sylvan was an 11-year-old boy almost as tall as his petite mother, Carla. Her son's anger and aggressiveness had created a nearly desperate situation in the family and school. Sylvan was acting out against other children, and he was constantly yelling at his mother and sister. Sylvan's father was absent most of the time, serving in Iraq. He had been wounded in battle, came home to recuperate for two months, then shipped out again.

Counseling with this family included my referral of Sylvan to a psychiatrist for assessment, which came back probable for ADHD. This was treated, and treatment helped somewhat, but as we explored the family dynamics more deeply, one confrontational session ended up being a break-through for Sylvan.

Gurian: You're scared of a lot of stuff and you won't admit it. You blame your mom, your teachers, your sister, and you won't ever see what's going on inside you.

(Silence. Sylvan's eyelids close half way, his jaw is moving under his cheeks, he is kneading his hands on his lap. We are twenty minutes into a session in which I have been relentless with him.)

Gurian: You're angry at me right now. You're angry at everybody except yourself, and your father. You notice that, Sylvan? Everyone's a screw-up except Sylvan, and Dad?

My dad's a hero.

Damn right he is. He's incredible. And you're never mad at him, even though he's the one who's gone. He's the one fighting over there and re-upping and scaring you every minute of every day.

(Quizzical expression--not just anger).

Gurian: Every time he leaves you, you get scared. You live in a constant state of fear, like you're getting attacked by all of Tron (his favorite video game). Any minute the news could come that he's dead. Any minute! And what did you do to save your dad? Nothing. You're a little kid stuck at home doing homework. You're no hero. Dad's the hero. But that means Dad can be killed—

Shut up!

I'll shut up, if you admit you're scared, every day, that you're dad's gonna die.

Shut up!

Will you admit it? Aren't you scared he's gonna die?

No!

No? (Silence for three beats.) You sure?

(Silence.)

Gurian: If I were you, I'd be scared. When my father left my mom for six months, I was scared to death, and my father wasn't fighting in a war. (Silence). You sure you're not scared your dad's gonna die?

(No words are needed for a moment—Sylvan's lower lip is starting to quiver.)

Gurian: Is it possible you're scared all the time?

(He fights back tears.)

Some people, when they get scared, they decide to be angry. Are you one of those people? Are you always angry because you're always scared you're Daddy's gonna die and you can't save him?

(He touches his fingers to his eyes.)

155

Your dad leaves you alone with your mom and your sister and your stupid school work, and you miss him and you're scared he's gonna die, and you're scared because you can't do a thing about it. Think about it: what scares you the most right now in this whole world?

(Silence.)

Isn't it the phone call or the soldiers coming to your front door?

(Sylvan fights back his tears successfully, his eyes brimming, but he nods.)

Don't you think all the time, "What if Daddy dies? What if he dies?"

(He nods.)

Gurian: It's the scariest thing in the world.

(Sylvan's face and body posture nod agreement even though he says nothing.)

You know what the word 'powerlessness' means, Sylvan?

(He makes no verbal or nonverbal response.)

It's an 11-year-old boy like you, who's smart and tall and strong and going to school and trying to love his mother and sister, and he wants his daddy around, but he can't make his daddy come home. It's a guy like you who can save the world in your video games but you can't save your daddy. That's powerlessness. It makes you really angry, so angry you can't see straight some times.

(He makes eye contact, his eyes wet.)

Does this stuff make sense, Sylvan? Does it make any sense, what we're saying here?

(He compresses his lips together, still battling tears, and nods his head. Then his hands rush upward to his face and he covers his eyes as he lets tears come through.

Gurian: It's okay, man, it's okay.

He turns away from me. I pass Kleenex toward him, which he doesn't use. As his tears subside, he wipes his nose and eyes with his fingers and his sleeve. When it is time to talk again, I say, "I'm sorry I pressed so hard, Sylvan."

He responds, "That's okay."

We talk for a while, then I suggest we get up and go out of the office for a walk, where we talk further about his fear and his anger, and how to be stronger and more brave, like his father is.

In the three successful cases I've presented here, assets with-in each male became available and more useful after confrontation occurred. Tom's case is emblematic: assets had already been made available to him, via previous therapy, but those assets had had little impact on Tom. He was moving toward dissembling his third mar-riage. Tom needed to be confronted, and therapists had not con-fronted him. He needed to admit his fear and, thus, his anger to his wife. He needed confrontation in order to become compassionate toward his wife regarding the fear and anger he was causing.

Fortunately, as couple communication helped him and his wife, his wife also admitted her faults to him, and admitted that, yes, she had pulled away from intimacy with him for some of her own reasons, too. Tom discovered that when he had the courage to admit fault with his wife, she gained the courage to admit hers. In this, Tom had a great deal of power, and felt "heroic." A coura-geous choice led to increased, healthy power for Tom in his mar-riage.

While not all confrontations go well in therapy, and while they do take from us, as practitioners, more energy than we might at first want to give to our days of seeing five or six clients in a row, the confrontations are often desperately needed by boys and men. If boys and men are not confronted and challenged by the people who care about them, and confronted in helpful, safe, life-changing ways, these males will have been let down by those of us who care for them. The full marriage, as it were, of patient and therapist, client and mentor, will not occur.

In talking about this, we can certainly say, "But girls and women have to be confronted, too." Yes they do. Females mix fear and anger; girls need to be taught how to have healthy relation-ships; women need to realize their own flaws. All this is true, for fear, courage, anxiety, resilience--these are part of human nature, not only a part of male or female nature.

Simultaneously, two points are also important. First, the biochemical base for males and females differs regarding confronta-tion and relationship. When males walk into our offices, their stress hormone levels are high, thus their adrenalin and testoste-rone is rising or has risen. They are primed for fight or flight. When females walk into our offices, their stress hormone levels are high, and thus their adrenalin and oxytocin rises. They are primed for tend and befriend strategies more than fight or flight strategies.

Second, males have utilized head-on confrontation for self-growth (generally via competition games) since the first year of their lives, whereas females have utilized more behind-the-scenes approaches to relational difficulties. Male babies are, in general, turned outward, even in the first weeks of life, more than female babies; male toddlers are, in general, more physically confrontational with the world than female toddlers; male schoolchildren, in general, seek more rough and tumble play than female children. Throughout life, males rely more on challenge-tests and direct-confrontation than females. Through confrontation, boys and men *feel more.* Through combat, they emote. Through challenge, they perform. Through being pushed down, they push back up.

Even with all exceptions always noted, we as mental health professionals are called, I believe, to integrate both the biochemical reality of male/female difference and the socialization differences that biochemistry has set up. If we do this, many boys and men in our practices will not feel less empowered for having been aggressively confronted—in fact, they will feel more empowered. They may well get from your therapy and counseling an environment that feels confrontationally safe and helpful.

From gradually adjusting your practice toward the way the male psyche grows, you may look back on many of your confrontations with males with professional satisfaction, for you will have confronted your own fears of pushing the envelope with males, and found your own courage to meet boys and men where they are—in their combative universe.

The Courage of the Therapist

Working with boys and men is not only a lesson in helping a boy or man gain courage; it is also a test of a therapist's courage, a somewhat different test than the test of courage that can occur when we work with girls and women. Boys and men constantly and unconsciously ask us the question. "In order to treat me, how brave will you be?" Boys and men often have defense systems in place that aggressively impugn others rather than allowing for breakthrough in the self. How brave will a therapist be in helping the client break through those aggression-based or anger-focused defenses?

Girls and women can be angry, aggressive, complaining, etc., but more often than with boys and men (and including all exceptions based on particular personality disorders), female defenses can dissolve more thoroughly through traditional talk therapy. With boys and men, quite often, a therapist must do some of the dissolving through action and confrontation. But we are not trained for this in school. In fact, we are trained to not interrupt, not force things, not fill in words for clients, not "tell them what they are feeling."

Thus, quite often, we as professionals may feel the dull fear of just not being adequate to the task of providing the kind of combative help that the male needs. We may feel the sharp dissatisfaction of knowing we need to press harder with the male, but of being scared to do so. We may sit and wait, in a kind of fear-paralysis of our own, for males to "open up" to us, even when waiting is not effective therapy—it is fear. These fears can add to the normal instinctive psycho-physiological fear of confronting a large, loud man alone in our small office, and we can find ourselves in a psycho-cultural inertia of fear rather than a courageous professional momentum that might move us toward fully helping the males in our care.

Boys and men enter our offices and our profession with many strikes against them already. Many of those strikes have overtly or covertly to do with their maleness being less understood than we realize. Our profession can better help boys and men if we are willing to delve deeply into the immense worth to humanity of the very male anger and aggression that we have gradually tried to remove from our quiet, sit-and-talk profession.

In saying this, I am not saying that we should all become constant confronters of every male. Many weeks of therapy can go by with different modalities working well, and many of these modalities specifically work because they do not force confrontations before the time is right. But even as we use these "safer, less aggressive, less angry" modalities, we might gain from realizing that we may have conveniently defined "safety" as quietness and calmness that may better fit the tend-and-befriend needs of more girls and women in crisis than boys and men. In defining our profession toward an unconscious female-centric mean, we may have signaled to half of our potential population that boys and men are not quite fit for therapy. This inadvertent ostracizing of "maleness" (especially including male anger and aggression) from therapy is destructive, not only to our profession but to all the children, women, and men who need us to mentor males with clarity and courage.

If we will each work to find, define, and act in new courage regarding confronting and nurturing maleness, more males will be retained in our practices and more boys and men will get the help they need. As with so many parts of the human experience, positive change starts with courage of individuals to change the way things are presently done. We have the chance, now, to look more closely than perhaps we have before at our psychological theories and practices. From this brave look will come, I believe, a new and productive gender balance in our profession.

Chapter 8: Working with Sensitive Boys and Men

"A man of genius is primarily a man of supreme usefulness."
--Alfred Adler

At the beginning of this book, we met Jeremy, age 14, and his parents, Chris and Tanya. Jeremy had begun to fail in school. By the time I met the family, he was getting F's in some classes, not doing homework, not handing in homework, lying to everyone, and gradually feeling more alienated and lost. A number of factors affected Jeremy's behavior. Two primary factors pertained to his personality's fit and lack of fit with the world around him.

Jeremy was a highly sensitive boy. As I worked with him, I could see that he cried easily, accessed his own feelings relatively easily, was directly empathic, lacked significant aggressiveness, and reached a state of over-stimulation easily. He was an only child of parents who were sensitive to his needs but did not realize the degree of sensitivity in his personality, and the level of his depression and anger now, at age 14. While a psychiatrist saw Jeremy and helped treat his depression with medication, I also helped Jeremy see that he was purposely failing in school out of anger at the school and toward his parents, and the whole family worked together to set a new course for this boy.

That course began in understanding Jeremy's fragility, and the effects upon that fragility of the first five years of his life. During those years, his mother had suffered from chronic fatigue syndrome and/or Lyme's disease (the diagnosis was difficult to pin down, she said, especially in the early 1990s). Tanya said that while she bonded well with Jeremy, she was also bedridden much of the first five years of his life. For Chris' part, his job took him away from home a great deal, and when he was home, "I was trying to take care of Tanya and trying to help with medical issues."

The first five years left scars of abandonment on Jeremy. As I worked with him and his family, he and his parents recalled moments of Jeremy sad in his room, or sitting beside his sleeping mother's bed, or wandering into the back yard, basically alone. Jeremy was a sensitive boy who needed a level of contact, bonding, attachment, and interaction he did not get; by puberty, the consequences were becoming clear. My best assessment was that a perfect storm of biology, difficulties in school, and bullying by older peers triggered Jeremy's depression, certain roots of which lay in the past. The triggers awakened his wounds of abandonment and fear, and stimulated Jeremy's rebellion against school work and parents, his lying, and his other family and school conflicts.

When Chris, Tanya, and Jeremy exhorted me in their first session to help them get at "more than feelings," they were saying, I believe, that they wanted help not only with the deepest wounds and most practical solutions their son, family, and school could discover, but also, they wanted help with male navigation of what Alfred Adler called *Gemeinschaftsgefuhl,* "fellow feeling," or "belonging in the mass." Jeremy had become an adolescent boy who no longer felt useful or needed, nor that he belonged anywhere, especially among other boys. Tanya put it this way: "He has no friends, to speak of. He doesn't do what normal boys do—he's lonely." Chris said, "I was a loner as a kid—Jeremy's got my personality— but with Jeremy it's worse than it was with me. At least I had a best friend. Jeremy doesn't even have that."

With all boys, and especially with sensitive boys like Jeremy, feeling-systems and emotional structures can sometimes feel deintegrated from fellow feeling within the mass of males. I believe this condition, alienation-from-male-hierarchy-development, is far more destructive to young males than we might at first realize. Over the last decade, significant studies have shown that males who occupy positions at the bottom and/or outside of adolescent and adult male hierarchies have higher than normal stress hormone levels. The heightened stress hormone, cortisol, can contribute to a cascade of "acting in" or "acting out" behavior, and include mental states from dysthymia to depression to dangerous, high risk activity to violence.

Male adolescence is a high-risk stage of life by its very nature, in which many of the risks taken are undertaken to perform well in the hierarchical world of males and masculinity. A certain level of performance is useful for basic survival and also for thriving in adolescence itself, then later on in life, when adolescent skill-building and hierarchical savvy can pay off with greater adult success. Like many sensitive boys, especially sensitive boys who struggle with their own personality's fragility in the mass of males, Jeremy was under significant stress regarding hierarchy and positioning that added to the stress of depression, bullying, lying, and bad grades.

The initial lens that the family counseling could use to explore Jeremy's deep issues was the developmental stress of the first five years of Jeremy's life. As we explored Jeremy's feelings of abandonment and powerlessness years ago, Jeremy's family could use this boy's innate sensitivity to help him "work on himself." And I as a male mentor was able to work with him to make sure he did not feel abandoned, as a sensitive boy, in his peer groups, male group activities, and adolescent male maturation systems. Focusing both on early abandonment trauma and now on its replay through Jeremy having become ostracized ("abandoned") by the mass of males, we together helped Jeremy not only to reconnect with his family, but also to deal with the bullying and other external sufferings he was experiencing at school and among boys.

Jeremy is a success story in large part due to the fact that he received a wide array of assets—appropriate medication, words/feelings connections, emotional narratives that had been unseen in the family of origin before, use of nontraditional counseling practices (such as presented in Chapter 6), constant mentoring in ways to reconnect with parents and the school, and ways to provide himself, throughout the rest of his life, with insights and practices that led to confident self-care, life-purpose, and integration of his sensitivity into the very real and very tough male world. Identifying his "sensitivity" as a little boy, then helping his family and community understand how to nurture that male sensitivity now, among male peer groups, were emboldening of his counseling, and his progress.

In all of this, there are two elements I would like to explore with you in this chapter: 1) the highly sensitive male personality itself; and 2) the importance of working with males, families, and communities to make certain that boy develops a sense of usefulness and fellow feeling (hierarchical savvy rather than male isolation) as the boy grows through adolescence.

The Sensitive Boy and the Bridge Brain

Assisting us in looking at the first element is the work of psychologists Elaine Aron and Ted Zeff. Zeff, author of *The Strong Sensitive Boy,* writes: "The highly sensitive person has trouble screening out stimuli and can be easily overwhelmed by noise, crowds and time pressure. The HSP (highly sensitive person) tends to be very sensitive to pain, and the effects of caffeine and violent movies. Highly sensitive people are also made extremely uncomfortable by bright lights, strong smells and changes in their lives. According to Dr. Elaine Aron, the HSP trait is equally divided between males and females. In other words, approximately twenty percent of all boys are sensitive." (Many autism-spectrum boys could be categorized as HSPs, though they may not be "sensitive boys" as we shall mean that term when we discuss bridge brains. For the placement of autism-spectrum boys on the brain scan spectrum, see Simon Baron-Cohen's *The Essential Difference*).

Zeff's and Aron's analysis is echoed by other research of Simon Baron-Cohen, Daniel Amen, and JoAnn Deak that we looked at in Chapters 2 and 7. It appears that somewhere between 15 and 20 percent of males fall near the middle of the gender-brain spectrum as "bridge brains"—males whose brain scans might bridge the genders by showing more female brain traits than the majority of male brains. Dr. Amen has provided these brain scans from his clinical practice. The bridge-brain, or "sensitive male's" scan, appears in the middle.

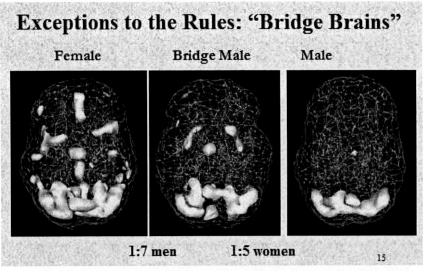

Exceptions to the Rules: "Bridge Brains"

Female   Bridge Male   Male

1:7 men   1:5 women [15]

Brain Scans Provided by Daniel Amen, M.D.

From looking at these brain scans, you can see that the female brain on the left is very active, even in a "rest" (zone-out) state. On the right, the male brain has very little activity in the rest state—it shows basic survival activity but far less activity than female brains show in memory, emotion, and word centers, creating significant brain difference between female and male.

The male brain in the middle, as Dr. Amen has noted, "shows activity in memory and emotion centers, even in the rest state." Most male brains will look like the one on the right, but some look like the brain in the middle—a bridge between male and female. This pictorial assessment is not a final word, but I hope that in seeing the contrasts you will join me in relating to the "sensitive boy" and "sensitive man" in this chapter.

Based on the statistics provided by Amen, Baron-Cohen, and Deak, and in hearing their echo in the research from Aron and Zeff, I try to keep in mind, with both males and females, that there are "exceptions to the rule," and those exceptions create yet another layer of gender effectiveness to be marshaled in my practice. It is important for me, as a practitioner who works with boys and men, to always be mindful of bridge brains, "20 percenters," and "sensitive/highly sensitive boys and men." As Zeff writes, "All of the highly sensitive males in my survey indicated that they were usually or always: intuitive, gentle, responsible, a peacemaker and good at counseling people." Zeff also notes that these sensitive males often feel like misfits in the larger world of males.

Thus, when I work with these males, I keep in mind three things regarding their "maleness":

1. Sensitive males may do better than other males with traditional sit-and-talk modalities; if these males are "bridge brains," they may gain more from sit-and-talk than might the majority of males.

2. Simultaneously, they possess male biochemistry, so these boys and men are also, by nature, hungry for my use of nontraditional strategies, including peripatetic counseling, that can feel novel to them, and can broaden my ability to work effectively with them.

3. Most of these sensitive boys (and men) are often starved for mentoring that help them understand how to manage male hierarchies, experience "fellow feeling," "a sense of belong-

ing in the mass of males," "power in the mass," "personal usefulness in hierarchies."

My meta-thinking regarding sensitive boys and men does not lead to success in every case, but it has worked well with many. The final point, regarding fellow-feeling among the mass of males, has been borne out by Zeff's and Aron's research in North America, which found that highly sensitive boys who played group sports with peer boys were more rarely teased at school for being sensitive. On the other hand, the highly sensitive boys in their research groups who had never played team sports indicated that they were usually or always teased at school.

Learning from mentors and therapists how to navigate traditional male systems can be very useful to sensitive boys, as an augment or addition to traditional therapy, and as an augment to support from both parents and other mentors for the boy's sensitivity itself. This was certainly the case with Jeremy. Joining a karate class and gaining personal development and friendships there had a positive effect on his growth in general.

Shortly, I will provide further and specific practical strategies you can use to help with all of the factors we've just defined. First, however, let's look at another specific population of males who are in significant need, and with whom those strategies can be highly useful.

Gay, Bi-Sexual, and Transgender Boys and Men

Males for whom the issues of "sensitivity" and need for safety in the mass of males can be amplified are gay, bi-sexual, and transgender males.

In nearly every professional presentation I give, this question is asked: "Is there brain research to indicate what is happening with gay, lesbian, and transgender brains?" The subtext of this question is often, "Is it natural to be gay or lesbian?" Because I speak in various settings, from clinical conferences to faith communities, I know that in some settings the questions are asked for purely clinical reasons, and in others, for religious or political reasons.

My answer is that there is a growing body of research, especially spurred by medical research into transgender individuals, showing that approximately 5 to 10 percent of human and primate brains may be preset in utero for homosexuality. Thus, a number of studies have posited brain and genetic bases for gay and lesbian neural development. These are controversial, but their science is important.

If you research "the gay brain" or "the gay gene" or other similar phrases, you will find fascinating research references (as well as counter-references). They provide additional understandings for any of us who work with boys and men—bringing science into the picture, even if a person does not necessarily agree with the scientific conclusions made in the study.

Beyond asking practitioners to look at brain research in this field, I can also observe through wisdom-of-practice in my counseling practice that:

*Gay, bisexual, and transgender boys and men often (though not always) fit the category of "sensitive boys." (In this chapter, for linguistic flow, I will use the word "gay" to include all three groups). As a practitioner working with gay males, I ask questions immediately of the gay client to try to ascertain the extent to which this individual fits or does not fit with the "sensitive" category. I find that having dialogue with the client about "sensitivity" is a strong starting place for working together, no matter where the dialogue ends. I believe this positive outcome occurs not only because the client and I build rapport around understanding the client's personality and assets, but also because we can immediately look at the client's history regarding his alienation from the mass of males.

*With greater frequency than in the heterosexual population, gay males tend to fit in the category of "bridge brains." I show clients the brain scans and ask them about their history and personal narrative from a brain-based perspective. For many gay males, this tack has been emotionally moving. Most people are not aware that brain scan technology can be discussed in a counseling office. Many gay males I have worked with did not know before counseling that there may be growing neurobiological research on the gender spectrum of male and female brains. Gay clients have often said, "You know, I sensed my brain was different, but just didn't know how." Emboldening this feeling of "belonging" is a powerful way to build therapeutic rapport.

*Many of the traditional therapy models that lean toward sit-and-talk and verbal-emotive functioning succeed, on average, with more frequency among gay boys and men than, on average, straight boys and men. With all exceptions noted, and with the caveat that this is a generalization, I have found that many gay males are able to work with me verbally and emotively on sensorial memories and narrative threads regarding relational memories with more fluidity than many straight males. If sitting and talking is working well, I don't explore too many other options. From success comes comfort; if there is no clinical failure in the verbal-emotive environment of my office, there is little necessity to alter traditional therapeutic practice.

*Simultaneously, innovations such as peripatetic counseling have worked very well with the gay boys and men in my practice. Even nitty-gritty changes to a therapy practice, such as giving clients squeeze balls and/or using music, graphics, and the arts, can help gay males flourish in therapy. The boy-friendly and male-friendly therapeutic practices I suggest in this book, including the tactical confrontation techniques, can work well with gay males.

With a higher-than-average suicide rate, gay males often develop depression in reaction to aggressive and violent attention from males that not only affects their individual psyches negatively, but also destroys their sense of fellow feeling in the mass of males. When counselors, whether male or female, become the kinds of mentors we described in Chapter 3, we can do a great deal to facilitate three family systems and male mentoring relationships for these boys and men.

Working with Sensitive Boys

Many of us who provide therapy, counseling, and mentoring to sensitive children and adults were and are sensitive children and adults. As such, we have good instincts as to what is needed to help such patients. Often, following these instincts, we put ourselves primarily in the position of good listener and direct empathy provider. We ask questions, listen to stories of bullying, fear or depression, and help with reframing and catharsis. With sensitive boys, HSPs, and gay males, these are crucial strategies.

At the same time, it is also important to remember the "maleness" of even the sensitive male client. This is a "boy" with a "male frame" for "belonging." Often, he is raised with too little fathering. Two areas of focus might thus differ somewhat for us in working with sensitive boys, as opposed to, say, sensitive girls.

1. The sensitive boy is experiencing his difficulties in the world of *boys*—it is in a boy's world that he is trying to navigate his feelings of not-belonging, his loneliness, his alienation. Even if he has female friends, he still may feel an inchoate alienation from the world of males, which causes significant stress, and amplifies all other presenting personality and social adjustment issues.

2. Even though this sensitive boy might be more "female" on the gender/brain spectrum (more directly empathic, more verbal-emotive, less physically aggressive), he still carries within his psyche his male predilections to crisis response—specifically, fight or flight—as he seeks to develop a sense of meaning and purpose in a world of other males; through that world he will unconsciously or consciously measure himself.

Overall, if we keep in mind the depth and subtleties of the drive for male fellow-feeling in all males (the drive that has provided an under-layer to a great deal of what I am saying in this book), and if we further keep in mind that sensitive males feel a deep need for, but also a disconnection from, that drive, we can continue to add successful tools to our toolboxes, no matter the sensitive male in our care, and no matter where he fits on the gender brain spectrum.

Here are specific tools I have found to be effective in my practice. I hope you'll consider adding them to your toolbox, or amplifying their use should they already be tools you use.

*Mentor the sensitive boy toward focus on one or two activities/jobs he is good at—focus as much of his energy there whenever possible and, meanwhile, help his family delete extra or gratuitous (and hyper-stimulating) daily activities.

*Make sure the retained activities carry a great deal of potential "usefulness"—to the boy, to his family, to his community, especially through male mentoring. So, if the boy is trying to be good at five things and failing, help him do well enough at three but brilliantly at two, and let one of those two involve a male coach, teacher, family member, or other male mentor.

*Educate parents about the sensitive boy's overstimulation, high stress, etc. If the sensitive boy's parents are pushing him into many activities—and pushing for the highest possible performance in all of them—mentor the parents regarding sensitive boys, their personality vulnerabilities, the dangers of over-stressing them, and alternative success paths.

If a boy is like Jeremy, naturally inclined toward higher math and science but not to writing and reading, we may have to teach his parents how to help him use more graphics in his writing tasks so that his writing can become good enough to get at least a B; while simultaneously focusing on finding programs, camps, and challenges in math and science where he can especially flourish. As always, throughout this process, we need to keep an eye on whether there are male mentors available in his "favorite" activities, including increasing his time with his father or father-figure male.

The "activity emphasis/de-emphasis" part of this suggestion is useful in:

1) *de-stressing* the boy on the areas in which he is not as competent (thus, de-stressing these areas by improving them with new strategies and also allowing for slightly lower performance expectations in those areas, in exchange for higher expectations in his "favorites.");

2) *boosting his self-esteem and self-confidence* via concentration on better performance in the areas in which he is already "a natural"; and

3) *increasing his time with male mentors* who can help him, through the activity and through general social interaction, to improve his performance, not only in the activity itself, but in the world of males.

*Even if the previous suggestions do not apply, i.e. the sensitive boy in your care is not overloaded with activities but is doing just fine in school or in his activities, the need for *male mentoring* is still, usually crucial. Sensitive boys are as hungry for male mentoring as any boy. Thus, in working with any sensitive boy, you can help the boy, his mother, and his family to take on one or more new male mentors within the extended family or through agencies like Boys Scouts of America or through faith communities, schools, and other assets.

*Help the highly sensitive boy's parents develop a "new daily plan" for technology use. To do this, you often have to help the boy and family develop bedtime rituals in which the television, cell phone, and computer are turned off by one-half hour before the boy should be asleep. De-stimulation helps create a lifestyle in which the highly sensitive boy (or girl) is not constantly over-stimulated by people, places, and electronics that heighten his stress levels and impede him from focusing on discovering inward equilibrium, especially before sleep time.

*Mentor the sensitive boy to keep a journal, in written or electronic form, in which he details his personal development. As the boy grows, his record of his journey can be useful to his continued development. Without such a record, he may measure himself against others and the world in a constantly one-down position. With this record as his own, however, he can gradually see his individual male journey, with all its high moments and low moments, as a journey toward meaning, one that he himself has been making, with his own power. Especially powerful during the time you are counseling the boy and his family: segments in this journal can become grist for emotionally moving dialogue with the boy.

I have made these suggestions for "sensitive boys," but all can work with sensitive men (whose lives we will explore in a moment). If we make sure to connect sensitive boys and men with mentors and activities that are natural to them, and if we help them experience and even record their own usefulness to the world, we help them find a secure place in the world. In facilitating its secure development, we are helping boys find mentors who will teach them personal survival skills, a deeper faith in themselves, more self-confidence in all spheres, how to take risks with relative safety, and how to remain moral and ethical, even in the face of bullying and pain.

When Sensitive Boys Are Bullied or Abused

When sensitive boys are bullied, they can become lethal. Nearly every counselor or therapist will work at some point with a young male who is or has been bullied. These males can kill themselves, shoot up schools, kill classmates, or drop grenades on their parents while their parents sleep.

During the era of Columbine and the school shootings, my book *A Fine Young Man* came out; also released were William Pollock's *Real Boys* and *Raising Cain,* by Dan Kindlon and Michael Thompson. Other titles and studies were published as well. All of us were involved in a public dialogue, mainly via academic conferences and the media, regarding various boys, including sensitive ones, who became violent.

That dialogue was instructive, and, since this American era, the study of bullying has continued on many fronts. For my part, I have come to believe that the two common ideologies taught to children regarding bullying—" walk away and tell an adult" and "use your words"—can certainly be effective in helping sensitive boys (and all children) who have been bullied, but they are not enough assistance for many bullied males in our counseling practices. A deeper understanding of males, bullying, and male culture can help us add further tools to our toolbox.

With sensitive boys who are bullied, the boy has generally been abused, attacked, targeted by one boy or, quite often, a group of boys. The bullies have challenged this sensitive male in ways similar to the ways they challenge many other males—on issues of *territory and power.* Unlike some of the other males the bullies challenge, the sensitive boy lacks internal assets (at least initially) to deal with aggressive male hierarchy challenge. He is over stimulated and overwhelmed by it; feels weakened by confrontation, rather than emboldened; does not know how to stand up to and use aggression; experiences male aggression's escalation into full-fledged violence and bullying; gives up territory and psychological boundary; relinquishes power—and, often, gains no measure of safety from the survival strategies adults have obliquely taught him. He keeps being abused and bullied, and may finally become so isolated from his family, the mass of males, and from humanity, that he becomes highly violent himself.

If we, as helping adults, mainly mentor this boy to "go get help when you're bullied," or "try to walk away," or "use your words," we risk the continuation of the bullying for so long that the sensitive boy becomes acutely dysthymic or severely depressed. I will never forget a dysthymic and frightened 11-year-old boy who came to me after being bullied for three months at and after school. He had tried everything he had been told to do in the school's anti-bullying curriculum. Now, he said, "They're going to kill me. Maybe I should kill them. What should I do?"

This sensitive boy felt abandoned by the systems that were set up to help him—school and family. This boy needed success skills that helped him deal with the male hierarchy challenges such as we've described throughout this book. He sensed that "male" approaches to life in the mass of males underlay a great deal of the bullying he was experiencing, but he could not articulate how and why. All he could do was continue, in desperation, trying to survive long enough for someone to teach him the skills that would help him navigate the mass of males. And because he was a sensitive boy who hung out with other sensitive kids, he did not learn adequate success skills from his peers. Furthermore, he had no father in the home and was not close to other elder males. Essentially, he was a young, sensitive boy lonely and depressed in the mass of males. He knew that he needed help in determining how to stand up to the bullies rather than constantly capitulating. When I met him, all he could think to do was reach out of his sadness and shame with vengeance, violence, or withdrawal into self-destruction.

The Elephant in the Room

In the professions attached to the field of psychology, we have pushed for "just walk away and get help" and "use your words" strategies to combat bullying. These have been very useful, and they will always be important parts of creating a more peaceful coexistence for diverse population in schools and communities.

At the same time, by advising zero tolerance of other less confrontational strategies, our profession has inadvertently created more suffering than we may have expected. We have hoped that normal (and sometimes cruel) hierarchy management among males would dissipate or disappear if we could direct as many people as possible toward becoming increasingly verbal-emotive and directly empathic. Not understanding the male psyche, most anti-bullying programs try to move the bullying framework to a non-confrontational/non-aggressive response array, without understanding males.

In using and teaching a diminished response array, we forget that many, if not most, of the bullied boys are already sensitive, directly-empathic, verbal-emotive boys—already nonaggressive when the bullying begins. They are already naturally inclined to use submissive words, walk away, get help. The bullying of these boys is constant or increasing in our schools and culture—our approach to bullying is not working as well as it could. Thus, I will argue here that while our recent approaches to bullying are an important part of a mature response array for bullying, bullied boys (and schools and families) need other tools to help them deal with male aggression. There is an elephant in the room—our neglect of a holistic approach to male development—as we in the psychology profession suggest, develop, and encourage anti-bullying policies to schools, families, and sensitive children.

With Jeremy and his family, I kept the elephant-in-the-room in mind, hoping to support extent anti-bullying strategies and curricula in the school and family, while also providing an expansive, holistic approach. As I do with all bullied children, I began my work with Jeremy and his family by listening, getting the facts, asking questions, discovering what anti-bullying measures Jeremy, his family, and his school had taken up to now, and simultaneously, helping Jeremy process his shame and his seething, repressed rage.

I told Jeremy my own stories of having been beaten up and bullied as a boy—stories of being held down on the ground and getting my nose stretched with pliers in Laramie by boys who wanted to see if my big Jewish nose would grow; of getting called a fag and geek and many other names throughout my school years; of staying home from school in Honolulu on "kill-haole-day" to avoid being beaten up by the bigger, local boys; of taking karate when I was 11 in order to gain self-defense skills; of standing up to a bully in seventh-grade by physically fighting him after school. With a boy like Jeremy, I am honest that fighting the bully actually made us friends, and ended the bullying. The sensitive boy I am working with most often needs to hear my undiluted, honest story of my own bullying in order to believe I really know how to help him.

The following is a rendition of a conversation with Jeremy that might illustrate some of what I am delving into here. My approach with Jeremy is not necessarily "politically correct," but as you can tell from this book, I am hoping that we can increase our usefulness to males by pushing into and then beyond political correctness. To save our nation's sons, especially some of the most sensitive boys among us, we need to take some risks.

Gurian: Take "kill-haole-day" in Hawaii, for instance. I was a weakling 10-year-old, sensitive boy, who had no muscle, was bad at sports, and only had one asset—my brains. This kill-haole-day happened in the schools about once a year in Hawaii in the '70s—it was a day when the local kids beat up or hassled white kids ("haole" means foreigner, and white kids were the foreigners). I was a target of the bigger boys.

So, what did you do?

I talked to my parents and teachers and the principal. I did everything I was supposed to do so I wouldn't be bulled.

Did it work?

Somewhat, but I still needed to figure out what else to do.

So, what did you do?

A father of a friend of mine heard about the bullying and told me to keep my eye out for an alpha male to do homework for. So I kept my eyes out. Do you know what an alpha male is?

Yeah. The leader of the group.

Right. There was a big Hawaiian-Samoan guy who pushed me into my locker a few times, but didn't seem to hate me. One day in class I saw him looking over at my test. That taught me something—*this guy needed me*. Growing up as a sensitive boy is a lot about seeing where you can fit or be needed in the hierarchy of males around you. You know what hierarchy is, right?

Yeah.

What is it?

Like, you know, whether you're popular or not.

Something like that. Yes. It's the pecking order, like the ladder each boy is on—some boys are at the top, some are in the middle, some are at the bottom. The boys at the top have the most power.

Yeah.

So I figured my friend's father was right—I could trade homework with this alpha male, the guy at the top of the pecking order, for protection against getting beat up. So, the next time the guy bumped me, I said, "Hey, if I do your homework for a week, will you talk to the guys about not messing with me?" He laughed and pushed me against my locker. I assumed I was gonna get beat up the next day, but instead, the next day, he came up to me at the bus stop and said he had thought about what I said, and if I helped him, he'd help me. And things got better for me, then. He and I entered into a transaction that got him what he needed and got me what I needed. I automatically moved up the hierarchy, and did not get beat up as much.

(Jeremy nods, seeing the logic of this). Why don't adults talk to us about this stuff?

(We talk about this for a while, then he says): You think I should find someone like that at my school?

(Honestly): Cheating is punished severely these days, more severely than in the '70s, so I'm not telling you to cheat. What I am saying is that here, in this office, and on our walks, we can look at all options. You need to look closely at *your* school and your situation. Look around and ask: "Is there someone older than me who has the respect of other kids, someone I can be useful to, and align myself with? Someone who might need the assets I have." Like, for instance, is there a particular coach of the bullies who your dad and you can go talk to? Or ask: "Is there a kid who needs me to do something for him—maybe not homework, but maybe helping him with his computer? Is there a team I can join, even though I don't think I'm very athletic? Is there a way I can be more brave and courageous than I'm being, a way I can stretch myself toward activities I think I'm not good at, but activities that might help me with a group of guys?"

Those are the kinds of questions to ask, Jeremy, because you're a sensitive kid like I was, and you need to learn how to handle boys and men who are going to hassle you. And believe me, they will hassle you all your life. They will try to break you down in order to make sure you become strong. If you learn how to handle them, you will get more protection, and more strength. You'll also be growing up—you'll be figuring out how to maneuver and manage other boys and men you'll meet in your life. As an adult male—a man—you aren't going to succeed very well unless you figure that out.

And remember, this is true of every guy, even the most sensitive, even an artist like Michelangelo, even a ballet dancer or fashion designer. No matter what you do, you have to develop strong character. You're 14—does what I'm saying make sense to you?"

Jeremy nodded. He was a smart boy—he knew exactly what I meant by those words. And he was male: he understood all of this at a visceral level.

He asked for more suggestions, and I said, "Okay, another thing you can do is study the packs and groups at your school. What crowd or pack can you get into now—even if it's a new pack of geeks and nerds—so you're never alone? Bullies tend to pick on sensitive, weaker kids who are alone or can be driven, through shame, to become alone. So, let's look at whether you can start walking to the bus with two or three other guys (and girls) so you have a crowd with you all the time?"

In this vein, various parts of our sessions became work sessions in which we developed an action plan for Jeremy and his family by which to approach particular bullies and groups. Various other parts of our sessions became teaching sessions in which I helped Jeremy, as a sensitive boy, understand *how male systems work*. In some sessions, we looked at how his previous practices had been successful, and which ones failed. I made sure Jeremy understood that just because he tried a new strategy, there was no guarantee of success. He would still experience failures.

By including from early on in counseling sessions my rendering of my own story to Jeremy and other boys, and by working with the boy and his family on a multifarious action plan, I believe I am helping bullied boys expand the tools in their toolbox—especially the tool of expanding their relationships. Having been a somewhat sensitive boy myself, I went through the phase of trying to rely only on submissive words or body postures to help me. Both helped me somewhat, but they were not enough to solve all the issues I faced. I needed a subtle reframing, which, fortunately, I got from mentors in my second decade of life, a reframing I pass on to bullied children now.

This reframing is one I hope boys like Jeremy, as I have, will remember later in life—that the mentor helped him see his bullying in a context of his larger life journey as a male; that in that larger male journey, he is seeking to learn who he is in all facets of his life, even the ones that are most stressful and painful; and that, like every male, he must discover courage in the mass, rather than avoiding his own usefulness to the mass, even if that usefulness ends up being rebellion against the mass later, or even, ironically, his becoming, in adulthood, the alpha male himself—something that does indeed happen to some bullied boys.

Bullying is a part of childhood that needs case-by-case analysis and individualized approaches from therapists, social workers, and other mentors. I hope you will consider, if you are not practicing these already, the addition of at least some of the following practical strategies to your already powerful skills, and the already established anti-bullying curriculum in your practice and community.

*Tell your own story of how you survived bullying (or were the bully or witness), what you did, what worked, what didn't. Be completely honest, even about things you did that now you look back on shamefully. This can significantly increase a therapist-client bond of trust with sensitive, bullied boys. That bond of trust can work wonders in counseling these boys.

*Work with the family to help sensitive, bullied boys get into self-defense programs, such as karate or other martial arts, as soon as possible. Such programs accomplish not only skills-development in physical and mental self-survival, but also help boys form new relationships with alpha males and females, and with empowering "packs" and social groups of males and females.

　　*During your sessions with the boy, role-play a number of ways to stand up to a bully. Stand over the boy, get in his face, call him the names he has been called by bullies. Then take the other side—be the bullied boy who is bullied now by your patient. Use words in powerful ways; model effective verbal responses to the bully. Clinical re-creation of bullying from both viewpoints creates opportunities for the boy to use words in strong, prepared ways, and feel prepared for the stress of the bullying.

　　*Ask fathers and other men into therapy to talk with the boy about how they were bullied (or were the bully or the witness). As they tell their stories to the boy, and as the boy asks questions of them, help the boy feel carried by these men into a male community of alignments and mentoring. Work out action plans with these men, so that the mentoring continues well beyond the time you will be the boy's therapist.

　　*Have a realistic response to male questions about "fighting back." Almost inevitably, a boy will ask whether he should fight back, physically, when bullied. When I am asked this question, I am honest to say that in most cases the consequences of fighting are going to be potentially negative these days—expulsion from school, etc.—but that if fighting back is necessary, it is necessary. I disclose the power that my fighting back against the bully in seventh grade gained me. I gained the respect of the bully and many of his friends. The bullying stopped immediately.

"When is it necessary?" the boy will ask.

"When you can't survive without it," is my answer.

There are risks to this honesty. A mother took her son out of counseling with me when she discovered from her son that I had said that fighting back might one day become necessary and useful. The father said, "But he's right!" The mother said, "He's telling my son to do something illegal and immoral." I was suggesting self-defense, which is not illegal, but her position made complete sense from her point of view. She did not see bullying in the same male-hierarchy context that her father and I, as males, saw it.

So there are risks for us in being honest about all aspects of bullying and fighting, but to not be honest with a boy, to not say what he already knows, which is, "At some point, you may have to fight back if you are to survive and thrive in the mass of males," has its own negative consequence. At both a micro and macro level, this neglect of male reality shows the boys and men in our care that we cannot be trusted. If a therapist can't be trusted to tell the truth, there is little hope for therapy with him.

Working with Sensitive Men

In working with Jeremy and others regarding bullying and the mass of males, I think often of what position a woman therapist might take on these points. I have been in dialogue about this with many women therapists and have not discovered any singular female response; rather, some women therapists believe there is something real and true about this perspective, while others do not; some say they are willing to try nearly anything useful in order to help bullied boys, while others are not so inclined. I am a man working with bullied boys, so my story is a male story, and that does afford certain advantages during counseling of these boys.

Yet, as we've said in previous chapters, there is no zero-sum on who can and can't be effective with sensitive boys and bullied boys and, for that matter, any boy or man. While it is essential that our profession recruit more men into it, as per our discussion in Chapter 1, it is also essential that women therapists receive training in how to work with the mass of males rather than in alienation from its often cruel hierarchical initiations of adolescent boys into adulthood. As more women therapists take more risks in working with males, I believe that women therapists will feel empowered by new depth of understanding of male hierarchy. When anyone, male or female, understands male hierarchy and the tribulations of sensitive boys within it, nearly any of the strategies I listed above can be practiced, no matter the practitioner's gender.

Similarly, when working with men in general, and sensitive men in particular, much of what we have already said in this chapter applies well, not only to adult male clients, but also to both male and female practitioners. Sensitive men were most likely sensitive boys, and what we've posited about "bridge brains" can work in dialogue with them. All innovative practices in this book can work with them, from peripatetic counseling, expressive arts therapy, and tactical confrontation to verbal-emotive dialogue.

At the same time, these men are men, not boys, so let's add further developmental material to our overall point that sensitive males are still very "male" and, thus, need gender-specific help, from both women and men therapists, as they seek to belong in the mass of males, and their adult relationships.

Carlos and Rosa Marie came to my office in search of marital help. They had been married sixteen years and had two sons, 10 and 8, and a daughter, 7. They had lost their house, and now lived in a small rental home. They had taken their children out of Catholic school and placed them in a low-performing urban school. They had difficulty earning enough money to make ends meet. They were in constant tension as a couple.

Research has generally found a trend of male dominance in many Latino couples, and often that research is corroborated in our clinical practices. With this couple, however, as with so many others, "male dominance" did not adequately capture the various domains of dominance in the marriage. In the case of Carlos and Rosa Marie, Rosa Marie deferred to Carlos in many areas of the family, and even deferred to him when he raised his voice and got angry, but at most of the other substrata levels of relationship, she was dominant.

When, for instance, she felt stress, she called Carlos names, verbally attacked him for not performing better at work, attacked his manhood, and directed her negative comments to his inability to provide for the family. Rosa Marie worked a forty-hour work week, so her attacks were not based on a lack of financial independence—they were a stress response that had an effect on her husband that she did not understand, a stress that would affect any man, but especially affected a highly sensitive man.

Through getting to know this couple, I learned about Carlos' relationship with his mother, which was a very close one; I learned that his mother had protected him from bullying in his family and elsewhere. Four years before, Carlos had grieved her death deeply (and during her dying process, he slept with her hospice nurse for a one month period). In speaking with Carlos in my office, and in meeting him outside my office and walking and talking with him, I came to understand that Carlos was, as so many men can be, a "sensitive" who had developed both an ethnically socialized and personally honed "macho," "tough" exterior—but he possessed a very sensitive personality.

The status of Carlos as a sensitive male was not an excuse for his affair. When I discussed this with Carlos and Rosa Marie, I was confrontational with Carlos. The affair had occurred four years before, and a great deal of our couple counseling was about helping Carlos take responsibility and helping Rosa Marie forgive.

In the area of verbal shaming and his sensitivity, however, Rosa Marie needed assistance. Initially, she did not see her own shaming practices as dangerous to the marriage, and she could not quite understand what importance "sensitive man" played in the marriage. Fortunately, she was open to receiving assistance.

To Rosa Marie I said, "I believe you think of Carlos as a traditional tough guy of Latino culture. But actually, when you shame him, the verbal tongue-lashing you think a tough guy can take is actually doing its part to destroy your marriage. It is destroying his sense of being a man. Carlos can't take it—he shuts down in order to survive it and/or turns away from it for survival, including doing things that are bad for your marriage."

It took a number of sessions to help her see who her husband was, and it took a number of sessions to help Carlos see his dependence on sex for self-esteem, and the need for him to develop a different kind of strength in dealing with this very strong woman he had, years ago, married for love, and still loved.

In working with this couple, I was lucky to have in my practice two people who did not wish to get divorced. This kept them fighting for their complex marriage for the period of time it took to help them. The core-theme of *duty* was one that Carlos could relate to well, and I worked with him to deepen his memory of how the men in his family had performed their collective duty to be the best husbands and fathers possible. Because his father had had affairs, there was deep work in this area for Carlos, some of which occurred in sessions with Rosa Marie, and some of which occurred in solo sessions.

On Rosa Marie's part, anger and rage dominated her family past. Her verbal shaming of her husband's maleness covered, as one would imagine, a lack of self-confidence. It also masked her lack of understanding of the male psyche. One of the most moving things Rosa Marie said in a session was this: "I didn't know a man could be so complicated. Now, I am thinking about all the men in my family differently." Comments like Rosa Marie's embolden me as a counselor to keep pressing clients to understand the hidden elements of gender in their personal lives and cultures, especially as regards boys and men, the "tough guy" and the often hidden "sensitive male."

Overall, in working with couples like Rosa Marie and Carlos, I find myself operating in some ways in sync with common psychological wisdom and in some ways not. On the one hand, I find it crucial to help men break through macho stereotypes to get at the hidden power of a well-expressed emotional life. On the other hand, I find that male toughness (like female) is also crucial to emotional and relational survival. What do I mean: Males, like females, have the psychological right to guard their feelings when needed for survival. Rosa Marie came to realize that her constant attacks on Carlos for not sharing enough of his feelings with her were just as dangerous as attacking him for not providing well enough for his family.

A Shamed Man

In my work in men's groups, I have been moved to hear how consistently men talk about their difficulty functioning in a marriage or divorce when they are constantly verbally shamed. Especially when the shaming occurs in front of children, as it often did with Carlos and Rosa Marie, the effects can be dangerous. And when it continues in counseling offices—men shamed for not feeling enough, not expressing feelings enough, or not fulfilling a partner's feelings-expectations enough—we lose male clients.

An African-American man in a men's group said, "Black women think they can say anything they want, diss us anyway they want. Selena (girlfriend for the last year) calls me every name in the book. She even does it when we're with friends. I swear to God I don't know how much longer I can take it. We went to counseling a year ago, and the therapist just took her side all the time. I walked out. It sucks."

Women often do not know how afraid a man is of female anger, especially female anger against maleness, masculinity, and men. Women often don't realize how fragile a man is in the face of verbal shaming, especially verbal shaming that destroys his sense of maleness and belonging in the mass of males. Without our realizing it, by more often "taking the woman's side than the man's," our profession has joined in providing further opportunity for attacking males.

If we are going to expand our psychological assistance to couples in need, it is essential that we not let therapy "take her side" without also "taking his side." If males feel like the second or other sex in counseling, the therapist has emboldened the counseling process to push males even further down (or out), which in the end becomes an abandonment of half of our counseling population—males.

This point came through in the comment by the black man in the group, and it comes through in comments from men who are told they are inherently defective because they are not as emotionally cognizant as their spouses are. Men in relationships with verbally shaming women often desperately need a therapist's help in realigning the verbal-emotive interactions of the relationship. Men are often not able to see how to encourage this re-alignment themselves, especially because they become overwhelmed by a woman's verbal-emotive power, and can only practice fight-or-flight in the face of it.

The New World

Boys and men are more sensitive than we may realize, and in ways our therapy profession is just beginning to discover. Boys and men are emotionally sensitive, spiritually sensitive, sensitive by personality, sensitive to hierarchies, sensitive to changes, sensitive to women's needs, sensitive to the fact that they as males in today's world often feel lost. Males are sensitive to hurt feelings and they are sensitive to the need to move beyond hurt feelings, if possible. One great thing about boys and men is that, quite often, they don't hold grudges for long, especially if they are apologized to and shown a new course in life.

Boys and men are also more sensitive to the needs of others than we realize, even though males don't always act in the exact ways other people, including their spouses, wish they would. Boys and men are sensitive to the emotional lives of girls and women, even though they constantly make mistakes in showing that sensitivity. They are sensitive to the needs of other males, even though, at times, they may be seen as trying to bring out of other males too much of one quality—usually, hierarchical toughness—and too little of another—tenderness.

Sensitive, loving, empathic, fragile—boys and men are highly complex; and, too, there is a natural simplicity to males, one that the most sensitive among them displays clearly: every boy and every man wants to be understood by and "belong with" the people tasked with helping them. Boys and men want to carry forward values such as duty, honor, heroism, sacrifice—values that give them challenge and hope. They want to learn ever new ways to become better partners to women. They want our therapy profession to be a place where they can belong, too.

To the extent that our therapy profession has acted as a female-centered medium for social change, it has neglected boys and men. Jeremy and Carlos are just two of the males who love women and female culture. They have a need for female culture, male culture, and our whole therapeutic culture to be willing to risk saying out loud, "Males need more male-friendly help and understanding than we have realized. They are creatures of nurture and nature who want what we all want: to belong, to succeed, and to be loved, unconditionally, for who they are."

Epilogue: the Future of Boys and Men

"Old definitions, which might once have limited us, break apart like dried crusts."

--Rainer Maria Rilke

I hope this book has challenged you to expand your thinking and practice. I hope it has added tools to your toolbox. I hope I have pressed you toward even greater service to all of humanity. I hope you will re-engage with this book and with me as needed in the future.

As we all know at some level—and as boys and men and girls and women need for us to help them understand—life is a journey of nature, nurture, fate, difficulty, joy, obstacles, happiness, adversities, and much more. Most of life we cannot control, no matter how hard we try. But we can control our own choices. In fact, quite often, they are the only thing we can control. A hero (or heroine) is nearly always the person who, by the end of the fairy tale, movie, or myth, has learned self-control. Woman or man, we are all seekers after a life of controllable choice, even as we learn to live in spontaneous radiance and joy.

With boys and men in your traditional therapy practices, you may have felt that the therapy was "going nowhere" or was "not as helpful as it could be." In traditional therapy, a practitioner has less control over his or her own therapeutic choices than many boys and men need for us to have. Traditional therapy is so sit-and-talk and so verbal-emotive, it is alien to many males; it begs us to take control of therapy and social work, and move these fields in new directions. We must break old definitions with our own hands—we must break the crusts.

Boys and men face the same core human issues of identity, autonomy, morality, and intimacy that girls and women face, but the genders face them in different ways. How fortunate we are in the new millennium that we can see the choices human beings make with more clarity and equality now than ever before. We can see nature and nurture with more clarity than in previous eras, even those that began in the '60s and '70s, could. Now, in the new millennium, we can see our changing gender roles with more equality than ever before.

With this good fortune comes the responsibility to be fully gender equal—which means including equality for males. In this latter context, I hope you will use the theories and practices in this book to foment social change. As an arbiter of personality, morality, marriage, human development, and human culture, you are essential to the journey of choices boys and men make. You can now do battle with and for these males in a world in which some males, such as our presidents and legislators and the CEOs of most of our companies, are doing, it appears, quite well, but also in which millions of males are desperate for us to see their difficulties, and expand our theories to include "boys and men" in our therapeutic discussions.

The future is hopeful for our profession and for its subjects if we open ourselves to meet boys and men where they are. What we in the field of psychology do defines culture—through our influence on academics, media, and social networking. Thus, a reframing of our practices and our field to break down old crusts is a matter of purpose and meaning to our children's future.

Thank you for all that you are doing for all your clients, both female and male. Thank you for reading this book, and please contact me through the various websites as you are so moved. What you do is life-changing, and we must support each other in this work if we are to fulfill ourselves in this very difficult and awe-inspiring new millennium.

Notes and Resources

Introduction

Over the years, I have been asked about my academic background, which does not include a degree in the field of psychology, and about how I ended up providing counseling services. Let me respond here, with my story.

When I first started researching and writing about gender science, I was teaching writing at Gonzaga University, and had no vision of becoming a therapist or counselor. However, when my first book on the father-son relationship, *The Odyssey of Telemachus,* was published in 1989, I was asked to lead workshops on male development. During and following the workshops, I got requests from mothers of sons, couples, women, and men to provide them with counseling. I told them I was not a counselor, nor did I have a degree in the therapy or psychology field (my terminal degree was an MFA, Masters in Fine Arts), so I could not counsel them.

Simultaneously, a friend, Jo Stowell, who was also a marriage and family therapist, informed me that I could register as a counselor—after finishing state ordered AIDS training—and then could legally act as a mental health counselor. This information was corroborated by a friend and colleague, Herm Ryans, who was a registered counselor at an agency, Treatment Alternatives to Street Crime (TASC), through which I later provided training and contract counseling at a federal prison.

As I looked into registering as a counselor with the state of Washington, I continued to receive calls and referrals from psychologists and therapists. "I have a family with two boys," a therapist said. "Can you give me your perspective?" A psychologist said, "I have a patient, a young man, who is floundering. What I'm doing isn't working. Can you work with him?" A counselor said, "I'm working with more than one couple in which the man is unreachable. What do you suggest? Have you thought about starting men's group and a counseling practice in Spokane?"

During that time, I developed a gender course on nature-based theory, which I later taught at Eastern Washington University and Gonzaga University. In 1991, I fulfilled the requirements to register as a counselor with the state of Washington and began a client load and a number of men's and couple groups. The need was so high for someone to focus on reaching boys and men in Spokane, my home, that I ended up with a fast-growing counseling practice.

I left Gonzaga University in 1994 to focus on counseling, writing, and lecturing. I worked as a contract counselor at Geiger Federal Prison through TASC, and provided gender training for the Washington State Department of Ecology, publishing books with a therapeutic and Jungian perspective, including *The Prince and the King* and *Mothers, Sons, and Lovers.* In 1996, I published *The Wonder of Boys*, which developed nature-based theory regarding boys' development. That book's material, like this book's, relied heavily on my client caseload, and called on the larger American culture to focus on boys' needs more fully than it had.

In Spokane, by 1996, my practice had grown into one that served not only males, but also girls and women. Everything I had learned about gender differences affected girls as much as boys, and women as much as men. This evolution from writer/teacher to counselor included further development of theory and practice in nature-based strategies for both genders, as well as the pursuit of constant training from other professionals in both counseling theory and practice.

If you are interested in more on the nature-based focus on boys, I hope you will explore the books *A Fine Young Man, The Good Son,* or *The Minds of Boys*

For more of a focus on men's lives, see *What Could He Be Thinking?, The Prince and the King,* and *The Invisible Presence.*

For more on applications of nature-based theory to school environments, see *Boys and Girls Learn Differently!, Strategies for Teaching Boys and Girls: Elementary and Secondary Levels,* and other books and workbooks by our Gurian Institute team.

For more on girls and women from the nature-based perspective, I hope you'll explore *The Wonder of Girls* and *Leadership and the Sexes.*

How Do I Help Him? is my twenty-sixth book, and eighteenth in the field of nature-based theory and gender science. I am one of those people who developed a psychological theory as much outside academe as within it, and learned my therapeutic practices more on-the-job than in-school. This is not a course of career I suggest for everyone, but it has led, I believe, to a life of service that I hope provides practitioners, academics, and policy makers with outside-the-box thinking and exciting results.

Now (2011), I am in my twenty-first year as a mental health counselor with a private practice that serves boys and girls, and women and men.

Chapter 1

Benedict Carey, "Need Therapy? A Good Man Is Hard to Find," *the New York Times*, May 21, 2011.

Because websites are included in the text of the statistical analysis, I won't repeat them here. And again, for more statistics and analysis, check out the multiple sources in the "Proposal to Create a White House Council on Boys to Men." Thirty-four thought leaders in gender issues and male development worked over a two-year period to create this scholarly literature review. Six of us were tasked with writing the final document. You can access our full document and Notes and References on www.whitehouseboystomen.com. Click the "Proposal" button.

More of Tom Mortenson's statistics appear at www.theboysinitiative.org. He can be reached at the Pell Institute.

Hoff-Sommers, C. H. *The War Against Boys.*New York: Simon & Schuster. 2001

Gurian, M. and Stevens, K. *The Minds of Boys.* Jossey-Bass/John Wiley: San Francisco, CA. 2005

Kleinfeld, J. "The State of Boys in America." *Gender Studies.* 2009

Whitmire, R. *Why Boys Fail.* AMACOM: New York, N.Y.2010.

In *How Do I Help Him?*, you'll note that I refer to various titles among my own published books as well as books published by my co-authors at the Gurian Institute. For a full list of these books and publishers, see www.michaelgurian.com.

Chapter 2

In order to further study nature-based theory and male/female difference through the lens of gender science, you might begin with a review of the following resources. These are some of the books and peer reviewed articles that provide a scholarly base for nature-based theory, thus they provide the scientific points and distinctions I make in this chapter and the further reference to those points and distinctions in later chapters. You can find an even longer list of science-based gender studies in the Endnotes to *Leadership and the Sexes* (Jossey-Bass/John Wiley, 2008). You can also find a more comprehensive list of primary studies on www.michaelgurian.com (click About, then click Research).

My scholarly and philosophical method in developing nature-based theory and its gender applications include:

*Scholarly reading and literature review of primary research with animals and humans, including brain scan research (PET, fMRI, SPECT).

*Observation of clients and others, including private practice, and wisdom-of-practice and action research through Gurian Institute programs.

*Scholarly reading of anthropological, psychological, and sociological research, both historical and contemporary.

*Holistic integration of the cross-discipline scholarship and observations into a theoretical and practical framework for working with both genders.

Albers, H. E., K. L. Huhman, and R. L. Meisel. "Hormonal Basis of Social Conflict and Communication." In D. W. Pfaff, A. P. Arnold, A. M. Etgen, S. E. Fahrbach, and R. T. Rubin (Eds.), *Hormones, Brain, and Behavior*, Vol. 1 (pp. 393–433). New York: Academic Press, 2002.

Arletti, R., A. Benelli, and A. Bertolini. "Oxytocin Involvement in Male and Female Sexual Behavior." *Annals of the New York Academy of Sciences* (1992), 652 (1): 180–193.

Amen, D., interview with Michael Gurian, 2006. Brain scans provided by the Amen Clinics (www.amenclinics.com).

Amen, D., M.D. *Making A Good Brain Great.* New York: Three Rivers Press, 2006.

Bales, K.L., et al. "Both Oxytocin and Vasopressin May Influence Alloparental Care in Male Prairie Voles." *Hormones and Behavior,* (2004) 45:361-454.

Blakemore, J.E.O., et al. *Gender Development.* New York: Psychology Press, 2009.

Brizendine, L., M.D. *The Female Brain.* New York: Broadway Books, 2006.

Carter, C.S. "Neuroendocrine Perspectives on Social Attachment and Love." *Psychoneuroendocrinology,* 23, 779-818.

Carter, R. *Mapping The Mind.* Los Angeles: University of California Press, 1998.

Christiansen, K. "Behavioral Effects of Androgen in Men and Women," *Journal of Endocrinology* (2001),170 (1).

Clawson, M. A. *Constructing Brotherhood: Class, Gender, and Fraternalism.* Princeton, N.J.: Princeton University Press, 1989.

Compaan, J. C., et al. "Vasopressin and the Individual Differentiation in Aggression in Male House Mice." *Annals of the New York Academy of Sciences* (June 1992), 652: 458.

Cordero, M. E., C. Valenzuela, R. Torres, and A. Rodriguez. "Sexual Dimorphism in Number and Proportion of Neurons in the Human Median Raphe Nucleus." *Developmental Brain Research* (2000), 124: 43–52.

Decapua, A., and D. Boxer. "Bragging, Boasting and Bravado: Male Banter in a Brokerage House." *Women and Language* (Spring 1999), 22 (1).

De Lacoste, M., R. Holloway, and D. Woodward. "Sex Differences in the Fetal Human Corpus Callosum." *Human Neurobiology* (1986), 5(2):93–6.

Diamond, M. "Male and Female Brains." Lecture for Women's Forum West Annual Meeting, San Francisco, CA, 2003.

Dragowski, E.A. et al., "Childhood Gender Identity ... Disorder? Developmental, Cultural, and Diagnostic Concerns." Journal of Counseling and Development. (Summer 2011) 89:360-366.

Eals, M., and I. Silverman. "The Hunter-Gatherer Theory of Spatial Sex Differences: Proximate Factors Mediating the Female Advantage in Recall of Object Arrays." *Ethology and Sociobiology* (1994), 15, 95-105.

Frederikse, M., A. Lu, E. Aylward, P. Barta, and G. Pearlson. "Sex Differences in the Inferior Parietal Lobule." *Cerebral Cortex* (1999), 9:896–901.

Gryn, G., A. Wunderlich, M. Spitzer, T. Reinhard, and M. Riepe. "Brain Activation During Human Navigation: Gender-different Neural Networks as Substrate of Performance." *Nature Neuroscience* (April 2000), 3 (4): 404–408.

Gur, R. C., et al. "Sex Differences in Brain Gray and White Matter in Healthy Young Adults." *Journal of Neuroscience* (1999), 19.

Gur, R. C., Ph.D., et al. "Sex Differences Found In Proportions of Gray and White Matter in the Brain: Links to Differences in Cognitive Performance Seen." Study: University of Pennsylvania Medical Center, May 18, 1999. [www.sciencedaily.com/releases/1999/05/990518072823.htm]

Gur, R., et al. "An fMRI Study of Sex Differences in Regional Activation to a Verbal and Spatial Task." *Brain and Language Journal* (2000), 74.

Halpern, D. F., C. P. Benbow, D. C. Geary, R. C. Gur, J. S. Hyde, and M. A. Gernsbacher. "The Science of Sex Differences in Science and Mathematics." *Psychological Science in the Public Interest* (August 2007), 8 (1).

Hamann, S., et al. "Men and Women Differ in Amygdala Response to Visual Sexual Stimuli." *Nature Neuroscience*, 4, 2004.

Hines, M. "Prenatal Testosterone and Gender-Related Behaviour." *European Journal of Endocrinology* (November 1, 2006), 155 (Suppl. 1): S115—S121.

Jensen, E. *Enriching the Brain.* San Francisco: Jossey-Bass, 2006.

Jessel, D., and A. Moir. *Brain Sex: The Real Difference Between Men & Women.* New York: Dell, 1992.

Joseph, R., Ph.D. *Neuropsychiatry, Neuropsychology, and Clinical Neuroscience*, 3rd ed. New York: Academic Press, 2000.Killgore, W., M. Oki, and D. Yurgelun-Todd. "Sex-Specific Developmental Changes in Amygdala Responses to Affective Faces." *NeuroReport* (2001), 12: 427–433.

Killgore, W.D., and D.A. Yurgelun-Todd. "Sex-related Developmental Differences in the Lateralized Activation of the Prefrontalcortex and Amygdala During Perception of Facial Effect." *Perceptual and Motor Skills Journal* (2004), 99.

Kilpatrick, L.A., D. H. Zald, J. V. Pardo, and L. F.Cahill. "Sex-Related Differences in Amygdala Functional Connectivity During Resting Conditions." *NeuroImage* (1 April 2006), 30 (2): 452-461. [http://today.uci.edu/news/release_detail.asp/key=1458]

Kimura, D. *Sex and Cognition.* Cambridge, MA: MIT Press, 1999.

Kimura, D. "Human Sex Differences in Cognition: Fact, Not Predicament." *Sexualities, Evolution & Gender* (2004), 6, 45-53. Simon Fraser University, B.C., Canada.

Knickmeyer, C., and S. Baron-Cohen. "Fetal Testosterone and Sex Differences." *Early Human Development*, 82 (12): 755-760

Liu, L. "Keep Testosterone in Balance: The Positive and Negative Effects of the Male Hormone." *WebMD*, January 2005.

Marcozzi, G., V. Liberati, F. Madia, M. Centofanti, and G. de Feo. "Age- and Gender-Related Differences in Human Lacrimal Fluid Peroxidase Activity." *Ophthalmologica* (2003), 217: 294-297 (DOI: 10.1159/000070638).

Pedersen, C.A. and Boccia, M.L. "Oxytocin Links Mothering Received, Mothering Bestowed and Adult Stress Responses." *Stress,* (2002), 5: 259-267.

Rhoads, S. E. *Taking Sex Differences Seriously.* San Francisco: Encounter Books, 2004.

Sandstrom, N., J. Kaufman, and S. A. Huettel. "Males and Females Use Different Distal Cues in a Virtual Environment Navigation Task." *Brain Research: Cognitive Brain Research* (1998), 6: 351-360.

Saucier, D., et al. "Are Sex Differences in Navigation Caused by Sexually Dimorphic Strategies or by Differences in the Ability to Use the Strategies?" *Behavioral Neuroscience* (2002), 116: 403-410.

Sax, L. *Why Gender Matters.* New York: Doubleday, 2005

Schlaepfer, T. E., G. J. Harris, A. Y. Tien, L. Peng, L. Seog, and G. D. Pearlson. "Structural Differences In the Cerebral Cortex of Healthy Female and Male Subjects: A Magnetic Resonance Imaging Study." *Psychiatry Research: Neuroimaging*(29 September 1995),61 (3) : 129-135.

Science Daily. "Intelligence in Men and Women is a Gray and White Matter." *ScienceDaily,* 22 January 2005. [www.sciencedaily.com/releases/2005/01/050121100142.htm]

Shors, T. J. "Significant Life Events and the Shape of Memories to Come: A Hypothesis." *Neurobiology of Learning and Memory* (2006), 85: 103–115. [www.rci.rutgers.edu/~shors/pdf/Significant/life/events/2006/Shors/article.pdf]

Shors, T. J. "Stress and Sex Effects on Associative Learning: For Better or for Worse." *The Neuroscientist* (2001), 4: 353-364.

Shors, T. J., and G. Miesegaes. "Testosterone in Utero and at Birth Dictates How Stressful Experience Will Affect Learning in Adulthood." *Proceedings of the National Academy of Sciences* (15 October 2002), 99: 13955-13960.

Silverman, I., and M. Eals. "Sex Differences in Spatial Abilities: Evolutionary Theory and Data." In J. Barkow, L. Cosmides, and J. Tooby (Eds.), *The Adapted Mind: Evolutionary Psychology and the Generation of Culture* (487-503). New York: Oxford University Press, 1992.

Thornhill, R. & Gangestad, S. *The Evolutionary Biology of Human Female Sexuality.* New York: Oxford University Press. 2008.

Uvnas-Moberg, K. "Oxytocin May Mediate the Benefits of Positive Social Interaction and Emotions," *Psychoneuroendocrinology*(1998), 23: 819-835.

Valla, J.M. and Ceci, S.J. "Can Sex Differences in Science be Tied to the Long Reach of Prenatal Hormones?" *Perspectives on Psychological Science.* (2011). 6:134-146

Vilain, E., K. McElreavey, F. Richaud, and M. Fellous. "Isolation of the Sex-Determining Gene in Men." *Pathologie et biologie* (Paris) (1992), 40(1): 15-7.

Weiss, L. A., M. Abney, E. H. Cook, and C. Ober. "Sex-Specific Genetic Architecture of Whole Blood Serotonin Levels." *The American Journal of Human Genetics* (2005), 76: 33-41.

Wood, G., and T. J. Shors. "Stress Facilitates Classical Conditioning in Males, But Impairs Classical Conditioning in Females Through Activational Effects of Ovarian Hormones." *Proceedings of the National Academy of Sciences* (1998), 95: 4066-4071.

Wood, W., and A. H. Eagly. "A Cross-Cultural Analysis of the Behavior of Women and Men: Implications for the Origins of Sex Differences." *Psychological Bulletin* (2002), 128 (5): 699–727.

Zhumkhawala, S. "Dolls, Trucks, and Identity." *Children's Advocate* (Nov-Dec. 1997). Action Alliance for Children, Oakland, CA. [www.4children.org/news/1197doll.htm]

The July 2008 *Anesthesia & Analgesia Journal* is devoted to the topic of Sex, Gender, and Pain Response. Fifteen clinical studies comprise the volume and make powerful reading for anyone interested in how men and women respond to pain differently. Volume 107: 1. My thanks to Lloyd Halpern, M.D., for calling this volume to my attention.

Also, see the work of Jay Giedd, M.D., at the National Institute of Mental Health (nimh.gov). He and his lab team have posted some of their brain scans on their site, some of which show differences in the male and female brain. According to the NIMH website, "The lab studies sexual dimorphism in the developing brain (especially important in child psychiatry (where nearly all disorders have different ages of onsets, prevalence and symptomatology between boys and girls) by exploring clinical populations that have unusual levels of hormones (congenital adrenal hyperplasia, familial precocious puberty) or variations in the sex chromosomes (Klinefelter's syndrome, XYY, XXYY)."

Baron-Cohen, S. *The Essential Difference.* New York: Basic Books, 2003

Taylor, Shelley E. *The Tending Instinct.* Times Books. New York. 2006

Tang, Y., Zhang, W., Chen, K., Feng, S., Ji, Y., Shen, J., et al. (2006). Arithmetic processing in the brain shaped by cultures. Proceedings of the National Academy of Sciences, USA, 103, 10775-10780.

In Chapter 8 of *Leadership and the Sexes,* you will find data showing how useful gender science has been in helping women advance in corporations such as IBM and Deloitte & Touche.

On www.gurianinstitute.com/Success, you will see the success data of boys mirrored for girls in schools we have worked with.

Need for Further Study

In presenting the science-based and clinical material in this book, I am also hoping my anecdotal research will be studied further via academic research. What I do with clients is anecdotally proven to work through my own action research (and some of my practices are echoed in the work of colleagues such as William Pollock, Michael Thompson, Ted Zeff, Gary Plep, and others), but if an academic or educational institution studied the strategies and practices as have other institutions studied the Gurian Institute's school-based gender innovations, the dialogue on best practices with boys and men would only increase, even if the success of some of the innovations prove to be un-replicable in certain general or institutional settings.

For that academic study to occur in a comprehensive way, some things might have to happen differently in our present academic and funding climate related to gender/brain difference information and its applications to boys and men. In presenting and working with the brain-based material in the area of gender, I have noticed a tacit fear of gender science among some academics, scientists, reporters, and politicians. Sarah expressed that academic fear, and also a resultant sense of condemnation of gender science.

As you move forward in this book, I want to be honest with you about some of the critiques I've heard and answered. I am a practical philosopher not a lab scientist, and I hope the following answers will give you a head start in gaining insight and innovation from this book in whatever is your profession. The critiques I've heard are:

"You and others like you are not scientists—why should we believe anything you tell us that uses science?"

"There are more differences between two boys (or two girls) than there are between boys and girls (or women and men)."

"Okay, yes, maybe there are some hard-wired gender differences, but they are minor compared to the power of socialization on boys and girls."

"If you talk about gender differences in families, schools, communities, etc., it will lead to dangerous gender stereotyping and a return to the patriarchy."

In my experience, most people (I would estimate 95 percent) who read a book like this, or take knowledge of gender differences into their practice, community, family, school, agency, or business, do not react negatively. Most people quickly realize that they already knew, instinctively, that there are profound differences between the genders, but didn't know there was science to reflect their knowledge.

But the fear of gender science is real for some, and needs response. Any theory or practice that looks carefully at innate brain differences (or even inculcated cultural differences) between males and females is going to take some hits. If you are thinking some of the things I listed above, or if you are preparing to use this work in the world and know that you will get some of the critiques I listed, here are answers I have discovered over the last two decades.

Q: You and people like you are not scientists—why should we believe anything you tell us about brain science?

A: My colleagues and I check what we do with scientists such as Tracey Shors, Ph.D., Daniel Amen, M.D., Harold Koplewicz, M.D. Please see the final pages of this book for comments from these and other scientists. And as noted in the body of Chapter 2: in books such as *Leadership and the Sexes,* you can find nearly a hundred primary scientific studies that clearly detail the structural, functional, chemical, and processing differences between male and female brains that this book uses as its science base. You can also go to www.michaelgurian.com for more of these studies (again: click About, then click Research.)

Albert Einstein said, "We mustn't leave science only to the scientists." By this, he meant: science must be made useful to everyone. My viewpoint on science is not as a scientist but as a practitioner utilizing and innovating in practical ways, with brain science and the standards of rigorous academic and in-the-field intelligence as my guides.

Q: There are more differences between two boys (or two girls) than there are between boys and girls (or women and men), so why pay attention to this junk science?

A: These comments indicate the destructive power of "scientific opinion" in a social dialogue. If you Google stories about my work or the work of others who utilize gender science, you may notice that opinions like these appear at the end of, or in the body of, some media articles on gender/brain differences. If the writer or interviewee of the story wants to claim that gender differences are meaningless, the pithy quote is used.

At the same time, opinions like these do not actually have much to do with the body of gender science information I am applying in this book. Between two boys and two girls, there are many differences; so, too, between a boy and a girl. Both are true. There are hundreds of peer reviewed studies proving differences between the male or female brain; there is no scientific basis, except opinion, to call gender science "junk science", or to deny its importance by saying that two boys and two girls can differ from one another.

Gender science elicits fear, and that fear can, at times, elicit opinions that undermine good work. With gender science, it is especially important to not believe everything you read on the Internet or in a short article. I encourage you to go to the primary studies themselves in order to get past thin opinions. I believe we will not reach many boys and men if we do not push through the fear of gender science. We will reach the talkative, sensitive, verbal-emotive boys through our traditional therapeutic strategies, but we will not reach the majority of boys and men.

Q: Okay, yes, there are some hard-wired gender differences, but they are minor compared to the power of socialization on boys and girls.

A: This position is taken by individuals who fear that admitting nature-based gender differences will lead to negative outcomes for girls and women. Simultaneously, since the researchers and reporters are aware of the plethora of applicable studies published by scientists in the last thirty years, they can't really insist gender science is junk science: so the stance taken is, "The gender/brain differences are minor," or "they're mainly socialized."

For those of us looking for a more accurate blend of nature and nurture, this reductionism is actually helpful. If you read articles that take the "gender differences are minor" or "nature doesn't matter" position, you will notice that the practical strategies these writers suggest for dealing with the "minor differences" are mainly the same innovations that grew previously from the work of practitioners and academics who understood how robust are gender differences in the brain.

Ultimately, whether one sees gender differences as a 50/50 blend of nature and nurture, as I do, or whether one sees gender differences as mainly nurture and a little bit of nature, the best practice innovations tend to be the ones that fit the 50/50 view, because these best practices constitute a group of innovations that succeed with boys and men across cultures.

Q: If you apply this gender work to families, schools, and communities, dangerous gender stereotyping will result, including a return to the patriarchy, and the further marginalization of girls and women.

A: This accusation makes for good copy but cannot be proven; most importantly, it has been disproven. Hundreds of organizations, schools, and corporations have applied gender science to help girls and women. IBM, Deloitte

&Touche, Nissan, Nike, NASA, and Microsoft are just some of the corporations that have retained and advanced more *women* in the companies by focusing on gender differences. The opinion that paying attention to gender differences leads to oppression of women (and a return to the patriarchy) is simply not true.

However, it is true that somewhere in this world there will be someone who will misuse gender science. Someone somewhere will use it to say, "You see, men are better leaders than women," or "women should stay home, have kids, and not work." We must all remain vigilant against these stereotypes. We must also remember that this kind of stereotyping can occur with any theory, whether Freudian or Jungian, object-relations or constructivist, family-of-origin, Piagetian or Kholbergian. Just as with these other theories, the existence of someone abusing a theory does not negate the fact that the science actually helps girls and women.

Chapter 3

Ladinsky, Daniel. *Love Poems from God.* (2002). Penquin Compass: New York.

McSolely, R. "Who's Training Whom," *Darshan*, (2002). Syda Foundation: Fallsburg, NY

Private Correspondence with Gina Cuen, 2011.

Garret, M.T. et al. "Crying for a Vision: The Native American Sweat Lodge Ceremony as Therapeutic Intervention." *Journal of Counseling and Development.* (2011). 89: 318-326

The whole issue of the magazine *Torah at the Center* involves Gender and Jewish Education (11:1, Fall 2007). This is just one of the faith-based publications that have, over the last five years, looked carefully at why boys and men are not as engaged in church, synagogue and other religious institutions as girls and women are. Another Jewish resource is *Fighting the Flight of Men* by Doug Barden (NFTB: New York, 2005).

My team and I have been involved in some of these dialogues, and while I don't know of a science-based study that has proven what the issues are, our observation is that many of the issues parallel the issues in this book. A strong book on this subject is David Murrow's *Why Men Hate Church*.

If you are Jewish and interested in a specific practical solution, see Chapter 8 of *The Purpose of Boys*. At the request of Rabbi Jacob Izakson and religious education director Adie Goldberg at Temple Beth Shalom in Spokane, Washington, I created a "Hineni" program for 15-year-old boys. It is explained in the book.

If you are a Christian, I hope you'll utilize *Following Jesus: A Boy's Quest for Heroic Manhood*, co-developed by Rev. Tim Wright of Community of Grace Church in Peoria, Arizona, and myself. This Confirmation/Rite of Passage program combines brain science and the Bible. We have also created *Following Jesus: A Wisdom Journey for Girls*. To learn more about these programs, and for more information on solutions-based gender programming for faith communities, see www.faith-communities.net.

Chapter 4

Amen, Daniel. *Sex On The Brain*. Bantam: New York. 2005
Baron-Cohen, Simon. *The Essential Difference*. Basic Books: New York. 2003
Taylor, Shelley E. *The Tending Instinct*. Times Books: New York. 2006
Gilmore, David. *Manhood in the Making*. Yale University Press: New Haven. 1990.
Sax, Leonard. *Boys Adrift*. Basic Books: New York. 2009.
Bly, Robert. *The Sibling Society*. Addison-Wesley Publishing: MA. 1993.
For further analysis of theories regarding male motivation, see the following resources, which can also provide further tools regarding the use of core themes with males.

If you are working with boys from birth to puberty, *The Wonder of Boys* (2006) provides core theme models, and ways to use them. For working with adolescent boys, *A Fine Young Man* (1999) and *The Purpose of Boys* (2009) provide core themes and implementation programs specific to working with males from age 10 to college age.

If you are working with young adult males in their late teens and 20s, *Nurture the Nature* (2007) provides thematic models for that age group.

If you are working on issues of male motivation specifically, *The Minds of Boys* (2005) can be especially helpful.

If you are working with men 25 and older, *The Prince and the King* (1991), *What Could He Be Thinking?* (2003), and *The Invisible Presence* (2010) are resources for adult male models. The first and the third provide guided meditations to help men explore their father-son and mother-son wounds.

For more on rites of passage, see the notes for Chapter 3.

Chapter 5

Sibert, K. "Don't Quit this Day Job," *the New York Times*. June 11, 2011. http://www.nytimes.com/2011/06/12/opinion/12sibert.html?nl=todaysheadlines&emc=tha212
Garbarino, James. (1999*) Lost Boys*. Simon & Schuster: The Free Press, New York.
Gilmore, David. (1990). *Manhood in the Making*. Yale University Press. New Haven.
Buss, David. *The Evolution of Desire*. Basic Books: New York. 2003.
The statistics and sources for the "Did You Know?" section are just the tip of the iceberg on analysis of the importance of the role of the father. For the Commission for a While House Council on Boys to Men Proposal, we gathered statistics from a broad literature review. In the area of Fathers' roles and necessity, Warren Farrell took the lead of the scholarship team. His team gathered these and many more statistics which you can access in full on

www.whitehouseboystomen.com. To join the efforts to advance the cause of the Proposal, contact Dr. Farrell at warren@warrenfarrell.com.

President's Advisory Council on Faith-Based and Neighborhood Partnerships: "A New Era of Partnerships: Report of Recommendations to the President," March 2010. Nearly 4 in 10 (36 percent) of Hispanic children, and nearly 1 in 4 (25 percent) of white children live in father-absent homes.

J. A. Martin, B. E. Hamilton, P. D. Sutton, S. J. Ventura, et al, Births: Final Data for 2006. *NationalVital Statistics Reports*: Volume 57:7. Hyattsville, MD: National Center for Health Statistics. 2009. The exact proportion is 38.5 percent Among white children, 26.6 percent are born out of wedlock.

Richard Koestner, C. Franz, and J. Weinberger, "The Family Origins of Empathic Concern – a Twenty-Six-Year Longitudinal Study." *Journal of Personality and Social Psychology*, Vol. 58, No.4, April, 1990, pp. 709-717.

See the discussion of empathy and its connection to fathers and life's happiness in Warren Farrell, *Father and Child Reunion*. New York: Putnam/Penguin, 2001. pp. 30-31.

M. Main and D. R. Weston, "The Quality of the Toddler's Relationship to Mother and to Father: Related to Conflict Behavior and the Readiness to Establish New Relationships." *Child Development*, Vol. 52, 1981, pp. 932-940.

Hjern Anders, et al., *ActaPaediatrica*. 99: 920-924, June 2010. DOI: 10.1111/j.1651-2227.2009.01638.x. *ActaPaediatrica* is a monthly peer-reviewed pediatric journal covering both clinical and experimental research. http://www.actapaediatrica.com.

U.S. Department of Health and Human Services, National Center for Health Statistics. Family Structure and Children's Health: United States, 1988. Vital and Health Statistics, p. 27. Table 13, Number of Children 3-17 Years of Age and Percentage Treated for Emotional or Behavioral Problems In the Past 12 Months, by Family Type and Selected Demographic and Social Characteristics: United States, 1988. In the previous 12-month period, 2.7 percent of children living with their biological mother and father, and 8.8 percent of children living with a formerly married mother and no father, were treated for emotional and behavioral problems.

U.S. Department of Health and Human Services, National Center for Health Statistics. Family Structure and Children's Health: United States, 1988, Vital and Health Statistics, p. 27, Table 13, Number of Children 17-years-of-age and Under and Percentage Who Had Frequent Headaches in the Past 12 Months, by Family Type and Selected Demographic and Social Characteristics: United States. 1988. In the previous 12-month period, 2.5 percent of children living with their biological mother and father, and 4.1 percent of children living with a formerly married mother and no father, had frequent headaches.

U.S. Department of Health and Human Services, National Center for Health Statistics. Family Structure and Children's Health: United States, 1988, p. 21, Table 7, Number of Children 17-years-of-age and Under and Percentage Who Had Chronic Enuresis in the Past 12 Months, by Family Type and Selected Demographic and Social Characteristics: United States, 1988. In the previous 12-month period, 2.3 percent of children living with their biological mother and father, and 2.9 percent of children living with a formerly married mother and no father, had chronic enuresis (bed-wetting).

U.S. Department of Health and Human Services, National Center for Health Statistics. Family Structure and Children's Health: United States, 1988, p. 20, Table 6, Number of Children 17-years-of-age and Under and Percent Who Had a Stammer or Other Speech Defect in the Past 12 Months, by Family Type and Selected Demographic And Social Characteristics: United States, 1988. In the previous 12-month period, 2.3 percent of children living with their biological mother and father, and 3.2 percent of children living with a formerly married mother and no father, had a stammer or other speech defect.

U.S. Department of Health and Human Services, National Center for Health Statistics. Family Structure and Children's Health: United States, 1988, p. 10. In the previous 12-month period, 39 percent of children living with their biological mother and father, and 55.3 percent of children living with a formerly married mother and no father, had one or more indicators of anxiety or depression.

U.S. Department of Health and Human Services, National Center for Health Statistics. Family Structure and Children's Health: United States, 1988, p. 10. In the previous 12-month period, 34.9 percent of children living with their biological mother and father, and 51.1 percent of children living with a formerly married mother and no father, had one or more indicators of hyperactivity.

John Guidubaldi, Joseph D. Perry, and Bonnie K. Nastasi, "Growing Up in a Divorced Family: Initial and Long Term Perspectives on Children's Adjustment" in Stuart Oscamp (ed.), *Applied Social Psychology Annual, Vol. 7: Family Processes and Problems*. Beverly Hills, CA: Sage Publications, 1987, p. 230.

Frank Mott, "When Is a Father Really Gone? Paternal-Child Contact in Father-Absent Homes." *Demography*, Vol. 27, No. 4, November 1990, pp. 499-518.

John W. Santrock and Richard A. Warshak, "Father Custody and Social Development in Boys and Girls." *Journal of Social Issues*, Vol. 35, No. 4, Fall, 1979.

The only factor more important than father involvement was the child's age. Robert H. Coombs and John Landsverk, "Parenting Styles and Substance Use During Childhood and Adolescence." *Journal of Marriage and the Family*, Vol. 50, May 1988, p. 479, Table 4. The factors considered were age, sex, ethnicity, social class, closeness to parent, parent trust, parental rules, parent strictness, etc. Age accounted for about 17 percent (.17 out of a maximum of 1) of the variation in drug use among the youth in their sample; positive father sentiment (closeness) accounted for another 10 percent, and no other factor accounted for more than 2 percent.

Carmen Noevi Velez and Patricia Cohen, "Suicidal Behavior and Ideation in a Community Sample of Children: Maternal and Youth Reports." *Journal of the American Academy of Child and Adolescent Psychiatry*, Vol. 273, 1988, pp. 349-356.

R. Dalton, et al, "Psychiatric Hospitalization of Preschool Children: Admission Factors and Discharge Implications." *Journal of the American Academy of Child and Adolescent Psychiatry*, Vol. 26, No. 3, May 1987, pp. 308-312.

H. S. Merskey and G. T. Swart, "Family Background and Physical Health of Adolescents Admitted to an In-Patient Psychiatric Unit, I: Principle Caregivers." *Canadian Journal of Psychiatry*, Vol. 34,1989, pp. 79-83.

Nicholas Davidson, "Life Without Father: America's Greatest Social Catastrophe." *Policy Review*, Winter, 1990, p. 42.

Fathers and Families of Massachusetts is a national organization devoted to seeing fathering issues from all sides and advocating for fathers in ways that balance needs with mothers. See www.fatherandfamilies.org. A Google search of Fathers and Families also elicits a number of other similar organizations at local levels.

Chapter 6

Bly, Robert, et al. *The Rag and Bone Shop of the Heart.* HarperPerennial: New York. 1990

Newell, Robert. *What Is A Man?* Harper Paperbacks: New York. 2001.

Neuroscientists Sara Moore and Gregory Berns, at Emory's Center for Neuropolicy, published their study in the Journal of Consumer Psychology. Their work was reported by Robert Lee Hotz in the Wall Street Journal, June 11, 2011. The article "Songs Stick in Teens' Heads" is a useful one to give parents. It is written in a way any layperson can read easily, and it helps explain why teenagers seem so "obsessed" with their music.

Comments I've made in this chapter regarding pornography were directed to normal developmental trajectories of males. I am not an expert in sexual addiction or deviance. If you are working with sex addicts or deviants, I hope you will discuss with more knowledgeable colleagues whether the use of visual-graphics is useful or detrimental for those populations.

To help you further explore expressive arts therapies, see one of more of these very useful websites:

International Expressive Arts Therapy Association, www.ieata.org
National Coalition of Creative Arts Therapies Associations, www.nccata.org
Focusing Institute: Expressive Arts Therapies, www.tinyurl.com/3argvul
ARTrelief, www.tinyurl.com/3kcvrj2
American Music Therapy Association, www.musictherapy.org
Music Therapy for Autistic Children, www.tinyurl.com/30dqhf8
American Dance Therapy Association (ADTA), www.adta.org
National Association for Poetry Therapy, www.poetrytherapy.org
Center for Journal Therapy, www.journaltherapy.com
National Association for Drama Therapy, www.nadt.org
American Society of Group Psycho-therapy and Psychodrama, www.asgpp.org

Chapter 7
Child, Lee. *Worth Dying For.* Dell: New York. 2011

Finder, Joseph. *Paranoia.* St. Martins: New York. 2004

Bosson, J.K. and Vandello, J.A. "Precarious Manhood and its Links to Action and Aggression." (2011). *Current Directions in Psychological Science.* 20;82-86

Benenson, J.F., et al. "Under Threat of Social Exclusion, Females Exclude More Than Males." (2011) *Psychological Science.* 22:538 – 544.

Stanton, S.J., et al. "Low- and High-Testosterone Individuals Exhibit Decreased Aversion to Economic Risk." (2011). *Psychological Science.* 22:447-453

Guesquirie, L.R., et al. "Life at the Top: Rank and Stress in Wild Male Baboons." (2011) *Science. 333:357-360*

Iggulden, Conn and Iggulden, Hal. *Dangerous Book for Boys.* Morrow: New York. 2007

Boy Scouts of America can be reached at www.scouting.org.

For more on the heroic impulse in males, please see:

Jung, Carl. *Man and His Symbols.* Dell: New York. 1968

Campbell, Joseph. *The Hero with a Thousand Faces.* New World Library: New York. 2008

Moore, Robert and Gillette, Douglas. *King, Warrior, Magician, Lover.* HarperOne: New York, 1990

Cannon, C. *Winning Back Our Boys.* TAG publishing, 2010.

Braden, W. R. *Homies: Peer Mentoring Among African-American Males.* LEPS Press, 1999.

Chapter 8

Adler, A. *Understanding Human Nature.* Reprint: Martino Fine Books. 2010

In my unorthodox career, I have found Adler's egalitarian, democratic approach very helpful. Adler believed that the work of understanding human nature should not be unique to psychologists; it should be pursued by lay people. He also believed it should be highly practical and practice-based in its orientation.

Brand, C.R., Egan, V.G. & Deary, I.J. (1993). "Personality and General Intelligence." In G.L.Van Heck, P.Bonaiuto, I.J.Deary& W. Nowack (eds.), *Personality Psychology in Europe* 4, 203-228. Tilburg University Press.

Gurian, M. *A Fine Young Man.* Tarcher/Putnam: New York. 1998

Pollack, W. *Real Boys.* Henry Holt: New York. 1998.

Kindlon, D. and Thompson, M. *Raising Cain.* Ballantine: New York. 1999.

Of the many worthy anti-bullying campaigns available to you, I will mention a new one that is somewhat unique in that the authors created both a secular and a Christian version. To learn more about *The Three Phase Bullying Solution* and the work of educator Frank Dilallo and his colleagues, see www.Peace2Usolutions.com.

Zeff, T. *The Strong Sensitive Boy.* San Francisco: Prana Publishing. 2010. You can learn more about this book at www.drtedzeff.com

Aron, A. *The Highly Sensitive Person.* New York: Broadway Books. 1997
For more on Dr. Aron's work, see www.hsperson.com. For more about Dr.
Zeff's work, as well as his analysis of connection between his ideas and Dr.
Elaine Aron's work, see www.drtedzeff.com.

For more about PREP (the Prevention and Relationship Enhancement Program), see www.smartmarriages.com.

Greytak, E.A., et al. (2009) *Harsh Realities: The Experiences of Transgender Youth in Our Nation's Schools.* New York: Gay, Lesbian, and Straight Education Network.

Karraker, K., et al. (1995) "Parents Gender-Stereotyped Perceptions of Newborns: The Eye of the Beholder Revisited." *Sex Roles.* 33: 687 – 701.

Schilt, K. & Westbrook, L. (2009). "Doing Gender, doing Heteronormativity: 'Gender Normal,' Transgender People, and the Social Maintenance of Heterosexuality." *Gender & Society.* 23: 440-464

Stryker, S. *Transgender History.* Berkeley: Seal Press. 2008.

Zhou, J, et al. (1995). "A Sex Difference in the Human Brain and its Relation to Transsexuality." *Nature.* 368:68-70.

Bibliography

Amen, Daniel (2005) Sex On The Brain. Bantam. New York

Arnot, Robert. (2001) The Biology of Success. Little Brown & Company. Boston, MA.

Baron-Cohen, Simon. (2003) The Essential Difference. Basic Books. New York.

Bear, Mark; Connors, Barry; Paradiso, Michael. (1996). Neuroscience. Williams and Wilkins. Baltimore, M.D.

Blum, Deborah. (1998) Sex On The Brain. Penguin Books. New York.

Brizendine, Louann (2007) The Female Brain. Three Rivers Press. New York.

Brott, Armin (2010) The Expectant Father. Abbeville Press. New York

Brott, Armin (2009) The Military Father. Abbeville Press. New York

Browne, Rollo and Fletcher, Richard. (1994) Boys in Schools. Finch Publishing. Sydney.

Bly, Robert. (1996). The Sibling Society. Addison-Wesley Publishing. MA.

Carr-Morse, Robin. (1998) Ghosts From The Nursery. Atlantic Monthly Press. New York

Carter, Rita. (1998) Mapping the Mind. U. of CA Press. Los Angeles, CA.

Deak, JoAnn (2003) Girls Will Be Girls. Hyperion. New York.

Faludi, S. (2000) Stiffed. Harper Perennial. New York.

Farrell, W. (2000). The Myth of Male Power. Berkeley. New York.

Flinders, Carol. (2002). The Values of Belonging. HarperSanFrancisco. San Francisco, CA.

Friedan, B. (1981/1998). The Second Stage (Cambridge: Harvard University).

Fogarty, Robin. (1997) <u>Brain Compatible Classrooms</u>. Skylight Professional Development. Arlington Heights, IL.

Garbarino, James. (1999) <u>Lost Boys</u>. Simon & Schuster: The Free Press, New York, NY.

Gilmore, David. (1990). <u>Manhood in the Making.</u> Yale University Press. New Haven.

Golden, T. R. (2000). <u>Swallowed by a Snake.</u> GH Publishing, LLC. Gaithersburg, MD.

Goleman, Daniel. (1995). <u>Emotional Intelligence.</u> Bantam. New York.

Gurian, J.P. & J. (1983) <u>The Dependency Tendency</u>. Rowman and Littlefield.

Gurian, Michael, with Kathy Stevens. (2005) <u>The Minds of Boys</u>. Jossey-Bass. San Francisco, CA

Gurian, Michael., et.al. . (2011)<u>Boys and Girls Learn Differently!</u> A Guide for Teachers and Parents. Jossey-Bass. San Francisco, CA., Tenth Anniversary Edition

Gurian, Michael. (2006) <u>The Wonder of Boys</u>. Tarcher-Putnam. New York, Tenth Anniversary Edition

Gurian, Michael. (2002) <u>The Wonder of Girls</u>. Pocket Books. New York.

Gurian, Michael. (1998) <u>A Fine Young Man</u>. Tarcher-Putnam. New York.

Harris, Judith R. (1998). <u>The Nurture Assumption.</u> Free Press. New York.

Hallowell, Edward and Ratey, John.(1994) <u>Driven to Distraction.</u> Touchstone. New York.

Jensen, Eric. (1995, 200 Rev.) <u>Brain-Based Learning</u>. The Brain Store. San Diego, CA.

Jessel, David and Moir, Anne. (1989) <u>Brain Sex.</u> Dell. New York, NY.

Johnson, Steven. (2004). <u>Mind Wide Open.</u> Scribner. New York.

Kandel Eric; Schwartz, James; Jessell, Thomas. (1995). <u>Essentials of Neural Science and Behavior.</u> Appleton & Lange. Norwalk, Connecticut.

Karges-Bone, Linda. (1998) <u>More Than Pink & Blue.</u> Teaching and Learning Company, 1204 Buchanan St., Carthage, IL 62321-0010.

Kipnis, Aaron. (1999) <u>Angry Young Men</u>. Jossey-Bass. San Francisco, CA.

Kimmel, Michael (2009) <u>Guyland.</u> Harper Paperbacks: New York, NY.

Kiselica, Mark; Englar-Carson, Matt; Horne, Arthur M. (Editors) (2007) <u>Counseling Troubled Boys.</u> Routledge Publishers: New York, NY.

Klindon, Dan. and Thompson, Michael. (2000) <u>Raising Cain</u>. Ballantine Books. New York, NY.

Kundtz, David. (2004). <u>Nothing's Wrong.</u> Conari Press: Boston, MA

Ladner, Joyce. (2003). <u>Launching Our Black Children for Success.</u> Jossey-Bass/John Wiley. San Francisco, CA.

Levine, Mel. (2002) <u>A Mind at a Time</u>. Simon & Schuster. New York.

Moir, Anne and Bill (1999). <u>Why Men Don't Iron.</u> Citadel. New York.

Moir, Anne and Jessel, David (1990) <u>Brain Sex.</u> Laurel. New York.

Murphy, Shane (1999) <u>The Cheers and the Tears: A Healthy Alternative to the Dark Side of Youth Sports Today.</u> Jossey-Bass/John Wiley. San Francisco/New York.

Newell, Waller R. (2000) <u>What is a Man?</u> Regan Books. New York.

Nylund, David. (2000) <u>Treating Huckleberry Finn.</u> Jossey-Bass/John Wiley. New York.

Payne, Ruby (2000) A Framework for Understanding Poverty. AhaProcess, Inc. Highlands, Texas

Pease, Barbara and Allan. (1999) <u>Why Men Don't Listen, And Women Can't Read Maps.</u> Broadway Books. New York.

Pollack, William. (1998) <u>Real Boys</u>. Henry Holt, New York.

Ratey, John and Eric Hagerman (2008) <u>Spark.</u> Little Brown. New York.

Ravitch, Diane. (2003) <u>The Language Police: How Pressure Groups Restrict What Children Learn.</u> Alfred A. Knopf. New York.

Real, Terrence. (1997). <u>I Don't Want to Talk About It</u>. Fireside: New York.

Rhoads, Steven E. (2004) <u>Taking Sex Differences Seriously</u>. Encounter Books. San Francisco, CA.

Salomone, Rosemary C. (2003) <u>same, different, equal</u>. Yale University Press. New Haven and London.

Siegel, Daniel J. (1999). <u>The Developing Mind.</u> Guilford Press. New York.

Slocumb, Paul. (2004). <u>Boys In Crisis.</u> Aha Process, Inc. Highlands, Texas.

Smith, Michael W. and Wilhelm, Jeffrey D. (2002) <u>"Reading Don't Fix No Chevy's": Literacy in the Lives of Young Men</u>. Heinenmann. Portsmouth.

Sommers, Christina Hoff. (2000) <u>The War Against Boys.</u>Touchstone. New York.

Sousa, David. A. (2001) <u>How the Brain Learns</u>. Corwin Press. Thousand Oaks, CA.

Sprenger, Marilee. (2002) <u>Becoming A "Wiz" at Brain-Based Teaching: How to Make Every Year Your Best Year</u>. Corwin Press. Thousand Oaks, CA.

Stephenson, Bret. (2004) <u>Slaying the Dragon. www.adolescentmid.com</u>. Stein, David. (1999) <u>Ritalin Is Not The Answer.</u> Jossey-Bass. San Francisco.

Sykes, Bryan. (2003) <u>Adam's Curse</u>. W.W. Norton & Company. New York.

Tannen, Deborah. (1991) <u>You Just Don't Understand: Women and Men in Conversation.</u> Morrow. New York.

Taylor, Shelley E. (2002). <u>The Tending Instinct.</u> Times Books. New York.

Verhaagen, David A. (2010). <u>Therapy with Young Men.</u> Routledge. New York.

Wexler, David (2009) <u>Men in Therapy.</u> Norton. New York.

Wolfe, Patricia. (2001) <u>Brain Matters.</u> Assoc. for Supervision and Curriculum Development.

Woody, Jane DiVita. (2002) <u>How Can We Talk About That?</u> Jossey-Bass. San Francisco, CA.

Zeff, Ted (2010) <u>The Strong Sensitive Boy.</u> Prana Publishing. San Francisco, CA.

About the Gurian Institute

The Gurian Institute, founded in 1996, provides professional development, training services, and pilot programs in gender diversity and gender dynamics. All of the Institute's work is science-based, research-driven, and practice-oriented.

The Institute staff, trainers, and coaches work with parents, mental health professionals, teachers, counselors, school districts, corporations, the legal system, medical professionals, and others who serve boys and girls, and women and men. The Institute has trainers throughout the world.

The Institute also provides products such as DVDs, books, workbooks, newsletters, and a user-friendly website at www.gurianinstitute.com.

Michael Gurian has personally developed training, consulting, and coaching programs specifically for therapists, social work professionals, corrections and law enforcement, and all other therapeutic professionals working in areas of male and female mental and social health. For training or consulting in this area—the area specifically referred to in *How Do I Help Him?*—see www.michaelgurian.com/how-do-I-help-him.html.

The Gurian Institute staff of certified trainers is committed to not only training professionals and parents but also to helping ensure that participant agencies, schools, corporations, organizations, and individual practitioners can be self-sufficient in their ability to provide ongoing assets to their communities.

The Gurian Institute Corporate Division provides training and consulting in gender diversity for businesses, corporations, and government agencies. This work has inspired the book *Leadership and the Sexes*, which looks at both women and men in our workforce from a gender science perspective. For more about this work, see www.genderleadership.com.

About the Author

Michael Gurian, MFA, CMHC, is the *New York Times* best-selling author of twenty-six books, in twenty-one languages. He has been a professional mental health counselor for over twenty years, and presently works in private practice at the Marycliff Center in Spokane, Washington. The Gurian Institute, which he co-founded, conducts research internationally, launches pilot programs and trains professionals. Michael has been called "the people's philosopher" for his ability to bring together people's ordinary lives and scientific ideas.

As a social philosopher, he has pioneered efforts to bring neurobiology and brain research into homes, schools, medical communities, workplaces, and public policy. A number of his books have sparked national debate, including *The Wonder of Boys, A Fine Young Man, Boys and Girls Learn Differently!, The Wonder of Girls, The Minds of Boys,* and *Leadership and the Sexes.*

Michael has served as a consultant to families, schools, corporations, therapists, physicians, community agencies, churches, criminal justice personnel, and other professionals, traveling to approximately twenty cities per year to provide keynotes at conferences and train professionals. He has presented at Harvard University, John Hopkins University, Stanford University, University of Missouri-Kansas City, UCLA, and many others.

Michael's philosophy reflects the diverse cultures (European, Asian, Middle Eastern and American) in which he has lived, worked and studied. From 1986 to '88, Michael taught at Ankara University, in Ankara, Turkey.

Michael's work has been featured in nearly all major media, including the *New York Times,* the *Washington Post, Psychology Today, Counseling Today, USA Today, Newsweek, Time,* the *Wall Street Journal, Parenting, Good Housekeeping, Redbook,* and on the *Today Show, Good Morning America, CNN, PBS* and *National Public Radio.*

Michael lives in Spokane, Washington, with his wife, Gail, a family therapist. The couple has two grown daughters, Gabrielle and Davita.

Michael can be reached on the worldwide web at www.michaelgurian.com.

Michael Gurian

Reviews of Previous Work

From the beginning of time, parents and sensitive teachers have observed differences in the behavior, learning styles, and focused interests of girls and boys. Defying the political correctness that is today's common wisdom, Gurian and the contributing authors (to *Boys and Girls Learn Differently!*) draw on emerging neuro-scientific data to justify these perceptions. While never allowing us to lose sight of the reality of individual differences, they suggest creative ways to modify the learning environment to encourage a broader spectrum of achievement in both gender groups.

—Edward Zigler, Ph.D., Sterling Professor of Psychology, Yale University; one of the original planners of the national Head Start program

Nurture the Nature is a beautifully written guide to raising children. It is as scientifically sound as it is humane. Michael Gurian provides invaluable insight into how understanding our children's unique core natures can help us raise happy, successful, and emotionally fulfilled children."

— Harold S. Koplewicz, M.D., Chair, Department of Child and Adolescent Psychiatry, New York University School of Medicine; and founder and director, the Child Mind Institute

I found *The Minds of Boys* enlightening not only as a neuroscientist but also as the mother of a young boy. It has absolutely changed the way that I think about boys (and men) and the ways in which they express their enthusiasm for life.

— Tracey J. Shors, Ph.D., Department of Psychology; Center for Collaborative Neuroscience, Rutgers University

Leadership and the Sexes is extremely valuable in two ways. Not only can everyone recognize something of themselves in it, but its numerous engaging examples of communication between women and men will help people interpret communication in the workplace more effectively.

—Sandra F. Witelson, Ph.D., Albert Einstein/Irving Zucker Chair in Neuroscience, Michael G. DeGroote School of Medicine, McMaster University

A Fine Young Man is filled with stories and practical advice for parents and teachers of adolescent boys. Michael Gurian takes a thoughtful look at nature and nurture and the role of culture and testosterone in the lives of boys. I recommend it to those who want to raise fine young men."
—*Mary Pipher, Ph.D., author of Reviving Ophelia*

There is no one who understands the development of boys better than Michael Gurian. In this insightful new book, *The Purpose of Boys*, Gurian offers useful advice about how to help boys succeed in the key challenge of today's world, finding purpose in life.
—*William Damon, Ph.D., Professor of Education, Stanford University; Author of The Moral Child*

It's a Baby Boy! is thoughtfully research-based, yet perceptively practical for any parent who has just been blessed by the gift of a boy. Parents will close the book truly understanding why boys and girls are different in so many ways, and how to nurture the nature of their son."
— *Fay E. Brown, Ph.D., Director of Child and Adolescent Development Program, Yale University*

I found the *The Wonder of Girls* to be a wonderful addition to the literature already available on raising girls. What I liked best was its constant correlation of developing biology in women to their psychological struggles, giving the authenticity that is sorely needed. I heartily endorse this new balanced way to understand how wonderful the capacities of girls and women are, and so vital to the nurturing of their infants, families and society. Bravo!
—*Deborah Sichel, M.D., author of Women's Moods: What Every Woman Must Know About Hormones, the Brain, and Emotional Health*
The Minds of Boys is a gift to parents, teachers and anyone else involved in raising or nurturing boys. It is filled with cutting-edge neuroscience, yet it has the warmth of a wise professional."
—*Daniel Amen, M.D., Founder of the Amen Clinics, University of California-Irvine; Author of Making Brain Great*

Leadership and the Sexes unlocks gender truths for the workplace. Every business-man or woman needs to read this book!

— Louann Brizendine, M.D., Neuro-psychiatrist and Clinical Professor, University of California-San Francisco; author of The Female Brain and The Male Brain

Michael Gurian is America's most passionate advocate for boys. In *The Purpose of Boys*, Gurian creates a rich reading experience and a clear recipe for helping boys to find purpose in their lives.

— Michael Thompson, Ph.D., author of It's a Boy! and coauthor of Raising Cain